New Dimensions of Chinese Foreign Policy

New Dimensions in Chinese Foreign Policy

Series Editor
Sujian Guo
San Francisco State University

New Dimensions of Chinese Foreign Policy

Sujian Guo and Shiping Hua

LEXINGTON BOOKS

A division of
ROWMAN & LITTLEFIELD PUBLISHERS, INC.
Lanham • Boulder • New York • Toronto • Plymouth, UK

LEXINGTON BOOKS

A division of Rowman & Littlefield Publishers, Inc.
A wholly owned subsidiary of The Rowman & Littlefield Publishing Group, Inc.
4501 Forbes Boulevard, Suite 200
Lanham, MD 20706

Estover Road
Plymouth PL6 7PY
United Kingdom

British Library Cataloguing in Publication Information Available

Library of Congress Cataloging-in-Publication Data

New dimensions of Chinese foreign policy / [edited by] Sujian Guo and Shiping Hua.
    p. cm.
  Includes bibliographical references and index.
  ISBN-13: 978-0-7391-1876-4 (cloth : alk. paper)
  ISBN-10: 0-7391-1876-5 (cloth : alk. paper)
  1. China—Foreign relations—1976- I. Guo, Sujian, 1957- II. Hua, Shiping, 1956-
JZ1734.N48 2007
327.51—dc22   2007013072

Printed in the United States of America

♾™ The paper used in this publication meets the minimum requirements of American
National Standard for Information Sciences—Permanence of Paper for Printed Library
Materials, ANSI/NISO Z39.48–1992.

Contents

Contents

List of Tables

Contributors

Michael Alan Brittingham, a visiting assistant professor in the Department of Political Science and International Studies at McDaniel College. He has previously taught at the University of Louisville. In 2005, he completed his dissertation entitled, "Reactive Nationalism and Its Prospects for Conflict: The Taiwan Issue, Sino-US Relations, & the 'Role' of Nationalism in Chinese Foreign Policy" in the Department of Political Science at the University of Pittsburgh. His current research interests include international relations theory, Chinese foreign policy, and nationalism.

Sujian Guo, director of Center for US-China Policy Studies and associate professor in the Department of Political Science at San Francisco State University, editor of the *Journal of Chinese Political Science*, and president of Association of Chinese Political Studies. His areas of specialization include Comparative Politics, International Relations and Methodology. His research interests include Chinese/Asian politics, communist and post-communist studies, democratic transitions, and the political economy of East and Southeast Asia. He has published more than 30 articles both in English and Chinese. His books include *The Political Economy of Asian Transition from Communism* (2006), *China's "Peaceful Rise" in the 21st Century: Domestic and International Conditions* (2006), and *Post-Mao China: from Totalitarianism to Authoritarianism?* (2000).

Shiping Hua, Associate Professor of Political Science and Director of the Center for Asian Democracy at the University of Louisville. His single-authored books are: *Scientism and Humanism: Two Cultures in Post-Mao China (1978-1989)* and *Chinese Utopianism: A Comparative Study of Reformist Thought in Japan, Russia and China (1898-2000)*. He has edited/coedited five other books in English. His articles and presentations have also appeared in popular media, such as Wilson Quarterly, The New York Times, and The Voice of America. Dr. Hua is the general editor of a book series with University Press of Kentucky: "Asia in the New Millennium."

Catherine Keyser, associate professor of political science at Drew University, Madison New Jersey. She received her Ph.D. from Columbia University in the city of New York. She has published *Professionalizing Research in Post-Mao China: The System Reform Institute and Policy Making*, and has also frequently guest edited the journal *Chinese Law and Government*. Professor Keyser received a Fulbright Research grant to China for 2006-2007 where she is working on child welfare reform policy and the creation of new institutions for addressing social issues.

Han Lheem, assistant professor of political science at Fayetteville State University. His research areas include international political economy, international environmental politics, Asian democracy and cultures, and Western and non-Western political philosophies. He has previously taught at the University of Tennessee, and an adjunct fellow at World Citizenship Institute and Peacebuilding Institute of East Tennessee.

Chenghong Li, a Ph.D. candidate of the Department of Political Science at the University of South Carolina. His current research interests include theories of international relations and foreign policy analysis, Chinese foreign relations, Chinese politics, politics and economy across the Asia-Pacific area. Most recently, his paper on Taiwan's mainland China policy was published in *East Asia: An International Quarterly*.

Jing Men, professor in the Department of Political Science at the Katholieke Universiteit Brussel. She received her Ph.D. from Vrije Universiteit Brussel in 2004. She is specialized in Chinese foreign policy and external relations. Her major publications include "Chinese Perception of the European Union", *European Law Journal*, November 2006; "China's Peaceful Rise?", *Studia Diplomatica*, Nov.-Dec. 2004; and "International Relations Theory in China", *Global Society*, July 2001 (with Gustaaf Geeraerts).

Xiaoyu Pu, a Ph.D. candidate in the Department of Political Science at the Ohio State University. He received his BA and MA from Nankai University (China) and Kent State University. His research interests include IR theory, international security, political psychology, China and East Asia. His recent publications include "Framing Sino-American Relations under Stress: Reexamination of News Coverage on the 2001 Spy Plane Crisis," co-authored with Steven Hook, *Asian Affairs: An American Review* (forthcoming); and a book chapter on political psychology (in Chinese) that is published by Peking University Press.

Lin Su, associate professor of International Relations and Deputy Director of the Center for European Studies, School of International Studies, Renmin University of China. Her main teaching and research interests are history of international relations and European politics and external relations. Recent publication in English is *China's Foreign Policy Making: Societal Force and Chinese American Policy* (with Yufan Hao, 2005). Her recent Chinese publications include: *World Political Economy* (co-editor, 2004); *EU Common Foreign and Security Policy and EU-China Relations* (co-editor, 2002). She was a visiting scholar at School of English and American Studies at University of Sussex,UK; the School of International Service at American University in Washington, DC.

Contributors

Guoxin Xing, a PhD candidate at School of Communication, Simon Fraser University in Canada. Previously, he worked as a journalist for China's official Xinhua News Agency and stationed in Turkey and Egypt as a resident correspondent. Guoxin's research interests include political communication, national image building, international public relations, political economy of global communication, and corporate communication and internationalization of China's enterprises.

Guang Zhang, professor of public administration at the Zhou Enlai School of Government, and Research Fellow, Japan Studies Institute, Nankai University (China). He received his PhD from Kent State University. His research interests include political economy, public finance, methodology, Chinese politics and East Asia. His publications appeared in *Asian Survey, Journal of Chinese Political Science, Zhengzhixue Yanjiu* (Political Science Research, in Chinese), and other journals. He is the author of book *A Study of Japanese Foreign Aid Policy* (in Chinese, 1996). His recent publications include "The Determinants of Foreign Aid Allocation across China: The Case of World Bank Loans," *Asian Survey*, No. 5 (September/October 2004).

Wanfa Zhang, a PhD candidate in the Department of Political Science at the University of Alabama in Tuscaloosa. He was previously a lecturer at Beijing Foreign Affairs College in China and the author of several articles published in *China Journal of American History* and *Journal of Foreign Affairs College*. He was also a contributor of entries in the *Dictionary on China's Diplomacy* (Beijing: World Affairs Press, 1998). His research interests include militarized interstate disputes, contemporary Chinese politics and diplomacy, as well as security issues in Asia-Pacific region and research methods.

Zhiqun Zhu, assistant professor and program chair of International Political Economy and Diplomacy at the University of Bridgeport, Connecticut. He is the author of *US-China Relations in the 21st Century: Power Transition and Peace* (London and New York: Routledge, 2006). His research and teaching interests include international relations, international political economy, East Asian politics, and US-China relations.

Charles E. Ziegler, professor and chair of the Department of Political Science at the University of Louisville, and director of the Institute for Democracy and Development. He is co-editor of and contributor to *Russia's Far East: A Region at Risk* (University of Washington Press, 2002), and author of *The History of Russia* (Greenwood, 1999), *Foreign Policy and East Asia* (Cambridge University Press, 1993), and *Environmental Policy in the USSR* (University of Massachusetts Press, 1987). His articles have appeared in *Problems of Post-Communism, Asian Survey, Pacific Affairs, Comparative Politics, Political Science Quarterly, British Journal of Political Science*, and many other journals and edited books. The author would like to thank Igor Danchenko for his able research assistance on this project.

Acknowledgments

This book is a collection of papers from an Association of Chinese Political Studies (ACPS) annual conference entitled "China in the 21st Century: Challenges and Opportunities" held at the University of Louisville from April 2-3, 2006. The conference was hosted by the Institute for Democracy and Development (IDD) at the University of Louisville together with the McConnell Center for Political Leadership. The conference was supported through a generous grant from the McConnell Center for Political Leadership and the Mr. & Mrs. S.H. Wong Foundation, Ltd. Hong Kong. The authors would like to thank the above organizations for their generous funding for the conference.

Introduction

New Dimensions of Chinese Foreign Policy

Sujian Guo and Shiping Hua

Since the new leadership led by Hu Jintao assumed power, Chinese foreign policy has continued along the lines laid out by Deng Xiaoping. However, the new leadership demonstrates some new thinking in its foreign policy. China faces many international challenges arising from Sino-U.S. relations, Sino-Japan relations, Sino-Russia relations, Taiwan issues, and Northeast Asian security, particularly from the U.S. response to its rising power and increasing trade friction with the United States, EU, and the developing world. Facing a rising China, there is an increasing wariness, fear, and suspicion from the world, particularly the United States. The Bush Administration has been advised to adopt a new containment strategy to counterbalance the "China Threat."[1] In response to the "China Threat" and U.S. pressure, the Chinese leadership recognizes that it is in the fundamental interest of China to maintain a stable and peaceful international environment for China's modernization programs and it has proposed "peaceful development" (*heping fazhan*), which has become a new thinking (*xinsiwei*) in Chinese foreign policy under the Fourth Generation Leadership.[2]

In a recently published volume *"China's Peaceful Rise in the 21st Century: Domestic and International Conditions,"* the author elaborates on the "new thinking" in Chinese foreign policy.[3] Although the concept "peaceful development" foreign policy strategy is a continuity of Deng Xiaoping's concept *"taoguang yanghui"* (keep a low profile and never take the lead), it is a break away from Jiang Zemin's *"duoji shijie"* (multipolar world). Under Jiang, building a multipolar world implies to "multipolarize" the American unipolarity and counterbalance U.S. hegemony. This "peaceful development" foreign policy strategy is, in fact, to accept the unipolar structure of the international system and that the U.S. will continue to be the hegemonic power in the long term. It proposes that China must avoid direct confrontation with the U.S. in order to secure a favorable external environment for its rise, although China can adopt a multilateral and bilateral diplomatic approach in the unipolar world dominated by a single hegemon.[4]

Second, "peaceful development" seeks to reassure the U.S. and other countries that China's rise will not be a threat to peace and stability in the region and the world and that the U.S. and other countries can benefit from China's peaceful development. China's development is mutually beneficial to China and the world in the process of globalization. The new policy also seeks negotiated settlement of regional problems such as the nuclear crisis on the Korean peninsula and South China Sea dispute with Vietnam and Malaysia.[5]

Third, the new foreign policy stresses that China is a peace-loving, people-based (*yiren weiben*), cooperative, tolerant, confident, and responsible power. However, China also recognizes that its "soft power" can be used to enhance China's role as a rising power in regional and world affairs and to facilitate China's economic development and modernization.

Fourth, the "peaceful development" strategy also impacts Beijing's Taiwan policy. Beijing has quietly shifted its Taiwan policy to "*budu buwu*" (no independence, no war) – aimed at maintaining the status quo and putting aside the "*tongyi*" (unification) for the time being. Deng Xiaoping made the unification one of the central tasks for the Chinese government, and Jiang Zemin pressed Taiwan for unification by declaring that the resolution of the "Taiwan issue" would not be delayed indefinitely. However, Hu Jingtao declared during his visit to Canada in September 2005 that the resolution of the Taiwan issue is complicated and would take a long time, and that "*fangtaidu*" (struggle against the "Taiwan independence") would be a long fight – without setting a time table for the unification. This is a departure from Jiang's "*jitong*" (hasty unification) to a new thinking that seeks "peace," "reconciliation," "cooperation," and "win-win situation" (heping, hejie, hezuo, shuangying) across the Taiwan Strait that could lead to a future of "peaceful development" and "common prosperity."[6] In 2005, Beijing invited Taiwan's top two opposition leaders, Lien Chan (KMT) and James Soong (PFP), to visit mainland China, accompanied by Taiwanese legislators, politicians, businessmen and media leaders, and embarked on a historical dialogue and political interaction across the Taiwan-Straits since 1949. The new shift in the Taiwan policy is an integral part of Beijing's "peaceful development" strategy.

Apparently, the Chinese leaders have made clear to the world that China has no interest in seeking regional hegemony or a change in the existing world order and China is committed to "peaceful development." However, what are the new dimensions of Chinese foreign policy since Hu Jintao and the new leadership assumed power? This edited volume attempts to address this question.

This volume brings together specialists in Chinese foreign policy to introduce readers to some new dimensions of Chinese foreign policy, elaborate on the significance of these dimensions and issues, and present differing perspectives. Most of the contributors to this volume are Chinese scholars or Chinese American scholars and thus are sensitive to the changes in Chinese foreign policy and their implications for the world. The contributors deal with some dimensions of foreign policy, such as the changing ideology, new orientation of emerging elites, nationalism in foreign policy making, "soft power" building of foreign policy, new approaches to the nuclear issue on the Korean peninsula, Middle East challenges in China's foreign policy, and changing attitudes toward international regimes, and their implications for domestic politics and external relations. Their insightful contributions will help scholars understand how new dimensions of Chinese foreign policy affect foreign policy making behavior and the implications on Sino-U.S. relations.

In Chapter 1, "Changing Ideology in China and Its Impact on Chinese Foreign Policy," Jing Men argues that, since the founding of the People's Republic of China, ideology in China has been undergoing profound changes. The Chinese government has revised and added new elements to the official ideology of Marxism-Leninism-Maoism. The recent developments towards pragmatism in the effort to revitalize Chinese ideology have a strong impact on the formation and implementation of Chinese foreign policy. An examination of the close connection between Chinese ideology and Chinese foreign policy explains the formation of China's peaceful development policy and its implications for the international system.

In Chapter 2, "Understanding the Rise of China: Chinese Intellectual Perspectives," Catherine H. Keyser and Su Lin examine the debate on the nature of China's rise and its implications, particularly with focus on the contents of the thoughts on national responsibility in Chinese elites. Partly as a response to "China threat" theories, Beijing has proposed a "peaceful development" foreign policy. Although most of Chinese elites agree that a peaceful rise is the best choice for China's future, there still exist disagreements among Chinese elites on the nature of the rise of China. Conservatives, realists and liberals have differing concepts on the meaning of 'rise' of China. The causes for the different approaches toward the goal of China's rise not only derive from different theoretical assumptions, but also from different perceptions about the state and priorities of reform.

In Chapter 3, "China's Rising and New Foreign Policy Orientations: Perspectives from China's Emerging Elite," Xiaoyu Pu and Guang Zhang explore China's strategic intentions in the future by focusing on the following question: will China shift its currently moderate foreign policy to a more assertive approach as its power status changes in the international system? This chapter examines Chinese foreign policy orientations of emerging elites in China based on Q methodology. The respondents include Chinese diplomats, other central and local officials, recognized scholars of international studies, and students from China's foremost universities. The study focuses on participants' perspectives on current Chinese foreign policy and their appraisal concerning what Chinese foreign policy should be over the next two decades. The project serves two purposes: first, it provides alternative perspectives on current Chinese foreign policy orientation; second, it provides a window into the pattern of possible future Chinese policy orientations.

In Chapter 4, "China's Contested Rise: Sino-U.S. Relations and the Social Construction of Great Power Status," Michael Alan Brittingham examines the social construction of a great power status as China is rising, and the implications it has for Sino-U.S. relations. The impending rise of China as a great power has become a popular topic of discussion among academics, policy-makers, and the media. Yet predictions about China's rise are nothing new. Indeed, such concerns can be traced back decades, if not centuries, and seems to fade and reappear almost cyclically. This perpetual rise to power is due not just to China's struggles with modernization or the short attention span of the Western media, but to the nature of great power status itself. While it is certainly grounded in the material capabilities of a state, great power status is, like many political phenomenon, socially constructed – i.e., it is dependent on shared ideas and social norms.

In Chapter 5, "China's 'Soft Power' Tapping and Management in its Ascent and their Implications for the World," Wanfa Zhang argues that soft power building not only serves as a booster for China's peaceful rise, but also helps to integrate the country into the community of nations and eventually facilitates it to become a "stakeholder" who will share the responsibility as well as the peace dividend with other nations. Because of potential benefits to all, Beijing's effort in soft power building should be viewed positively by the international community and responded with welcome and encouragement rather than suspicion, fear and negative acts. This chapter is a study of the significance of China's "soft power" building and management in its rapid rise both in the short and long runs. By studying China's efforts in soft power tapping and management, historical and contemporary cases of successes and failures, the country's advantages and disadvantages, domestic and international environment, the author explores the implications of its soft power cultivation efforts for the future of China as well as for the world.

In Chapter 6, "China's Peaceful Rising and Its International Image Cultivating," Guoxin Xing argues that China has adopted "peaceful rising" as a new foreign policy strategy to assuage "China threat" propagated by the United States and some of its allies. By proclaiming such a slogan, China is cultivating its international image as a responsible status quo power in the world. This chapter examines China's efforts in international public relations and Western public opinion on China's peaceful rising strategy. The findings suggest that China still lacks of mechanism both in structural international PR and manipulative PR to cultivate its international image. As such, the public opinion in the rest of the world, especially in the United States and some of China's neighboring countries, is still suspicious of China's new foreign policy strategy.

In Chapter 7, "China's New Approach to North Korean Nuclear Issue: An Economic Interdependence," Han Lheem attempts to analyze China's new economic strategy to North Korea, which is looking beyond the six-party talks and the American approach. Unlike the U.S. approach of trying to squeeze Kim and forcing him to drop nuclear ambitions, the Chinese new agenda on North Korea are oriented towards massive investment and in gaining Kim's confidence. Chinese new engagement policy has influenced the North Korean leadership's perception of market reform policy. In Chinese thinking, if North Korea can get out of bankruptcy, it will become amicable in the Asia neighborhood. The Chinese new strategy is aimed at trying to do business with North Korea, while the U.S. approach seeks to resolve the nuclear issue as quickly as possible.

In Chapter 8, "China's Middle East Policy and Its Implications for U.S.-China Relations," Zhiqun Zhu examines Chinese foreign policy towards the Middle East since the early 1990s, with a focus on China's efforts in obtaining oil, trading with Middle Eastern countries, and its fight against terrorism/separatism related to the region. Based on empirical observation, the chapter explores how Chinese activities in the Middle East affect U.S.-China relations and if their interaction in the region will turn into a zero-sum game or a positive game for the two countries.

In Chapter 9, "the Energy Factor in China's Foreign Policy," Charles E. Ziegler argues that China's foreign policy behavior has been influenced by growing energy dependence. As a major importer, China can pursue energy security through strategies that result in conflict; alternatively, energy vulnerability might lead it toward cooperation with rival oil consuming nations through participation in multilateral organizations and other forums. After outlining the argument for the strategic nature of energy, China's increasing energy dependence is assessed, as are Beijing's efforts to shift China's energy balance. China's energy diplomacy with the Middle East, Russia and Central Asia, the Asia-Pacific, Africa and Latin America are examined, and Beijing's efforts toward greater energy security through multilateral organizations are discussed. The evidence supports the liberal hypothesis that economic interdependence promotes international cooperation. Energy demands have accelerated China's rise to global prominence, and appear to moderate conflictual aspects of Chinese foreign policy.

In Chapter 10, "Increasing Interdependence between China and the United States and Its Implications for China's Foreign Policy," Chenghong Li examines the increasing transnational dimensions of the Sino-U.S. relations and their implications for China's U.S. foreign policy. By positioning their theoretical and policy analysis from a kind of ideal-type thinking, scholars of both schools did not pay enough attention to the exact shape and content of the current Sino-U.S. relations, particularly the increasing transnational interactions across the pacific as well as their potential influence on the relationship between China and the United States. This chapter attempts to bridge the gap between realist and liberal understanding of China's rise and its challenges by exploring the increasing new dimensions of transnational and interdependent relations between China and the United States as well as their possible implications for China's foreign policy, especially toward the United States.

All ten chapters examine each of the new dimensions of Chinese foreign policy and address their significance for China's "peaceful rise" and its foreign relations with the U.S. and the rest of the world. All the factors involved in these new dimensions help to explain Chinese foreign policy behavior in the years to come, although this volume might not address all of the factors and issues that could affect China's future foreign policy development.

Notes

[1] Robert D. Kaplan, "How We Would Fight China," *The Atlantic Monthly*, vol. 295, no. 5, June 2005, pp. 49-64,
http://www.theatlantic.com/doc/prem/200506/kaplan

[2] Hu Jintao replaced the term "peaceful rise" with "peaceful development" also because of Jiang's opposition to the term "rise" (*jueqi*). Hu's final decision is that the rise of China should be discussed freely by scholars in their writings but the term of "rise" is no longer used in government statements.

[3] Sujian Guo, ed., *China's Peaceful Rise in the 21st Century: Domestic and International Conditions* (Ashgate Publishing, 2006), pp. 2-4.

[4] Xiaoxiong Yi, "Chinese Foreign Policy in Transition: Understanding China's 'Peaceful Development'," The *Journal of East Asian Affairs*, vol. 19, no. 1, 2005.

[5] Ibid.

[6] http://www.ccforum.org.cn/archiver/?tid-36534.html;
http://www.huaxia.com/zt/rdzz/05-020/2005/00303455.html;
http://news.xinhuanet.com/taiwan/2005-04/29/content_2895458.htm

Chapter 1

Changing Ideology in China and Its Impact on Chinese Foreign Policy

Jing Men

China has undergone dramatic changes since the Chinese Communists established their government in Beijing in 1949. From engaging in class struggle to building a harmonious society, from denunciation of Confucianism to resurrection of Confucianism, from world revolution to peaceful rise, China has been continuing to search for the road of development to realize national power and prosperity. "Power and prosperity" is the ultimate goal of state construction in China. The efforts made by the Chinese leadership during all these years have been aimed at building a strong and wealthy country, a country that is not taken advantage of by any other powers, a country that is respectable and independent in the international politics, a country that maintains justice and peace in the world.

While China's ultimate goal has never wavered, the means to pursue that goal have been constantly readjusted. In pursuit of the goal, ideology plays an important role. Ideology is a system of ideas through which national leaders learn to structure their environment and explain reality. It rationalizes policy choices by national leaders, offers direction of action and helps stimulate unity of thinking, builds a consensus of national identity, and supports social cohesion. Under ideological guidance, policies have been made to serve national goals. For more than five decades, the Chinese leadership has been refashioning and reinterpreting the ideological formation to legitimize the governance of the Communist Party of China (CPC) and to unify the people's mind. With the support of a system of ideas, Beijing aims to realize the goal of modernization.

The ideological content has been in a process of constant revision ever since Marxism and Leninism was introduced to China in the early twentieth century. Marxism advocates class struggle and believes in the inevitable collapse of capitalism and the ultimate victory of communism. Marxism holds that the exploiting class should be overthrown by force to establish a proletarian dictatorship. Lenin further developed Marxism by taking states as the leading protagonists in the revolutionary struggle and world politics. Leninism takes competing nation-states as the principal actors and points out that revolution would first be successful in those nation-states where imperialist control is the weakest. Mao Zedong was highly inspired by the revolutionary spirit of Marxism and Leninism. Applying the Marxist and Leninist ideas to the practical Chinese situation, Mao Zedong and his colleagues developed Mao Zedong Thought. Mao Zedong Thought was regarded as Chinese Marxism which helped the Chinese Communists defeat the Nationalist Party.

However, in the years of reform, the role of Marxism has been deteriorating. An increasing amount of capitalist elements have been allowed to put into practice in China. The liberation of mind has an unexpected side-effect on the ideological basis. The sublime status of Marxism has been shaken. In words of Brugger and Kelly, Chinese ideology has been developed into "Marxism without Marx."[1] Deng Xiaoping avoided the debate in the ideological field and sought to convince the Chinese people with the noticeable economic achievements. Jiang Zemin promoted the "Three Represents" to broaden the social base of the CPC from workers and peasants to the overwhelming majority of the people in China including capitalists. While recognizing the irreversible trend of reform, Hu Jintao focuses on correcting the problems brought by the reform and emphasizes the construction of a harmonious society to shorten the gap between the rich and the poor.

Ideology affects China's interpretation of world events and the making of Chinese foreign policy. Due to the continuous revision of ideological components in the past five decades and more, the ideological influence on Chinese foreign policy has been varied. The Communist idea inspired red China to join the socialist camp in the 1950s, and launched the campaign for world revolution in the 1960s. As a consequence of Mao's death and the reassessment of Mao's policy, the Chinese leadership has adopted a more practical foreign policy since the late 1970s. The domestic reform facilitates the deepening of China's interdependence with the world and motivates Beijing to implement a cooperative policy externally. The increasing acceptance of capitalist elements in Chinese society is parallel to the process of China's opening to the outside world, and to the improvement and strengthening of official relations between China and the other countries.

Since 1949, four generations of Chinese leadership have governed the country. Sharing the same goal of "power and prosperity," Chinese leaders nevertheless followed different roads. Mao Zedong attached great importance to class struggle and world revolution; Deng Xiaoping engaged in reform and opening up; Jiang Zemin deepened reform and strengthened China's ties with the outside world; and Hu Jintao focuses domestically on the scientific way of development and externally on the diplomatic policy of peaceful rise. Based on the transition of Chinese leadership, this study is divided into four parts. The first part studies the ideological engagement of Mao Zedong and examines how China was affected by the revolutionary ideas in its foreign policy. The second part reviews Deng Xiaoping's efforts to redefine and revise Mao Zedong Thought, and the consequences on Chinese foreign policy. The third part looks at the elaboration of ideological issues in Jiang's era, the resurrection of Confucianism as the basis of cultural essence in Chinese society, and the noticeable developments in China's relations with the outside world. The fourth part studies Hu's efforts in search of ideology and the new developments in Chinese foreign policy. This study aims to underline the fact that reform and opening policy has transformed China from a state which was ideologically-oriented and revolutionary to a state which is pragmatic and cooperative in the international political system. Laying aside ideological differences in Chinese foreign affairs has effectively contributed to the rise of China in the international society.

MAO'S ERA

China in Mao's era was strongly ideologically oriented. Marxism-Leninism-Mao Zedong Thought was taken as the guideline instructing socialist revolution and construction. Class struggle was applied to the Chinese society with the purpose to eliminating reactionaries. Externally, the revolutionary ideology directed China to join the socialist camp in its struggle against the capitalist camp, to launch the world revolution, and to engage in anti-hegemonism.

Regardless of its ideological inclination, the Chinese leadership gave primary consideration to national interest. They were believers of Marxism and eager to promote communism internationally. However, their support to the international communist cause was aimed at rebuilding and empowering China. In other words, the Chinese Communists were in the first place nationalists. Once the international revolution had a conflict with the domestic development, the Chinese leadership had to compromise their revolutionary principles to national interest. The capability to adapt itself to the changing situation demonstrated the pragmatism and flexibility of Chinese leadership, which is the key to understand the changes of policies in the diplomatic field.

Thus, in Mao's era, the Chinese foreign policy experienced an interesting shift, from trying to combine the international communist cause with the national mission to solely concentrating on the Chinese national interest and from being ideal and fanatic at the liberation cause of all the people on the earth to being down-to-earth and pragmatic at China's external relations. Such a shift of policy occurred at the moment that Beijing was facing the most serious security challenge ever since the PRC was founded. From then on, Chinese foreign policy has become more flexible and realistic. The influence of Marxist ideology on the making of Chinese foreign policy has gradually dwindled.

Ideological Formation

Marxist ideology served as an important instrument for the Chinese Communists to spare the country from colonial suppression, feudalist exploitation and imperialist aggression. While expressing faith in the guiding role of Marxism and Leninism, the Chinese did not stop by making a complete copy out of it. Mao Zedong further developed it on the basis of the Chinese situation. As the reactionary forces in rural areas were relatively weak, Mao Zedong proposed to encircle the cities from rural areas and then captured them. This proposal opened up China's characteristic revolutionary road to the Communists' final success in China. Mao Zedong developed the ideas including guerrilla war, class struggle and a united front in his revolutionary practice. His contribution to the formation and development of ideology in China was recognized by the Chinese leadership at the 7th Party Congress in 1945. For several decades, Mao Zedong Thought was put together with Marxism and Leninism as the ideological guidance for Chinese policy making. On the 10th anniversary of the founding of the PRC, the Head of State Liu Shaoqi declared: "China's lightning speed in developing its social productive forces cannot be matched by any capitalist country and it certainly could never be dreamt of in old China.... The Chinese Communist Party, which has led the Chinese Revolution to victory, is armed with Marxism-Leninism. This is epitomized in Mao Zedong Thought: the integration of the universal truth of Marxism-Leninism with the concrete practice of the Chinese revolution."[2]

The revolutionary victory in 1949 instilled a strong belief in the Chinese Communists that "Capitalism is decadent," and "Communism is superior to capitalism."[3] Communism seemed to offer an ideal path for the Chinese to restore prestige after being liberated from feudalism, colonialism, and imperialism. It appeared to promise an effective mobilization of the national resources that were dissipated by factionalism, disloyalties, corruption and inefficiency in the past. Moreover, it guaranteed to put an end to all the uncertainties and disputes on the path of economic and social development. Finally, its emphasis on social justice eradicated the exploitation which appeared to be endemic to capitalist economic systems.[4]

In order to bring socialism, and eventually communism to the world, the Chinese leadership practiced class struggle against those capitalists and reactionaries. Class struggle was regarded as an effective tool to purify China in particular and the world in general. The Chinese government carried out the proletariat dictatorship and highlighted the respectful status of workers and peasants who constituted the main forces to bring China into an independent status.

Guided by Marxism-Leninism-Mao Zedong Thought, China accomplished socialist transition in the early 1950s. Industry and agriculture were completely socialized; the middle class underwent ideological remolding. From the early 1950s till the death of Mao Zedong in 1976, numerous political campaigns were launched with the purpose of dispelling the reactionaries and the enemies. While clarifying that contradiction among the people with the non-antagonistic nature could be resolved by non-coercive political means, Mao's speech "On the Correct Handling of Contradictions among the People" delivered on Feb. 27, 1957 nevertheless stressed that the concept of class struggle between the proletariat and the bourgeoisie existed in the ideological field.[5] Distorted and exaggerated, this idea was applied in those political campaigns including the Cultural Revolution (1966-1976). He regarded all his opponents as either revisionists or reactionaries. Many of his colleagues were persecuted and disappeared from the political centre, while Mao himself was admired as "the greatest teacher and the most outstanding leader of the proletariat in the present era."[6]

External Expression of Official Ideology

The revolutionary ideology was the starting point for Mao Zedong to perceive China's position in the world as well as to make Chinese foreign policy. The three explicit doctrines of Chinese diplomatic affairs at the founding of the PRC were strongly revolutionary in nature. *Lingqi luzao*, "to set up a separate kitchen," expressed the resolve of the CPC to make a fresh start at its foreign relations. The CPC refused to recognize the diplomatic ties established by the Nationalist Party, and preferred to build relations with the other countries on a completely new basis. *Dasao ganjing wuzi qingke*, "to clean up the room before inviting guests," implied that before developing diplomatic ties with the others, the CPC determined to drive all the imperial forces out of the country. *Yibiandao*, "to lean to one side," indicated that China chose to lean to the socialist camp headed by the Soviet Union, and attempted to realize its national interest via the consolidation and enhancement of the socialist camp.

The choice of leaning to one side led the CPC to give more stress on the promotion and development of international communism. Such a policy not only promised a way to regenerate China, but also encouraged the Chinese leaders to strive to eliminate imperialism worldwide. Believing that communism was the right way of nation-building, the Chinese leaders promoted communism and supported communist struggles in the underdeveloped countries. By establishing its ties with the newly independent countries in Asia, Africa and Latin America, Beijing expected that such relationship would not only further legitimize the Chinese Communist government worldwide, but also strengthen the socialist influence in their competition against the capitalists. By supporting guerrilla movements to overturn the capitalist governments in some countries, offering moral and material assistance to the national liberation and development in Asia, Africa and Latin America, and developing close ties with some radical governments to challenge the international political system, the CPC honored its ideology of Marxism-Leninism-Mao Zedong Thought in the international arena.

The Bandung Conference held in 1955 was significant for China. Before 1955, Beijing had diplomatic ties with only 21 countries in total. After the Bandung Conference, Beijing seized the initiative to declare its full support to the newly independent countries and accorded swift recognition to most of them. From 1955 to 1959, China fostered diplomatic relations with 12 newly independent countries including 7 Asian countries and 5 African countries. From 1960 to 1964, China established official relations with 15 countries including one Asian country, one Latin American country, and 13 African countries. By 1964, 49 countries had diplomatic relations with Beijing. Among them, 34 were Afro-Asian countries. Cuba was the only one from Latin America.[7]

The Chinese believed that the working class should not be limited by national boundaries.[8] Class struggle in international affairs was exemplified by the possibility of war against the imperialists. Mao believed that war could not be abolished while classes continued to exist. "Even if a no-war agreement is signed, the possibility of war still exists. When the imperialists want war, no agreement can be taken seriously."[9] According to Mao, war was an inherent characteristic of imperialism and sooner or later such a war would break out between the Soviet Union and the United States. In the two decades after the PRC was founded, Beijing was highly alert to the imminence of war. People were motivated under the slogans as "prepare for an early war, a major war, and a nuclear war."[10] The hostile relationship with the United States started from the Korean War. The hostility escalated in the 1960s when the Americans increasingly involved themselves in the Vietnam War. China's sense of threat was particularly strong after the Soviet Union invaded Czechoslovakia. Aware of the Soviet military built-up at the Sino-Soviet border, Chinese leaders sounded a new note of alarm: "We must heighten our vigilance, intensify our preparedness against war and be ready at all times to smash any invasion launched by U.S. imperialism, Soviet revisionism and their lackeys, whether individually or collectively."[11]

Due to the deteriorating relationship with the Soviet Union in the 1960s, China's external security environment worsened. Prompted by an increasing international and domestic pressure, the Chinese leaders formulated more radical policies in international politics. Attacking the Soviets as revisionist, Beijing attempted to establish an alternative model of international communism which was more militant. China began encouraging the revolution worldwide.

By and large, the Chinese strategy of an anti-imperialist united front had mixed results. Based on the Chinese model of revolutionary armed struggle, China involved itself in the support of national liberation and revolution movements worldwide. Since such movements were often in direct conflict with the conservative and repressive governments, China's radical policy had a negative impact on its diplomatic relations.[12] Also by relying on the ideologically based strategies, China underestimated the degree of complexity of the link of these countries with one or the other of the two superpowers. Its fanatic enthusiasm for world revolution not only affronted foreign communist parties which preferred to follow their own national roads to socialism, but also alienated friends and neutrals until China stood virtually alone among its former communist allies.[13]

By actively encouraging and supporting opposition groups in many countries, China provoked and encountered diplomatic trouble in at least 32 countries.[14] The number of exchanges of delegations between China and foreign countries dropped from 1,322 in 1965 to 66 in 1969.[15] Nevertheless, China's revolutionary behavior had also a positive impact on China's image. China had succeeded in changing her image in the Afro-Asian world from a weak country to a rising power capable of challenging the international order established and maintained by the two superpowers. The influence of China was widely recognized by the Afro-Asian countries. Thus, when China readjusted its strategy to remove the radical features from its external relations, the normal diplomatic ties with these countries were quickly resumed.

As mentioned earlier, the Chinese leaders in Mao's era attempted to bring the national goal and the international goal in congruence in their foreign policy. By promoting the international communist cause, they intended to fulfill their mission of state building. However, their commitment to communism could not compete with their commitment to national interest. Rather than being an internationalist, Mao Zedong was a true nationalist in seeking China's status in the international politics.[16] China's shaky security situation at the end of the 1960s indicated to the Chinese leaders that their choice of policy was a mistake. The international communist cause had to be given up in face of the serious challenge to national security. Marked by its improved relationship with Yugoslavia, Beijing readjusted its guiding principles in the field of foreign policy. As Mao once said, "I am the one who 'would not change direction until he comes to the end of his wrong course' and 'once he turns, he turns 180 degrees.'"[17]

China repaired its diplomatic relations with Afro-Asian countries from 1969 on. Partly motivated by the Soviet security threat, and partly due to the fact that militant rhetoric or limited local revolutionary activity could only damage its diplomatic endeavor, China dropped revolutionary propaganda and the strategy of people's war, and paid greater attention to its defense needs. China sent new ambassadors abroad, and received an increasing number of visits from foreign countries. In 1970, more than 90 overseas delegations, of which around 30 were at governmental level, visited China, while over 50 Chinese missions, mainly economic and technical, were sent overseas. In the same year, Beijing obtained for the first time a simply majority (51 to 49) in favor of its admission to the UN.[18] Beijing was eventually accepted as a member of the UN at the 26th General Assembly of the UN on Oct. 25 of 1971.

Beijing's accession to the UN was a watershed event in Chinese history. As an acknowledged member of the international society, the PRC was obliged to behave within the framework of the existing system. The UN membership "immediately modified the nature of China's challenge, which now related more to reforming, rather than transforming, the existing international political and economic system."[19] By being involved in building and sustaining the existing international order, "revolutionary China under Mao had developed some stake in the existing order in the society of states, and recognized the privileges and prestige it could gain as a significant power by working along with that society."[20] The membership not only mitigated its initial hostility towards the international society, but also encouraged China to further multifaceted integration into the international society.

The changing external environment obliged Mao to revise his understanding of international politics. Marked by the Three World Theory in 1974, Mao Zedong held that the most important conflict in the world was not the conflict between the socialist and the capitalist countries, but the struggles of the two superpowers for world hegemony and the struggle of the other countries in the world to resist them. Mao welcomed the countries from the Second and the Third World to join the united front advocated by Beijing against the superpowers. By then, the theme of world revolution was transformed from the struggle between the haves and the have-nots to anti-hegemonism of the Second and the Third World countries against the First World countries. The adjustment of the Chinese foreign policy in the 1970s led to a great harvest in Chinese diplomatic relations. More than 60 countries established official relations with China in this decade.

Table 1.1 The Role of Ideology in Chinese Foreign Policy in Mao's Era

Content of ideology	Marxism-Leninism-Mao Zedong Thought
Nature of ideology	Radical and revolutionary
Role of ideology in making foreign policy	Important
Principles of foreign policy	Leaning on one side; anti-imperialism; anti-hegemonism
Nature of foreign policy	Confrontational, revisionist
Focus in foreign policy	Socialist camp; Third World countries
Approach in external relations	Bilateral, party-to-party relations were important

DENG'S ERA

Marked by the implementation of reform and opening up policy, China has chosen a road which has not ever been taken by any other socialist countries. Being made out of China's practical situation, the reform and opening up policy has demonstrated a far-reaching influence on China's ideological reformulation. First of all, in order to legitimize such a policy, the Chinese leadership advocated an ideological reform, and tried to eliminate the conservative influence of Mao Zedong Thought. The "Two Whatevers" promoted by Hua Guofeng, the personally chosen leader by Mao, was criticized by Deng Xiaoping. Second, in order to stimulate reform, Deng Xiaoping encouraged the introduction of some capitalist elements including private ownership and market economy into China. According to Deng Xiaoping, getting rich was glorious. Third, the reform and opening up policy gave rise to the problem of the understanding of socialism in China. In order to help unify people's mind, the Chinese leadership had some theoretical developments on the "primary stage of socialism" and the "socialism with Chinese characteristics."

Deng Xiaoping's ingenious move to deviate the country away from revolutionary ideology had a direct repercussion on the making of Chinese foreign policy. As suggested by Prof. Suisheng Zhao, China in Mao's era was a revolutionary state, whereas in Deng's era was a post-revolutionary state.[21] A revolutionary state is engaged in revolution. Mao's era emphasized revolutionary ideology and revolutionary objectives. Internally, it involved a series of political campaigns. Externally, the sensitivity to the threat to its sovereignty and national security often led to military reaction. The revolutionary ideology alienated China from the international society. In Deng's era, following the relaxation of external political situation and the emphasis on domestic economic modernization, Deng transcended Mao's fanatic revolutionary model in state construction as well as in international affairs. The government in Deng's era regarded economic strength as the propelling force of social progress, and encouraged China's openness to the outside world and international economic cooperation.

Although Mao's and Deng's policies were different, both of them had the same goal of national rejuvenation. Similar to Mao Zedong who devoted his life to regenerating the Chinese nation, Deng Xiaoping was also a nationalist, deeply committed to the preservation of national independence, the reunification of the country, and the attainment of national wealth and power.[22] On the first page of the book *Selected Paintings on Deng Xiaoping*, Deng said, "I am a son of the Chinese people, I deeply love my country and my people."[23] Although Deng's government was no less nationalistic than Mao and his supporters, the ideological fervor had subsided, radical features were eliminated, and pragmatism was stressed.

Revision of Mao Zedong Thought

The end of the 1970s was a transitional period in Chinese history. Under Deng Xiaoping's leadership, China underwent a series of political and economic reform that gradually opened the country to the international community. Domestically, after experiencing the havoc of the Cultural Revolution, the Chinese national economy urgently needed to be rehabilitated, and social order needed to be resumed. Starting from 1978, the far-reaching reform policy was implemented.

For several years after Mao's death, Chinese politics was still strongly colored by Mao's influence. Hua Guofeng rigidly carried out Mao Zedong Thought and preached that Chinese leaders should resolutely defend whatever policies Chairman Mao had formulated, and unswervingly adhered to whatever instructions Chairman Mao had issued.[24] In the ideological contest against Hua Guofeng's "Two Whatevers," Deng Xiaoping advocated "seeking truth from facts." He pointed out, "Neither Marx, nor Lenin, nor Mao Zedong himself ever mentioned any 'whatever,' we must accurately and completely apply Marxism-Leninism-Mao Zedong Thought in the guidance of our party, our army and our people."[25] The 3rd Plenary Session of the 11th Party Central Committee held at the end of 1978 re-evaluated the ideological system and concluded that "People's mind should be emancipated" and "Mao Zedong Thought should not be treated rigidly. Instead, the CPC should actively revise it to suit the changing situation."[26] Emphasizing that truth could only come from objective reality, the *Communiqué* of the Session pointed out the limitations of Mao Zedong as a human being and negated the absolute correctness of Mao Zedong Thought. Due to the importance of the *Communiqué*, the 3rd Plenary Session of the 11th Party Central Committee became a milestone in the CPC's history.

By launching the campaign of "emancipation of the mind" in China, Deng Xiaoping intended to "break spiritual shackles" from Mao's words and deeds.[27] The article "Shijian shi jianyan zhenli de weiyi biaozhun" (Practice is the Only Criterion to Test Truth) became well known due to its innovative move in the field of ideology.[28] The article argued, "Truth is objective, it is the authentic reflection from people's mind to the objective world and its principle. . . Simply making use of the existing theories of Marxism and Mao Zedong Thought to limit the ever changing and rich reality is a wrong attitude."[29] Mao Zedong's contributions were further re-evaluated on the 6th Plenary Session of the 11th Party Central Committee in June 1981. The CPC downgraded the former socialist theory which took class struggle as the basic principle. The "Resolution on Certain Questions in the History of Our Party since the Founding of the PRC" admitted that the Cultural Revolution was "a mistake comprehensive in magnitude and protracted in duration," and criticized Mao for his political campaigns and his "erroneous left theses" which led to the Cultural Revolution. The document also pointed out for the first time that China was in the primary stage of socialism.[30]

Although Deng Xiaoping disagreed with Mao's ideas and policies in many respects, he was unwilling to totally repudiate Mao Zedong Thought—for fear that this would lead to divisions in the party and result in the decline of the CPC's authority. In order to solve the problem, Deng Xiaoping redefined the concept of Mao Zedong Thought. Regardless of the fact that Mao was the main individual who articulated and summarized the Chinese revolutionary experience, Mao Zedong Thought was labeled as an accumulated wisdom from collective endeavors. Deng Xiaoping explained, "Mao Zedong Thought is a system of ideas, we cannot comprehend simply from some individual words and phrases. Only on the basis of a complete and accurate understanding of Mao Zedong Thought, will we not isolate, misinterpret, and damage Mao Zedong Thought."[31]

Deng's efforts allowed two further steps in framing a new orthodoxy. First, the Chinese leadership gained much leeway in the interpretation of Mao Zedong Thought. Since not everything Mao said or wrote was necessarily part of the official ideology, it became possible for Deng to claim that some of Mao's views were inconsistent with the general idea of Mao so that Deng could renounce many of Mao's ideas related to the Cultural Revolution. Second, such revision provided great flexibility for Chinese leaders to add new ideas to the guiding ideology. The orthodoxy could continue to adapt and grow. In this way, it became easier for Deng to provide ideological explanations for new policies and practices, to give responses to new conditions and experiences, without being restrained by former ideological precepts.[32]

Together with the ideological reform, Deng's leadership developed the theory of Primary Stage of Socialism in China. The 12th Party Congress in September 1982 announced that China was still in the primary stage of socialism—both of its material civilization and spiritual civilization were underdeveloped. Deng Xiaoping, at his opening speech for the Congress, used for the first time the expression of "constructing socialism with Chinese characteristics." By emphasizing Chinese characteristics, he meant that Chinese modernization should start from its practical situation; a complete copy of other country's experience would not be successful.[33] Following the deepening of reform, the CPC further elaborated the concept of primary stage. On the 3rd Plenary Session of the 12th Party Central Committee held in 1984, the *Communiqué* of the CPC stated, "commodity economy development is an insurmountable stage as well as an indispensable condition to realize our economic modernization."[34] Two years later, on the 6th Plenary Session of the 12th Party Central Committee, Deng Xiaoping stated, "Our implementation of reform and open policy need to take in some useful elements from the capitalist system as a supplement to the development of our social productivity."[35]

The idea of primary stage was essentially developed in the report of the 13th Party Congress in 1987. As a concept, the primary stage of socialism in China is the stage to gradually get rid of poverty and backwardness; to transform from an agricultural state to an industrial state; to develop from natural economy and half natural economy to highly developed commodity economy; to establish and develop socialist economic, political, and cultural system; and to revitalize the Chinese nation.[36] The 13th Party Congress also pointed out, "It is impossible for us to return to the closed state of the past, which forbade the people to come into contact with different kinds of thoughts. Nor is it possible to avoid that the people come up with different sorts of ideas in the course of construction and reform."[37]

As the general designer of the reform, Deng was spoken of highly by the Chinese public. The Chinese media praised that he made the most significant theoretical breakthrough in the post-Mao era. According to *Beijing Review*, Deng managed to "answer the fundamental question of how to build a modern socialist country in China, the biggest developing nation in the world. This was the problem to which Mao, the leading founder of the People's Republic, failed to find an answer."[38] Thanks to his efforts in the ideological development, Deng Xiaoping's Theory to construct socialism with Chinese characteristics was added to Marxism-Leninism-Mao Zedong Thought at the 15th Party Congress in 1997.

Readjustments in Foreign Policy

The revision of ideology, particularly the common understanding reached among the Chinese leaders that China is at the primary stage of socialism required the leaders to focus on economic modernization. Economic development since then has been given priority in Beijing's work agenda. The policy of reform and opening up was carried out to stimulate national development. This policy brought more flexibility to the making of Chinese foreign policy. The emphasis on the political and ideological issues in the diplomatic field was replaced by the emphasis on the development of mutually beneficial economic relations. Deng discarded Mao's fanatical revolutionary model in China's external affairs. He clarified that "some believed that ideology in China was exploited as an instrument to overturn the Western governments such as the United States. This was not the perception of Chinese government either in the 1980s or in the 1970s, but rather in the years before."[39] Ideology was no longer the decisive element in considering the establishment of diplomatic ties with the other countries. Instead, economic diplomacy gradually became the primary concern.

Deng Xiaoping introduced new guiding principles in handling inter-party relations. He pointed out that there should be no interference and involvement in the affairs of the other parties in the other countries. "Since the success of Chinese revolution relied on the combination of the general principle of Marxism with our actual conditions in China, we should not require other developing countries to follow the Chinese model in their revolutions." He continued further, "We should respect other parties and peoples in the search and solution of their own issues. We resolutely object others to give orders to us, we should neither give orders to others. This is an important principle."[40] Hu Yaobang, the General Secretary of the CPC in the early 1980s, further developed Deng's idea and explicitly addressed four principles in his work report at the 12th Party Congress in 1982: the CPC should develop its relations with the communist parties or other working-class parties in strict conformity with "the principles of independence, completely equality, mutual respect and non-interference in each other's internal affairs."[41]

The four guiding principles uttered by Hu Yaobang were conducive to renovate the CPC's old ties and to establish the new ones with different parties of other countries. First, the CPC envisaged a new-style inter-party relationship wherein compatibility or homogeneity of ideology ensures no more than mutual political and moral support. Second, it acknowledged that inter-party relations should not in any way prejudice inter-state relations. The two relations should be strictly and carefully separated. Third, the CPC reiterated that revolution could not and should not be exported. The mutual support between the Communist and other "fraternal" parties should be strictly "political and moral." Fourth, in line with this principle, the CPC would never impose its will or policy upon the others. Nor would it let the others force their views and opinions on the CPC.[42]

With the help of the four principles, the CPC gradually disentangled itself from the old type of inter-party relations and in the mean time, made its efforts to develop interstate relations. Putting ideological differences aside, and based on the Five Principles of Peaceful Coexistence,[43] Premier Zhao Ziyang declared in his work report on the 7th Five-Year Plan in 1986, "China strives to establish, resume or expand normal relations with all the countries in the world, coexist in harmony, and engage in friendly cooperation with them. China does not determine its closeness with or estrangement from other countries on the basis of their social systems and ideologies.... China is opening to the world, both to the capitalist countries and the socialist countries."[44] Beijing's efforts were rewarded. Over two hundred parties and political groups had established or resumed formal relations with the CPC by the end of 1987, and these relations were strictly restricted to moral and ideological affairs.[45]

In 1977, considering the changes both internally and externally, the Chinese leadership concluded that capitalism and socialism had ceased to be useful analytical categories. The main contradiction was proclaimed to lie in between the two superpowers of the "First World" and all the "Second World" and "Third World" countries.[46] From the 1980s, as a consequence of diluting ideology in Chinese foreign policy and the improved relationship with the developed capitalist countries, the terms of both the "First World" and the "Second World" were dropped by the Chinese leaders. Only the expression of the "Third World" was kept in order to demonstrate China's standpoint in international politics. In words of Samuel Kim, the demise of the Three Worlds Theory indicated the shift of China from a system transforming to a system maintaining approach. The Three Worlds Theory, as a theory of struggle, became obviously incompatible with China's growing enmeshment in the capitalist world system.[47]

Disavowal of Mao's inevitability of war, Deng Xiaoping believed that war would not break out soon. Based on the Five Principles of Peaceful Coexistence, Beijing normalized its diplomatic relations with Washington and eased tensions with Moscow. The improvement in external security environment encouraged the Chinese leaders to revise their outlook on war. The world war was perceived to be possibly avoided and peace would likely be preserved in the coming decade. As Deng said in a talk with several leaders in the central government in 1983, "There is no possibility of great war. Don't be afraid of it, there is no risk of it. We used to worry about war and talk of its possibility every year. It seems that the worry was overdone. In my opinion, war will not break out in at least a decade."[48] Putting the danger of war aside was one of the most important contributions Deng Xiaoping made to China's military thinking. It facilitated an important change in grand strategy from Mao's era to Deng's era. Thanks to his analysis, the Chinese government turned its focus from the preparation for the forthcoming war to economic reform and modernization.

Compared to the foreign policy in Mao's era, there were both changes and continuities in Deng's era. Starting from Mao's anti-hegemonism, Deng made an important adjustment by adding another line to it: maintain world peace. Rather than advocating world revolution, Deng engaged in maintaining a peaceful environment. Thus "oppose hegemonism and maintain world peace" became a guiding principle in the foreign policy of Deng's era.

Serving as the basic line of Chinese foreign policy, the Five Principles of Peaceful Coexistence changed China's diplomatic behavior. China became more interested in what the UN system could do for its modernization.[49] Compared with the highly selective and symbolic participation throughout the 1970s in the UN, China showed more willingness to be engaged in this multilateral organization in the 1980s. For example, China participated in the Conference on Disarmament (CD) in 1982, the Human Rights Commission in 1982, and the International Court of Justice in 1984. China also readjusted its attitude toward the UN peacekeeping activities. Chinese ambassador Ling Qing stated in the General Assembly in late November 1981 that the Chinese government had decided to adopt a flexible attitude toward the UN peacekeeping, and starting January 1, 1982, China paid its share of the assessed expenses for the UN peacekeeping operations.[50] In 1986, the government work report defined for the first time that multilateral diplomacy was an integral part of China's foreign policy of independence.[51]

From the early 1980s on, China diverted its attention from a symbolic champion of the Third World cause to the cultivation of a triangular relationship with the United States and the Soviet Union. China refused to join the two leading Third World caucuses—the 129-member Group of Seventy-Seven (G-77) in global developmental politics and the 108-member Non-aligned Movement (NAM) in global geopolitics.[52] Although far less in power and capability in comparison to either the Soviet Union or the United States, China enjoyed its position that "when added to whichever superpower, would decide the outcome of an overall global confrontation between Washington and Moscow."[53] This pivotal role gave China much leverage in its relationship vis-à-vis the two superpowers. In words of a leading Chinese expert on foreign affairs, "Contemporary world politics is largely determined by the dynamics of the 'triangle' between the United States, China, and the Soviet Union."[54] Compared with the first two decades of the foundation of the PRC, the international environment was gradually developed in the direction favorable to China by the end of the 1980s. Rather than being obliged to react to the challenges and pressure from the outside world, China was able to take initiatives to develop its relations with the superpowers, and to exploit the opportunities brought by the competition of the two to make its voice heard in their strategic rivalry.

Free from ideological constraint and guided by pragmatism, China diassociated diplomatic relations from the considerations of political systems or ideologies. The revolutionary, transformative rhetoric was shelved in favor of a language of accommodation to the prevailing world system. Beijing reversed from hostility toward the existing international political system to an increasing accommodation to international rules and norms, and normalized its diplomatic ties with a large number of countries. It was in China's interest to lessen pressure on China's defense demand, to promote a peaceful and cooperative international environment, and to increase participations in the world economy.

Table 1.2 The Role of Ideology in Chinese Foreign Policy in Deng's Era

Content of ideology	Marxism-Leninism-Mao Zedong Thought-Deng Xiaoping Theory
Nature of ideology	Pragmatic, seeking truth from facts
Role of ideology in making foreign policy	Less important
Principles of foreign policy	Anti-hegemonism; maintaining world peace
Nature of foreign policy	Less confrontational, more accommodative
Focus in foreign policy	From Third World countries to triangle relations with the Soviet Union and the United States
Approach in external relations	Mainly bilateral, importance was given to state-to-state relations

JIANG'S ERA

Deng Xiaoping's reformulation of the official ideology paved the way for the reform and opening to the outside, liberated people's minds, but weakened the importance of socialist ideology in China. After the Tiananmen incident in 1989, the Chinese leaders attempted to address the accumulated ideological problems of the past decade. Their endeavor to update ideology was demonstrated in the following aspects. First, the economic reform policy was confirmed. Further steps were taken to develop from a planned economy to a market economy by increasing the percentage of private ownership in national economy and significantly improving people's living standards. The government attempted to gain wide support from its people with noticeable economic achievements. Second, patriotism was re-emphasized among the people within China. Patriotic education was strengthened in all kinds of forms from rewriting school textbooks to the propaganda in journal articles and movies. Third, Mao's condemnation of traditional Chinese culture was replaced by the post-Tiananmen leadership's revived interest to it. The leadership attempted to take traditional Chinese culture as the integrating and cohesive force, which could unite the people around the CPC. The relaxation of Marxist ideology and the regression to traditional Chinese culture mark the endeavor of the leadership in the search of a systemic body of ideas to facilitate the central position of the CPC in China. By claiming itself as "the guardian of national pride,"[55] the CPC intended to find a new basis of legitimacy. Meanwhile, the searching process facilitated China's accommodation to the international society, making the interaction with the outside world a motivation to further converge China into the prevailing international system. The evolution of ideological content introduced salient changes in Chinese foreign policy. Thanks to the deepened reforms and increasing emphasis of pragmatism, Chinese foreign policy indicated a greater degree of openness and flexibility. The diplomatic task is to create a long-term stable, friendly and peaceful international environment for China to realize its domestic goals.

Further Ideological Reformulation

When Jiang Zemin was chosen to be the General Secretary of the CPC in 1989, the political climate in China had changed tremendously. The so-called "socialism with Chinese characteristics" seemed only to rationalize the existence of capitalist elements under the socialist umbrella. The introduction of the concept of "primary stage of socialism" and the promotion of capitalist elements in Chinese economy accelerated the erosion of the Marxist-Leninist-Mao Zedong Thought. Deng Xiaoping's original intention was to eradicate all the ideological and psychological obstacles to economic reform, but it resulted in the demise of Marxist ideology. The decay of ideology threatened to undermine the central role of the CPC, producing not simply a crisis of faith but also a crisis of power.[56] At an internal party meeting in early 1987, Zhao Ziyang was said to put forward the proposition that socialism should be abandoned on the grounds that nobody knew any longer what socialism or the socialist road really meant.[57] The crisis in belief partly attributed to the large-scale Tiananmen demonstrations in 1989.

In order to further justify the reform policy, Jiang Zemin systematically summed up the theory of socialism with Chinese characteristics in his report at the 14th Party Congress in 1992: "While following the socialist road, we emphasize that we choose our own way. We can neither take the textbooks as a dogma, nor copy foreign models. Instead, we should take Marxism as guidance, and practice is the only criterion to test the truth. We should liberate our mind, seek truth from facts, respect the creative spirit of the people, and build socialism with Chinese characteristics."[58] The definition of socialism with Chinese characteristics legitimized the reform policy and offered greater flexibility to Chinese leaders in their decision-making. It also explained why socialism could survive in China while it failed in Eastern Europe and the Soviet Union.

In order to maintain the coherence of ideology, Jiang Zemin spoke highly of Deng's contribution to the ideological development and said that "Deng Xiaoping's Theory is the combination of Marxism with current Chinese practice. It has inherited and developed from Mao Zedong Thought in the new historical situation. . . The reform of nearly twenty years has proved that we do not abandon socialism, on the contrary, we are steadily building socialism to revitalize China."[59] By emphasizing the continuity of Deng's socialist theory from Mao Zedong Thought, Jiang Zemin attempted to get rid of the suspicion and anxiety inside the leadership on the nature of the reform. He added further, "It is significant to improve the ownership structure in which the public ownership as the principle part develops together with many other forms of ownership."[60] Jiang Zemin's speech paved the way for the rise of non-public ownership in national economy, and turned on the green light for the non-public economy to become an indispensable component in the socialist market economy.

While literally adhering to socialism, Jiang's leadership could not turn a blind eye to the changing reality within China. Wang Yu, Chinese economist and chairman of Chinese Market Economy Association, anticipated, "As Chinese socialism is to make people get rich together, proletarians will be replaced by a property class in Chinese society in the coming decades when market economy becomes mature."[61] To adapt to social changes, Jiang Zemin revised the nature of the CPC and put forward "Three Represents" in February 2000. The CPC, understood for eight decades as "the vanguard of the Chinese working class, the faithful representative of the interests of the Chinese people of all the ethnic groups, and the core of leadership over the socialist cause of China" has now become "the faithful representative of the requirement to develop advanced productive forces, an orientation towards advanced culture, and the fundamental interests of the overwhelming majority of the people in China."[62] Jiang's "Three Represents" eliminated words such as "class" or "socialism," and purportedly diluted the color of ideology. Jiang went further to revise the principles for accepting the CPC members. Jiang Zemin's speech on

July 1, 2001 symbolized a dramatic change in the CPC's history. The middle class people, who used to be the targets of class struggle in Mao's era, have since then been permitted to join the CPC.

The modification of the representative nature of the CPC and the revision of the CPC's admission principle reflected the changing situation within China as a result of over twenty years' reform. While Mao Zedong stuck to his proletarian revolutionary line and emphasized the important role of workers and peasants in socialist struggle against capitalism, the post-Mao leaders believed that the weakness of China came from its backward economy. The focus on economic interest stimulated the leaders to drop the class differences and to stress the interest of the people as a whole. The working class and the peasantry, which formed the basic parts of the CPC in the revolutionary period, have been replaced by those people who have got rich in the reform. As the CPC's reform comes in line with the interest of the middle class people, the admission of these people would help further promote the reform, which would in turn legitimize the leading role of the CPC.

While blurring the class differences in Chinese society, the CPC attaches an increasing importance to Chinese nationalism. The general loss of confidence in communism, caused by the internal capitalist-oriented reform and the global collapse of communism, forced the CPC to rely on nationalism to fill the ideological vacuum.[63] Nationalism appeared as a spontaneous public reaction inside China to foreign pressures in the post-Cold War era. The wounded national pride and the resentment to foreign interference motivated the rise of nationalistic discourse in China in the 1990s. In face of the sanctions against China by Western countries after the Tiananmen incident, the Chinese government mobilized its propaganda machinery to recall China's humiliated past by the Western countries. At the 150th anniversary of the Opium War in 1990, Jiang Zemin stressed that "the Opium War was the beginning of China's humiliation forced by the Western countries and even today the hostile forces in the Western countries continued to attempt to subvert socialist China through 'peaceful evolution'."[64] The official media broadcast extensively the scenes of chaos in Eastern European countries in order to demonstrate to the Chinese that the Western so-called human rights and democracy would bring disunity and disorder, which would result in new humiliation to the country. In this way, the government attempted to convince the people that a strong central government was vital for the stability of the country.

In the rising tide of nationalism, the CPC positioned itself as the representative of the Chinese nation. The failure in the bid to host the year 2000 summer Olympic Games in Beijing provoked popular Chinese resentment directed at foreign countries, particularly at the United States.[65] The CPC channeled nationalism into patriotism. Propagandized by *People's Daily*, "Patriotism requires us (the Chinese) to love the socialist system and road chosen by all the nationalities in China under the leadership of the Communist Party."[66] In the promotion of patriotism, the CPC deliberately blurred the lines between nationalism, socialism, and communism. As Jiang Zemin said, "In China today, patriotism and socialism are unified in essence."[67] Patriotism replaced communism as "the common spiritual pillar" of the Chinese people and "the powerful spiritual force that supports the Chinese people."[68]

To build patriotism among the Chinese people, the CPC sought help from traditional Chinese culture. With the declining influence of Marxism-Leninism-Mao Zedong Thought in Chinese society, traditional Chinese culture seemed to be the ideal substitute to act as a foundation of solidarity among the people and to serve the purpose of social stability. As a Chinese leader said, "China's national culture is long-standing, well-established, rich, profound and influential…. Our ancestors have bequeathed us extremely rich and extremely precious cultural legacy, which we should cherish, protect and explore."[69] Confucianism, as the main body of traditional Chinese culture, has been regarded as the foundation of the new nationalism since the 1990s.[70] China's Ministry of Posts and Telecommunications issued a set of stamps to memorize Confucius at his 2,540[th] anniversary in 1989. This gave the leadership a chance to demonstrate to the public that it is proud of the glorious Chinese tradition. The respect to traditional culture was revealed further in 1991 when the State Education Commission issued a nationwide program aimed at promoting modern and contemporary history.[71] The program offered a detailed list of requirements regarding the teaching of national culture and history. The Chinese leadership sought to encourage the development of patriotism based on Confucianism to meet the requirement of the changing socioeconomic environment, to better represent the interest of the people in the reform era, and to keep the Party's leading position unchallenged.

Further Developments in Foreign Policy

The major contribution of Jiang Zemin to the ideological refashioning was the articulation of Three Represents. Three Represents were developed to recognize the social changes in China and to forge a common understanding of developments among the Chinese. The addition of Three Represents to Chinese ideology officially transformed the nature of the CPC from the advocator of the international communist cause to the representative of national interest. National interest served as the core of foreign policy making. Motivated by national interest, Chinese foreign policy was developed in a down-to-earth style. Chinese foreign policy in Jiang's era, readjusted to be more pragmatic and flexible, focused on two themes: peace and development. "Peace" refers to the international environment and "development" refers to the domestic modernization. Domestic modernization as the central task of the Chinese government is essential to build China into a rich and powerful country. Centered on domestic modernization, China made diplomatic efforts to maintain a peaceful and favorable environment. China was successful in breaking the international isolation after the Tiananmen Incident, in developing its membership in most of the international governmental organizations, in accomplishing the strategy of great power relations and the formation of great power identity, and in strengthening neighborhood relations.

At the end of the 1980s, the Chinese leadership was not well prepared for the dramatic changes in the international political system. Beijing anticipated that the struggle between the international hostile forces and the socialist countries would still exist for a long time.[72] The fact that the socialist countries in Eastern Europe almost disappeared overnight shocked the Chinese leadership. To make things worse, China lost its bargaining chips with the United States as a consequence of the collapse of the Soviet Union. The end of the U.S.-Soviet superpower rivalry meant that Washington did not need Beijing to counterbalance Moscow any more. China "ceased to be an independent factor in the management of the strategic relations between the Soviet Union and the United States."[73] Against the will of the Chinese, the American-led coalition achieved an overwhelming victory in 1990-01 Gulf War. A unipolar world dominated by the American hegemony emerged in the post-Cold War period.

While the strategic changes in the world were unfavorable to China, the end of bipolarity also provided China a previously unimaginable possibility for development. East-West relations improved radically, Moscow and Washington overcame their mutual animosity.[74] The disappearance of the hostility between the two camps, the relaxation of ideological differences, the enhanced commercial and business relationship, enabled China to enjoy the best external environment and to concentrate on economic growth.[75] China's increased cooperation and exchanges with other countries not only improved its security environment, but also strengthened its foreign trade relations with others, and introduced a growing amount of foreign investment and advanced technology to China.

With the increased experience in the international society, China gradually realized the importance of setting up a positive image in its relations with the outside world. The general pattern and direction of China's international behavior has been a slow but steady movement from conflict to cooperation. China has accepted the basic international norms and governing procedures in the multilateral arena.[76] China has gradually honored its international commitments by joining a number of international regimes. To name a few of them, China joined the Non-Proliferation Treaty (NPT) in 1992. It signed in 1993 and ratified in 1997 the Chemical Weapons Convention (CWC). It signed the Comprehensive Test Ban Treaty (CTBT) in September 1996. It joined the Zangger Committee in 1997, which requires that its members allow nuclear exports that are safeguarded by the IAEA. It signed in 1997 the International Covenant on Economic, Social and Cultural Rights (ratified in 2002), and in 1998 the International Covenant on Civil and Political Rights. Most noticeably, China joined the World Trade Organization (WTO) in 2001 after fifteen years of negotiation. The accession to the WTO marked China's further step to integrate itself in the international regime. The growing confidence of the Chinese leadership in the international politics encouraged more cooperative behavior from China, making the country more willing to accommodate and more eager to be a responsible power.

In order to create a stable and peaceful international environment for China to concentrate on its economic modernization, the Chinese leadership endeavored to develop big power relations. Although it disliked the hegemonic behavior of the United States, Beijing successfully improved its relations with Washington in the 1990s and a constructive partnership was established between the two sides at Jiang's visit to the United States in 1997. In the mean time, in order to promote the formation of a multipolar structure in world political system, Beijing was actively forging all kinds of partnership with all the other influential powers including Russia, Japan, and the European Union and its member states. The fostered partnerships had a positive impact on the maintenance of world peace and the development of mutually beneficial economic relations between China and these countries.

While downplaying the importance of the Third World countries in general, China attached great importance to its relationship with the neighbors. The development of a good neighborly relationship was one of the key tasks in the diplomatic field. After establishing the diplomatic relations with South Korea in September 1992, China supported a dialogue between the two Koreas and attempted to help reduce tension in the Korean Peninsula. China used behind-the-scenes pressure to restrain the North Korean regime from confrontation with the West.[77] In Southeast Asia, the end of the civil war in Cambodia and the normalization of relations with Vietnam was another achievement in China's foreign affairs. Since the late 1980s, China had used its status as a permanent member of the UN Security Council to push for peaceful negotiations among the four parties[78] in the Cambodian civil war.[79] The Sino-Vietnamese peace agreement was signed in Paris in 1991. Indonesia re-established its diplomatic relations with Beijing in 1990. Singapore established the official ties with Beijing in the same year and Brunei followed suit in 1991. By then, Beijing has developed formal diplomatic relations with all of the members of ASEAN.

China started its relationship with ASEAN in 1991 when Chinese Foreign Minister Qian Qichen expressed China's interest in strengthening cooperation with this regional organization. Through several years' negotiations and joint efforts, China was accorded full dialogue partner status of ASEAN at the 29th ASEAN Ministerial Meeting in Indonesia in 1996. In South Asia, while consolidating good relations with Pakistan, China also made progress in its relations with India. The Sino-Indian relations improved after the disintegration of the Soviet Union. Both sides reaffirmed the Five Principles of Peaceful Coexistence which had been put forward by the leaders of the two countries in the 1950s, and agreed to establish a constructive cooperation relationship. Since its founding, the regional organization "Shanghai Five" including China, Russia, and the three Central Asian States Kazakhstan, Kyrgyzstan, and Tajikistan, has played an important role in battling the terrorist threats emanating from Afghanistan and ensuring regional stability. In June 2001, "Shanghai Five" grew to be six by inviting Uzbekistan to join the group, and officially adopted a name as Shanghai Cooperation Organization (SCO).

Chinese foreign policy in Jiang's era brought great changes to the country's relations with the outside world. Compared with the 1950s when Beijing had very limited ties with the outside world, the beginning of the 21st century saw that it had successfully established a wide contact with the largest number of countries and the international institutions ever possible in its history. Its international influence has been much expanded, and its image as a great and responsible power is rising. China's interaction with the outside world has gradually transformed the country in many aspects.

Table 1.3 The Role of Ideology in Chinese Foreign Policy in Jiang's Era

Content of ideology	Marxism-Leninism-Mao Zedong Thought-Deng Xiaoping Theory-Jiang Zemin's Three Represents; patriotism based on national culture
Nature of ideology	Pragmatic
Role of ideology in making foreign policy	Unimportant
Principles of foreign policy	Maintaining peaceful environment
Nature of foreign policy	cooperative status-quo, flexible and pragmatic
Focus in foreign policy	Big power relations and neighborhood relations
Approach in external relations	Both bilateral and multilateral

HU'S ERA

When Hu Jintao became the General Secretary of the CPC in 2002, the achievements brought by the reform and opening policy had largely increased China's state power and international status. However, problems appeared in the process of reform including corruption, social unrest, income gap between the rich and the poor, development differences between the eastern and the western parts of China. Facing the new situation, Hu on the one hand, continuously deepens the reform and market economy, and on the other hand, attempts to address the problems so as to facilitate a sustainable development. In the ideological field, to confront the contradictions between Marxism and market reform, reeducation campaigns have been prompted to revive Marxist ideology in China, to improve the party image and authority, and to strengthen the CPC's leading position.

Keeping a favorable external environment for China in order to concentrate on its domestic development continues to top the work agenda of Hu's leadership. Foreign policy has been made to guarantee an international environment amicable to its national development. Moreover, from the 1990s on, China's booming economy has made it increasingly dependent on imported oil and raw materials. China has strengthened its ties with African and Latin American countries due to its search for strategic resources. Noticeably, Hu's government become more pragmatic and strives to develop an all-round cooperative relationship with all the possible countries and international organizations in the world.

Ideological Redirection

For Hu Jintao, building a common ideological aspiration is crucial for the social and economic development in China. In less than two years' time, Hu paid two visits to Yanan, the cradle of Chinese revolution. His gesture sent a clear signal to the Party members that the CPC in the background of reform and opening up should keep a humble attitude and a hardworking spirit of Yanan, to resist the temptation of excessive material enjoyment. At the 4th Plenary Session of the 16th Central Party Committee convened in September 2004, "Resolution on Strengthening the Construction of the Party's Governance Ability" was passed by the Central Committee. According to the resolution, the Party must make efforts to build its ruling capacity in order to meet the demands of the changing situation. The resolution summed up the fifty-five years of the CPC's ruling experience and emphasized that "the Party must adhere to Marxism and Leninism, Mao Zedong Thought, Deng Xiaoping Theory and the important thought of 'Three Represents' as its guiding ideology, while keeping on exploring the new horizon for the development of Marxist theories in its new practice." Furthermore, it clarified that "Only socialism can save China, and only with socialism with Chinese characteristics can we develop China." Therefore, the Party "must continuously promote the self-improvement of socialism to add vigor and vitality to socialism."[80] Hu pointed out at the 5th Plenary Session of the 16th Central Party Committee that "Marxism still suits China," but in the mean time called for new ways of looking at Marxist doctrine to bring it into line with China's changing reality.[81]

In order to tackle the chasm between official discourse of socialism with Chinese characteristics and the growing reality of often "unbridled capitalism,"[82] and to make the Party's ideological and theoretical work more creative, convincing and influential, the CPC planned to strengthen the research of Marxist theory by allocating one hundred to two hundred million yuan to produce new translations of Marxist literature and to update texts for high school and university students. More than three thousand theoreticians and scholars all over China would participate in the work to compile one hundred to one hundred and fifty books on the study of Marxist doctrines.[83]

Also included in the campaign of reeducation, the Party members are required by Hu Jintao to keep the advanced nature of the CPC in the new era. As indicated in his speech at the 82nd anniversary of the CPC in 2003, Hu stressed the theme of "building a Party that serves the interests of the public and governs for the people." Developed from this theme, he called on the Party members "to work in accordance with the trend of the times and in the interests of the people to play a leading role in pushing social development."[84]

Together with the educational campaign, Hu proposes a scientific way of development, gives emphasis on solving social tensions caused by a growing rich-poor gap and corruption, and advocates the construction of a harmonious society in China. Featuring democracy, the rule of law, equity, justice, sincerity, amity and vitality, the new task stresses the basic concepts of "people first" and "government for the people." As a further development of Jiang's "Three

Represents," Hu attaches an increasing importance to the interest of the people, not only people who have got rich, but also people who have been left behind in the reform process. By paying attention to people's needs and serving the people, the CPC intends to rebuild its credit in Chinese society.

In the CPC's search of a new ideological base that would rally the support of the people, the mix of communism and Confucianism is taken as a remedy for social conflict and sustainable development. The "people first" approach seems to be closely related to traditional Chinese culture, which stresses the important role people play in maintaining the stability of the country. As a matter of fact, the idea of "people first" was an essential part of Mencius' thoughts. Mencius, an important representative of Confucianism, pointed out that "the people are the most important to a state, whereas the ruler is the least important (*mingui junqing*)." The construction of a harmonious society also seems to get some inspiration from the Confucian values. The features marking the harmonious society are surprisingly comparable to the basic virtues promoted by Confucianism such as humanity (*ren*), justice (*yi*), ethics (*li*), resourcefulness (*zhi*), and sincerity (*xin*). The state of harmony was advocated by Confucianism more than two thousand years ago in order to create a peaceful and harmonious society.

The importance attached to traditional Chinese culture is also demonstrated by the high-profile International Confucius Cultural Festival held annually in Qufu, the hometown of Confucius. Dated back from 1989, the festival has got an increased degree of exposure in recent years due to the resurrection of Confucianism. In 2004, China held a public memorial service to mark the 2555th birth anniversary of Confucius, which was the first official public memorial service ever since the founding of the PRC in 1949.

While trying to blend communism and Confucianism in the search of an ideological framework, Hu's leadership emphasizes that patriotism is the core of national spirit which "encourage(s) our people of generations to come to make concerted efforts for a prosperous and strong China."[85] The education of patriotism has been specified in the form of the "Eight Glories and Eight Shames" proposed by Hu Jintao in March 2006. Among the eight aphorisms, the first is to urge the people to "love the motherland, do not harm it."[86] Composed of both traditional Chinese values and modern virtues, the eight rules have been promoted by Hu to serve as the code of social conduct and moral standards.

Compared to the former Chinese leaders, Hu faces a more demanding task in deconstructing and rebuilding the components of Chinese ideology. Both Deng and Jiang disentangled themselves from the restraint of communist ideology. However, the introduction of capitalist idea and the reemphasis of traditional Chinese culture in the ideological field, to a large degree, shook the foundation of the original revolutionary ideology and posed a serious challenge to the construction of faith in Chinese society. Hu's proposal of scientific way of development with the "people first" approach is aimed at strengthening the leading role of the CPC and unifying people's mind. Whether the efforts made by the current leadership are effective or not will need to be seen, but what seems to be clear so far is that pragmatism has been used by the Chinese leaders as a criterion for both domestic and international activities.

More Sophisticated and More Adept in Foreign Policy

In order to ease the anxiety of other countries at the rise of China, Beijing searched for a new initiative in its foreign policy which stresses China's peaceful rise. From the end of 2003 to the early months of 2004, this newly developed idea had been gradually in shape. The term "peaceful rise" was first proposed by Zheng Bijian, Vice President of the Central Party School at the Boao Forum for Asia in 2003. Since then, the Chinese leaders expressed in many occasions that China will take the road of a peaceful rise. This idea demonstrates Beijing's avowed efforts to develop good neighborhood relations, to take global responsibility, and to ease the anxiety of other countries. Distinct from the former rising powers in history, the Chinese government intends to convince the world that China's rise is to "build an all-round well-off society" internally and to "maintain world peace and promote common development" externally.[87]

The most notable feature of the "peaceful rise" strategy is peace and development.[88] Nevertheless, after half a year of promoting this new strategy in Chinese foreign policy, the Chinese leaders were afraid that the revisionist interpretation of the word "rise" would give a wrong impression to the other countries. From the latter half of 2004, the term "peaceful rise" gradually descended in official documents. Instead, "peaceful development" was adopted as the official term of China's new strategy. In his speech published in *China Daily*, Chinese Foreign Minister Li Zhaoxing pointed out: "China's development cannot materialize without the world. And a stable and prosperous world also needs China. So long as we hold high the banner of peace, development and co-operation, and hold on to the path of peaceful development, we will surely make new contributions to world peace and development."[89] The efforts paid by Beijing to the choice of the terms in the new strategy indicate that China cares about the reaction of the international society. As a rising power focused on national development, China is willing to demonstrate to the world its interest in maintaining world peace and stability.

Inspired by its glorious past and its pursuit of an influential status in world politics, China is in favor of a multipolar structure in the international politics in the post-Cold War era. The Chinese policy of multipolarity can be traced back to Deng Xiaoping, who in one of his speeches claimed, "Nowadays the old structure is in the process of transformation, and the new structure is not yet formed.... No matter how many poles there will be in the world, three poles, four poles, or even five poles.... for the so-called multipolarity, China should be counted as one of the poles."[90] Although by no means hiding its craving for multipolarity, China has quietly revised its understanding of multipolarity in recent years. Before 2003, Chinese Foreign Ministry held that multipolarity "helps weaken and curb hegemonism and power politics, serves to bring about a just and equitable order and contributes to world peace and development."[91]

Without mentioning the name of the United States, China made it clear that such policy of mulipolarity was to counterbalance against it: "At present, by virtue of its economic, technological and military advantages, an individual country is pursuing a new 'gunboat policy' in contravention of the United Nations Charter and the universally-acknowledged principles governing international relations in an attempt to establish a unipolar world under its guidance."[92]

The interactions with the outside world exert a noticeable impact on China's diplomatic behavior. Beijing is gradually changing from exclusively focusing on the bilateral approach to an increasing reliance on the multilateral approach, from suspicion of multilateralism to be at ease with it. Such a change has also affected its interpretation of multipolarity. Starting from 2003, a new understanding of multipolarity has come into existence: "Our efforts to promote the development of the world towards multipolarization are not targeted at any particular country, nor are they aimed at re-staging the old play of contention for hegemony in history. Rather, these efforts are made to boost the democratization of international relations, help the various forces in the world, on the basis of equality and mutual benefit, enhance coordination and dialogue, refrain from confrontation and preserve jointly world peace, stability and development."[93] While multipolarity is still in use by the Chinese leadership, its implication has been quietly changing. In the new interpretation, the Chinese highlighted the elements of multilateralism such as democratization of international relations, and the strengthening of coordination and dialogue.

On the international affairs, Hu's leadership becomes more pragmatic in handling the North Korean nuclear crisis, the Taiwan Strait relations, the relations with the big powers, and neighborhood relations. China has become more active since 2002 in mediating between the parties involved in the Korean nuclear crisis, and played a crucial role in pushing the crisis towards a peaceful solution. The joint declaration in September 2005 by the U.S. and North Korea would have been impossible without the earnest mediation of the Chinese. In order to clarify its standpoint at the Taiwan issue, Beijing passed the anti-secession law in March 2005. In the following months, the leaders of both the Nationalist Party and the People's First Party received invitations from Hu to visit mainland China. As the first invitation given to the Taiwanese politicians ever since 1949, Hu's gesture has a far-reaching influence on the future Taiwan Strait relations. It not only shows his political wisdom and flexibility but also indicates to the international society his sincerity for peace.

Between China and its neighbors, deepened political trust and high level of cooperation were strengthened by China's accession to the Treaty of Amity and Cooperation in Southeast Asia (TAC) and the Joint Declaration on the China-ASEAN Strategic Partnership for Peace and Prosperity in 2003. These treaties and agreements serve as a crucial guidance for a comprehensive and sustained development of China-ASEAN relations in the future. The Tripartite Agreement for the Joint Marine Seismic Undertaking in the Agreement Area in the South China Sea reached by the oil companies of China, Vietnam, and the Philippines in Manila in March 2005 was hailed by the Philippines President Arroyo as "the breakthrough in implementing the provisions of the code of conduct in the South

China Sea among ASEAN and China" to turn it "into an area of cooperation rather than an area of conflict."[94] For a decade, China has been following the policy of "putting aside the dispute for common development" concerning the territorial disputes in the South China Sea. The progress in this area offers hope for the concerned countries to find a feasible solution for the territorial disputes in the coming years.

While the relationship with the other big powers is maintained positively, China has noticeably strengthened its political and economic ties with Africa and Latin America countries. Economic cooperation serves as the basis of the warming of the political relationship between China and these countries. The China-African trade volume increased from US$12 million in 1956 to US$39.7 billion in 2005. By far, China has US$1.18 billion of direct investment in Africa. In only six months' time in 2006, Chinese Foreign Minister Li Zhaoxing, Chinese President Hu Jintao and Chinese Premier Wen Jiabao visited Africa respectively. Furthermore, after the first policy paper the PRC had ever issued in its diplomatic history in 2003 on EU-China relations, Beijing published its second policy paper in 2006 which is on China-Africa relations. The Beijing Summit of the Forum on China-Africa Cooperation (FOCAC) was held in Beijing from Nov. 3-5, 2006 to boost the further development of diplomatic ties and the establishment of new China-Africa strategic partnership. More than 30 African heads of state or government attended the summit, which was the largest-scale meeting between China and African leaders since the founding of People's Republic of China. The unprecedented attention given to the African countries demonstrates the rising importance of Africa in Chinese external relations.

Different from most of the African countries which established their diplomatic ties with Beijing in the 1950s and 1960s, most of the Latin American countries only forged the official relations with Beijing since the 1970s. Nevertheless, these countries have already caught up the Africans in the cooperation with the Chinese. In 2004, the Sino-Latin American trade volume reached US$40 billion. China's total investment in Latin America has surpassed US$4 billion. In the background of economic globalization, the mutually beneficial economic relationship becomes the stimulus to promote bilateral cooperation and development. From 2004 to 2006, eight out of nine members of China Standing Committee of the Politburo visited Latin American countries, and many heads of state of these countries also paid their visits to China. The unhistorical frequent exchanges of visits between the two sides no doubt indicate the strengthening of bilateral relationship.

In Hu's era, Beijing has been more sophisticated and pragmatic in developing its diplomatic relations. It has learnt to use its foreign policy to serve national interest more skillfully. As Evan Medeiros and Taylor Fravel put it, China is "becoming a much more capable and adept player of the diplomatic game."[95] The state of harmony emphasized in Chinese society is corresponding to its peaceful policy externally. By pursuing peace and stability externally, the Chinese leadership pursues the goal of realizing power and prosperity for the country.

Table 1.4 The Role of Ideology in Chinese Foreign Policy in Hu's Era

Content of ideology	Marxism-Leninism-Mao Zedong Thought-Deng Xiaoping Theory-Jiang Zemin's Three Represents-Hu Jintao's view of scientific way of development; introduction of new content of ideology from Chinese culture
Nature of ideology	Pragmatic
Role of ideology in making foreign policy	Unimportant
Principles of foreign policy	Peace, development and cooperation
Nature of foreign policy	More cooperative, more flexible and pragmatic
Focus in foreign policy	All-round development of diplomatic relations with other countries and international institutions
Approach in external relations	Both bilateral and multilateral, with more attention given to multilateral diplomacy

CONCLUDING REMARKS

The review of the more than five decades of the PRC's history demonstrates both change and continuities in its ideological framework and the making of foreign policy. Up until now, China remains as one of the few communist countries, at least in name. Marxism stays as the main body constituting Chinese official ideology. Marxism and the CPC are mutually supportive. The CPC was founded under the guidance of Marxism. Marxism is given the lofty position in Chinese ideology because it legitimatizes the existence of the CPC in China. However, the changing domestic and international environment posed a serious challenge to the credibility and applicability of Marxism in China, and obliged the Chinese leadership to seek help from patriotism centered on the traditional Chinese culture. While Marxism was the belief of the Chinese Communists and served as the guidance of domestic and foreign policy in Mao's era, its influence gradually declined following the implementation of reform and open-up policy.

Another noticeable feature in the ideological field is that the Chinese leadership has been creative and pragmatic in dealing with the changing situation. From the time when Marxism was introduced to China, the Chinese leaders have been making respectable efforts to make it adaptable to the Chinese situation. As a consequence of their efforts, Marxism has been reformulated to contain Mao Zedong Thought, Deng Xiaoping Theory of socialism with Chinese characteristics, Jiang Zemin's articulation of Three Represents, and Hu Jintao's proposal of scientific way of development. In the searching process of ideology, the Chinese leaders have been remarkably pragmatic. Just like Deng Xiaoping said, "It doesn't matter whether it is a black cat or a white cat, as long as it catches mice."[96] No matter what approaches, strategies, and policies have been taken, they have to serve the same national interest: to bring the country power and prosperity.

From 1949 when the PRC was founded till 1971 when it became the sole representative of China in the UN, Beijing achieved a great success in legitimizing itself in international society. From 1986 when Beijing started the negotiation to join the General Agreement of Tariffs and Trade till 2001 when it became a member of the WTO, China completed its efforts to become a normal state. The theory of peaceful rise developed in Hu's era is another promise China gives to the world of its peaceful intention. With such an endeavor, it intends to establish an image of a responsible power and demonstrates to the world that the rise of China would not pose a security threat to others. As pointed out by Wang Yizhou, deputy director of the Institute of World Economics and Politics of China Academy of Social Sciences, China's foreign policy is transforming from inward-looking, mainly concerned about its own development, to outward-looking, concerned both about its own development and the development of the whole population in the world.[97]

Chinese foreign policy is made to maintain its national interest. In the five decades of its history, the approach to serve the national interest has been remarkably readjusted. Before the implementation of reform and opening policy in China, the Chinese attempted to fight against hegemonism and to redress the injustice in the international politics via revolutionary means. Currently, the Chinese national interest is served by staying inside the existing international political system and cooperating with the other countries. China pursues the grand strategy of peaceful development in order to serve the goal of becoming a rich and powerful country. As a whole, due to the great flexibility and pragmatism of the Chinese leadership, the making of Chinese foreign policy has been successful to help China turn from a weak, developing country to a strong, influential power in the world; from a revolutionary revisionist state attempting to overturn the international political system to a cooperative and peaceful status quo power accommodating to the rules and norms of the international regime and willing to maintain the existing international order.

Notes

[1] Bill Brugger and David Kelly, *Chinese Marxism in the Post-Mao Era* (Stanford, California: Stanford University Press, 1990), p. 171.

[2] See *Renmin ribao (People's Daily)*, Oct. 1, 1959.

[3] This communist belief was widely promoted in China. Till the 1990s, such propaganda still appeared in the textbooks of *Political Science* used by high school and university students.

[4] R. G. Boyd, *Communist China's Foreign Policy* (New York: Frederick A. Praeger, 1962), pp. 110-111.

[5] See Mao Zedong, "On Correctly Handling the Contradictions among the People" [Guanyu zhengque chuli renmin neibu maodun de wenti], Feb. 27, 1957, in *Selected Works of Mao Zedong (Mao Zedong xuanji)* (Beijing: People's Publishing House, 1977), vol. 5, pp. 363-402.

[6] Xinhua (New China) News Agency, "Advance along the Road Opened Up by the October Socialist Revolution" [Yanzhe shiyue shehuizhuyi geming kaichuang de daolu qianjin], Nov. 5, 1967, quoted in Chalmers Johnson (ed.), *Ideology and Politics in Contemporary China* (Seattle and London: University of Washington Press, 1973), p. 334.

[7] See "List of the Countries Establishing Diplomatic Ties with the PRC" [Zhonghua renmin gongheguo yu geguo jianli waijiao guanxi riqi jianbiao], available at http://www.fmprc.gov.cn/chn/lbfw/jjbiao/t9650.htm

[8] See Xiao Gongqin, "Nationalism and the Ideology in the Transtional Period in China" [Minzuzhuyi yu Zhongguo zhuanxing shiqi de yishixingtai], *Zhanlue yu guanli (Strategy and Management)*, vol. 5, no. 4, 1994, p. 23.

[9] Quoted in Michael Yahuda, *China's Role in World Affairs* (London: Croom Helm, 1978), p. 137.

[10] See Wu Xinbo, "China: Security Practice of a Modernizing and Ascending Power", in Muthiah Alagappa (ed.), *Asian Security Practice: Material and Ideational Influence* (Stanford, California: Stanford University Press, 1998), p. 118.

[11] *Beijing Review*, no. 40 (1968), p. 15, quoted in Michael Yahuda, *China's Role in World Affairs*, p. 207.

[12] Joseph Camilleri, *Chinese Foreign Policy: The Maoist Era and Its Aftermath* (Oxford: Martin Robertson, 1980), p. 93.

[13] Chalmers Johnson (ed.), *Ideology and Politics in Contemporary China*, p. 327.

[14] Michael Yahuda, *China's Role in World Affairs*, p.194.

[15] King C. Chen, *China and the Three Worlds* (London: The MacMillan Press Ltd., 1979), p. 28, and p. 35.

[16] Yongnian Zheng, *Discovering Chinese Nationalism in China: Modernization, Identity, and International Relations* (Cambridge: Cambridge University Press, 1999), p. 70.

[17] "Chairman Mao's Criticism of the Peng-Huang-Zhang-Zhou Anti-Party Clique" [Maozhuxi dui Peng, Huang, Zhang, Zhou fangeming jituan de pipan], quoted in Chalmers Johnson (ed.), *Ideology and Politics in Contemporary China*, p. 341.

[18] Joseph Camilleri, *Chinese Foreign Policy: The Maoist Era and Its Aftermath*, p. 112.

[19] Yongjin Zhang, *China in International Society Since 1949: Alienation and Beyond*, (Houndmills, Basingstoke, Hampshire and London: Macmillan Press Ltd., 1998), p. 60.

[20] Ibid., p. 92.

[21] Quansheng Zhao, *Interpreting Chinese Foreign Policy: Micro-Macro Linkage Approach* (Oxford: Oxford University Press, 1996), p. 41.

[22] Michel Oksenberg, "China's Confident Nationalism," *Foreign Affairs*, vol. 65, no. 3, 1987, p. 505.

[23] Quoted in Xiao Gongqin, "Nationalism and the Ideology in the Transitional Period in China", p. 25.

[24] Ma Licheng and Ling Zhijun, *Confrontation: Record of Three Times of Thought Liberation in Contemporary China* [Jiaofeng: dangdai Zhongguo sanci sixiang jiefang shilu] (Beijing: Today's China Publishing House, 1998), p. 22.

[25] Deng Xiaoping, "The 'Two Whatevers' does not Conform to Marxism"[Liangge fanshi bu fuhe Makesi zhuyi], May 24, 1977, in *Selected Works of Deng Xiaoping [Deng Xiaoping wenxuan]*, vol. 2, available at http://gd.cnread.net/cnread1/zzzp/d/dengxiaoping/2/010.htm

[26] "Communiqué of the Third Plenary Session of the Eleventh Central Committee of the CPC" [Zhongguo gongchandang dishijie zhongyang weiyuanhui disanci quanti huiyi gongbao], Dec. 12, 1978, available at http://www.people.com.cn/GB/shizheng/252/5089/5103/5205/index.html
[27] Ma Licheng and Ling Zhijun, *Confrontation: Record of Three Times of Thought Liberation in Contemporary China*, pp. 59-61.
[28] Ibid., p. 54.
[29] "Practice is the Only Criteria to Test Truth" [Shijian shi jianyan zhenli de weiyi biaozhun], *Renmin ribao (People's Daily)*, May 12, 1978.
[30] "Resolution on Certain Questions in the History of Our Party Since the Founding of the PRC" [Jianguo yilai ruogan lishi wenti de jueyi], July 27, 1981, available at http://www.people.com.cn/GB/shizheng/252/5089/5103/index.html
[31] Deng Xiaoping, "To Completely and Accurately Understand Mao Zedong Thought"[Wanzhengdi zhunquedi lijie Mao Zedong sixiang], July 21, 1977, in *Selected Works of Deng Xiaoping*, vol. 2, available at http://gd.cnread.net/cnread1/zzzp/d/dengxiaoping/2/012.htm
[32] Colin Mackerras, Pradeep Taneja, and Graham Young, *China Since 1978* (South Melbourne, Australia: Longman Australia Ltd., 1998), 2nd ed., p.102.
[33] See Deng Xiaoping, "Opening Speech of the 12th Party Congress"[Zhongguo gongchandang di shierci quanguo daibiao dahui kaimuci], Sept. 1, 1982, in *Selected Works of Deng Xiaoping* [*Deng Xiaoping wenxuan*] (Beijing: People's Publishing House, 1993), vol. 3, pp. 1-4.
[34] "On the Decision of Economic System Reform by CPC Central Committee" [Zhonggong zhongyang guanyu jingji tizhi gaige de jueding], Oct. 20, 1984, available at http://www.ccyl.org.cn/zuzhi/theory/dspws/page3/womende1.htm
[35] Deng Xiaoping, "Speech on the Sixth Session of the Twelfth Party Central Committee" [Zai dang de shierjie liuzhong quanhui shang de jianghua], Sept. 28, 1986, available at http://www.ccyl.org.cn/zuzhi/theory/dspws/page3/zaidang.htm
[36] Xiao Yan and Wang Ping (ed.), *Twenty Years' Theory Development* [*Ershinian lilun fengyun*] (Shenyang: Liaoning People's Publishing House, 1998), p. 328.
[37] Wan Li, *Selected Works of Wan Li* [*Wan Li wenxuan*] (Beijing: People's Publishing House, 1995), p. 525.
[38] *Beijing Review*, vol. 35, no. 41, October 12-18, 1992, p. 17.
[39] Deng Xiaoping, "The Principles and Standpoint to Develop Sino-American Relationship" [Fazhan Zhongmei guanxi de yuanze lichang], in *Selected Works of Deng Xiaoping*, Jan. 4, 1981, vol. 2, available at http://gd.cnread.net/cnread1/zzzp/d/dengxiaoping/2/049.htm
[40] Deng Xiaoping, "An Important Principle in Dealing with Relations Between Fraternal Parties" [Chuli xiongdidang guanxi de yitiao zhongyao yuanze], in *Selected Works of Deng Xiaoping*, May 31, 1980, vol. 2, available at http://gd.cnread.net/cnread1/zzzp/d/dengxiaoping/2/044.htm
[41] Hu Yaobang, "Comprehensively Create A New Situation of Socialist Modernization" [Quanmian kaichuang jianshe shehuizhuyi xiandaihua jianshe de xinjumian], work report at the Twelfth National Party Congress, Sept. 1, 1982, available at http://www.people.com.cn/GB/shizheng/252/5089/5104/index.html
[42] See Yongjin Zhang, *China in International Society Since 1949: Alienation and Beyond*, p. 122-123.
[43] The Five Principles of Peaceful Coexistence as promoted by China are: mutual respect for sovereignty and territorial integrity; mutual non-aggression; non-interference in each other's internal affairs; equality; and mutual benefit.

[44] Zhao Ziyang, "Report on the Seventh Five-Year Plan" [Guanyu diqige wunian jihua de baogao], March 25, 1986, available at
http://www.peopledaily.com.cn/item/lianghui/zlhb/rd/6jie/newfiles/d1140.html
[45] *Renmin ribao (People's Daily)*, Nov. 11, 1986, quoted in Zhimin Lin, "China's Third World Policy," in Yufan Hao and Guocang Huan (eds.), *The Chinese View of the world* (New York: Pantheon Books, 1989), p. 248.
[46] See Melvin Gurtov and Byong-Moo Hwang, *China under Threat: The Politics of Strategy and Diplomacy* (Baltimore and London: The John Hopkins University Press, 1980), p. 7.
[47] Samuel S. Kim, "China and the Third World in the Changing World Order," in Samuel S. Kim (ed.), *China and the World: Chinese Foreign Relations in the Post-Cold War Era* (Boulder, Colorado: Westview Press, 1994), p. 131.
[48] Deng Xiaoping, "Speech in Beijing after Coming back the Inspection in Jiangsu and Other Places" [Shicha Jiangsu dengdi hui Beijing hou de tanhua], March 2, 1983, in *Selected Works of Deng Xiaoping*, vol. 3, p. 25.
[49] Samuel S. Kim, "China and the United Nations," in Elizabeth Economy and Michel Oksenberg (eds.), *China Joins the World: Progress and Prospects* (Council on Foreign Relations, 1999), p. 46.
[50] See Samuel S. Kim, "China's International Organizational Behavior," in Thomas W. Robinson and David Shambaugh (eds.), *Chinese Foreign Policy: Theory and Practice* (Oxford: Clarendon Press, 1995), p. 421.
[51] Zhao Ziyang, *"Report of the Seventh Five-Year-Plan"* [*Di qige wunian jihua de baogao*], March 1986, available at
http://202.99.23.246/item/lianghui/zlhb/rd/6jie/newfiles/d1140.html
[52] Samuel S. Kim, "China and the Third World in the Changing World Order," p. 128.
[53] Yongjin Zhang, *China in International Society Since 1949: Alienation and Beyond*, p. 67.
[54] Huan Xiang, "On Current Situation," *World Economic Herald*, Oct. 14, 1984.
[55] Suisheng Zhao, "A State-led Nationalism: The Patriotic Education Campaign in Post-Tiananmen China," *Communist and Post-Communist Studies*, vol. 31, no. 3, 1998, p. 289.
[56] Steven I. Levine, "Perception and Ideology in Chinese Foreign Policy", in Thomas W. Robinson and David Shambaugh (eds.), *Chinese Foreign Policy: Theory and Practice*, p. 31.
[57] *Renmin ribao (People's Daily)*, editorial, July 22, 1989, quoted in Samuel S. Kim (ed.) *China and the World: Chinese Foreign Relations in the Post-Cold War Era*, p. 7.
[58] Jiang Zemin, "Quickening the Step of Opening-up and Reform and Socialist Construction, Achieving A Greater Success in the Socialist Cause with Chinese Characteristics" [Jiakuai gaige kaifang he xiandaihua jianshe bufa, duoqu you Zhongguo tese shehuizhuyi shiye de gengda shengli], Oct. 12, 1992, available at http://www.china.org.cn/ch-80years/lici/14/14-0/8.htm
[59] Ma Licheng and Ling Zhijun, *Jiaofeng: dangdai Zhongguo sanci sixiang jiefang shilu* p. 391.
[60] Ibid., p. 393.
[61] Wang Yu, "Three Stages in Chinese Economic Reform" [Zhongguo jingji gaige de sange jieduan], March 25, 2001, available at
http://dailynews.tyfo.com/news/financial/block/html/2001032500030.html
[62] Jiang Zemin, Sange daibiao (Three Representatives), available at http://www.people.com.cn/GB/shizheng/252/5303/5304/20010627/498370.html
[63] See Kang Xiaoguang, "The Course and Outlet of China's Modernization" [Gongguo xiandiahua de mailuo yu chulu], *Zhanglue yu guanli (Strategy and Management)*, no. 1, 1994, pp. 10-12.

[64] Editorial, "Hold High the Great Flag of Patriotism—In Commemoration of the 150th Anniversary of the Opium War" [Gaoju aiguozhuyi de weida qizhi—jinian yapian zhanzheng 150 zhounian], *Renmin ribao (People's Daily)*, June 3, 1990, p. 1.

[65] Suisheng Zhao, "A State-led Nationalism: The Patriotic Education Campaign in Post-Tiananmen China," p. 290.

[66] Quoted in Suisheng Zhao, "A State-led Nationalism: The Patriotic Education Campaign in Post-Tiananmen China," p. 291.

[67] Ming L., "Insist on the Unification of Patriotism and Socialism," *Qiushi (Seeking Truth)*, no. 9, 1990, quoted in Suisheng Zhao, "A State-led Nationalism: The Patriotic Education Campaign in Post-Tiananmen China," p. 296.

[68] Suisheng Zhao, "A State-led Nationalism: The Patriotic Education Campaign in Post-Tiananmen China," p. 296.

[69] Li Ruihuan, "National Culture Important for Literature to Flourish," *Beijing Review*, vol. 33, no. 9, 1990, p. 20.

[70] See Pi Mingyong, "Nationalism and Confucian Culture" [Minzuzhuyi yu rujia wenhua], *Zhanlue yu guanli (Strategy and Management)*, no. 2, 1996, pp. 51-7.

[71] See "General Program for Strengthening Education in Modern and Contemporary History and National Conditions" [Zhongxiaoxue jiaqiang jinxiandaishi ji guoqing jiaoyu de zongti gangyao], *Renmin jiaoyu (People's Education)*, no. 10, 1991, pp. 2-24.

[72] *Beijing Review*, vol. 32, no. 49, December 4-10, 1989, p. 17.

[73] Michael Yahuda, "Sino-American Relations," in Gerald Segal (ed.), *Chinese Politics and Foreign Policy Reform* (London and New York: Kegan Paul International Ltd., 1990), p. 183.

[74] Oleg N. Bykov, "Beyond Superpowership," in Armand Clesse et al. (eds.), *The International System After the Collapse of the East-West Order* (Dordrecht, Boston, and London: Martinus Nijhoff Publishers, 1994), p. 63.

[75] Mel Gurtov and Byong-Moo Hwang, *China's Security: The New Roles of the Military* (Boulder and London: Lynne Rienner Publishers, 1998), p. 1.

[76] Samuel S. Kim, "China and the United Nations," pp. 81-2.

[77] Alastair Iain Johnston, "International Structures and Chinese Foreign Policy," in Samuel S. Kim (ed.), *China and the World: Chinese Foreign Policy Faces the New Millennium*, p. 63.

[78] The four parties refer to the Vietnamese-backed Phnom Penh government, the communist Khmer Rouge, Sihanouk's supporters and a second noncommunist resistance group led by former Prime Minister Son Sann.

[79] Joseph Y. S. Cheng, "China's Foreign Policy in the Mid-1990s," in Joseph Y.S. Cheng (ed.), *China in the Post-Deng Era* (Hong Kong: The Chinese University Press, 1998), p. 228.

[80] "CPC Issues Document on Ruling Capacity," *China Daily*, September 21, 2004.

[81] "China Will Allocate More than Two Billion Euros to Revive Communism" [Zhongguo jiang bochu liangqian duo wan ouyuan chongzhen gongchanzhuyi yishixingtai], *Asia Times*, Jan. 20, 2006, available at http://www.asianews.it/view.php?l=zh&art=5174

[82] "China Confronts Contradictions Between Marxism and Markets," *Washington Post*, Dec. 4, 2005, available at http://www.washingtonpost.com/wp-dyn/content/article/2005/12/04/AR2005120400982.pf.html

[83] "China Will Allocate More than Two Billion Euros to Revive Communism."

[84] "Hu Calls to Keep the Party's Advanced Nature," *China Daily*, January 15, 2005.

[85] "Hu Jintao Calls for Unity of Chinese Nation," *People's Daily Online*, Sept. 3, 2005, available at http://english.people.com.cn/200509/03/eng20050903_206345.html

[86] Edward Cody, "Eight-Step Program for What Ails China," *Washington Post*, March 23, 2006, available at http://www.washingtonpost.com/wp-dyn/content/article/2006/03/22/AR2006032202042.html?nav=rss_world

[87] "The Rise of China Doesn't Exist Any Threat to Others" [Wen Jiabao: Zhongguo de jueqi bucunzai renhe weixie], March 15, 2004, available at http://news.creaders.net/headline/newsPool/14A196875.html

[88] Guan Wenhu and Li Zhenxing, "On the Image of a Responsible Power" [Lun Fuzeren de daguo xingxiang], *Tianfu xinlun (Tianfu New Ideas)*, no. 5, 2004, p. 20.

[89] Li Zhaoxing, "Banner of Diplomacy Stressed," *China Daily*, Aug. 23, 2005, p. 4.

[90] Deng Xiaoping, "International Situation and Economic Problems" [Guoji xingshi he jingji wenti], Marc 3, 1990, in *Selected Works of Deng Xiaoping*, p. 353.

[91] The Chinese official viewpoint on multipolarity was originally published on the website of the Ministry of Foreign Affairs before 2003. Due to the fact that the Chinese government revised its understanding on the concept, the Foreign Ministry removed the original version from its website. After some efforts, the author found this old version of multipolarity on one of the Chinese embassies' websites. Thanks to their slow pace of website upgrading, the readers could still get access to this version which is available at http://www.chinaembassy.se/eng/zgwj/jbzc/t100415.htm

[92] Ibid.

[93] China's official view on multipolarity, available at http://www.fmprc.gov.cn/eng/wjdt/wjzc/t24880.htm

[94] Speech given by the Philippines President during the Presentation of the Signed Tripartite Agreement for Joint Marine Seismic Undertaking between China, Vietnam and the Philippines and Awarding Ceremony for Outstanding Electric Cooperatives and General Managers, March 14, 2005, available at http://www.ops.gov.ph/speeches2005/speech-2005_mar14.htm

[95] Evan S. Medeiros and M. Taylor Fravel, "China's New Diplomacy," *Foreign Affairs*, vol. 82, Issue 6 (Nov./Dec. 2003), p. 23.

[96] Quoted in Hua Laoshuan, "Pride and Prejudice: 'Overall Westernization'" [Aoman yu pianjian he "quanpan xihua"], *Huaxia wenzhai (China News Digest)*, June 10, 1999, available at http://archives.cnd.org/HXWK/column/Opinion/cm9907b-3.gb.html

[97] "China's Diplomacy is Experiencing Quiet Changes" [Zhongguo waijiao qiaoran zhuanxing], March 1, 2004, available at http://news.creaders.net/headline/newsPool/1A195646.html

Chapter 2

Conceptualizing Foreign Policy: The "Peaceful Rise" Debate Among China's Scholars

Catherine H. Keyser and Su Lin

INTRODUCTION

"The focus of my speech today is to put forward a topic of a 'New Path for China's peaceful Rise," said Zheng Bijian to an audience of Asians present for the Boao forum on Asia in November of 2003. China's growing power is peaceful, he suggested, and he characterized it as a 'peaceful rise' (heping jueqi). That speech set off a long brewing debate among China's scholars and policymakers over how to understand China's dramatic rise. Up until Zheng's now famous speech most research centered on the impact of China's rise on the international order. But Zheng's speech ignited intense debate within China. A survey of recent articles, symposia, and speeches illuminates a variety of positions and thinking about the meaning of the term "peaceful," the role of peaceful in foreign policy making, and the relationship between discussing China's foreign policy and her domestic development. This chapter reviews how "rise" and "peaceful rise" are understood by Chinese scholars, and what principals guide their arguments on Chinese foreign and domestic policy. Finally, the debates over China's emergence in the global order further underscore a more general phenomenon that within Chinese intellectual circles there is a growing marketplace of ideas for crafting China's future. We argue that to fully appreciate the various dimensions of Chinese foreign policy in the 21st century it is critical to illuminate the process by which terms and concepts related to China's rise come to be understood within China and the nature of their relationship to Chinese perceptions of their place in the world. In short, we contextualize the politics of 'peaceful rise' as part of a process of leadership transition and the working out of new foreign policy strategies for the 21st century.

The notion of "peaceful rise" was always controversial and its short five month history came to a close by the middle of 2004 when official documents and speeches had replaced peaceful rise with peace and development (heping fazhan). In addition to discussing the contents of the debate we also ask why official discussion of peaceful rise emerged when it did. Why was the idea 'peaceful rise' then dropped suddenly as an official expression? And finally, what is the landscape of perspectives among China's international relations scholars and policy advisors that help us understand the trajectory of this debate and new thinking about China and the world?

The debate among China's scholars over the meaning and feasibility of a peaceful rise provides insight into the development of thinking about international relations in China. In addition to the above questions, one goal of this chapter is to bring into English Chinese scholars' views and approaches. As Wang Chaohua recently noted, "while Chinese works of literature have earned growing international recognition since the eighties as deserving translation into other languages in a timely and comprehensive fashion, this has yet to be the case for contemporary intellectual debates, which as a rule remain accessible only through scanty and intermittent coverage by news media."[1] This essay seeks, in part, to address the lacunae by articulating the intellectual debates in foreign policy. To proceed, we place discussion of China's relations with the world into the larger intellectual context of China's more than twenty years of reform. We then look specifically at the nature of the debate over China's rise and the possibility of its being peaceful focusing on key questions to which the Chinese authors addressed their writing. We then step back and place the debates in a larger political context asking why did they emerge at that time? Finally, we discuss what the internal debate among China's international relations (IR) scholars tell us about how the Chinese intellectual community and the Chinese party-state perceive China's role in the world in the coming decades. First, however we need to put Chinese intellectual and scholarly activities in the context of post 1949 China.

CHINESE SCHOLARS AND THE STATE IN THE REFORM ERA

Not since the establishment of the PRC in 1949 have scholars been independent from the interests and the control of the Chinese party-state. While at critical times the interests of the scholars and the state have parted ways with usually repressive results, in general intellectuals across the disciplinary spectrum have proceeded through what Wang characterizes as two very different 'reform decades.' For our purposes, the 1980s saw less critical thinking on Chinese perspectives about international relations and foreign policy in part because this period represented an intensive learning era. During this time Chinese international relations scholars were busy translating IR theory into Chinese as well as 'catching up' on understanding the international order about which China was only just beginning to think after the isolationist period under Mao. But by the mid-nineties, there had been remarkable development within international relations as IR scholars began to think more critically about the international arena. For China's intellectuals in general, "(i)f the eighties were principally a time of assimilation, the hallmark of the nineties has been a more sophisticated exploration of wider range of foreign influences, and the creative tension with them."[2] The idea of creative tension, one can argue, extends to Chinese international relations specialists' consideration of the nature of China's growing international power in increasingly theoretical ways.[3]

Unlike other intellectual arenas, however, foreign policy poses intense challenges for scholars because of the political sensitivity surrounding how China will present herself to the world. The necessity of a united front has always been important and isn't unique to China. But the role of democratic centralism as an organizing principle in communist political systems means that unlike other political systems a policy directive, or as in the case of foreign policy, the national image is not open for unsanctioned discussion. This sensitivity is reminiscent of the early debates over the nature and pace of economic reform in the early to mid-1980s. Thus, when discussing China's rise it is important to appreciate the political sensitivity surrounding the nature of China's development. This sensitivity is due, in part, to official constraints on any wide ranging discussion of the government's intentions, or on any specific government policy that might criticize the official position, even if that position isn't clear as is the case with the term peaceful rise. Moreover, the peaceful rise discussion has evolved into a discussion over domestic issues but the party-state is less comfortable with discussions that include analysis of domestic issues because of an underlying fear of instability. Finally, as with other arenas, and similar to the process of the 1980s, open discussion of a policy or approach can only proceed once the general idea or slogan has been articulated by a leader which provides political sanction and some sense of the boundaries for discussion. In the 1980s those boundaries were pushed beyond the ability of the leadership to tolerate them. And similarly there has been greater political control over the written word in the 1990s. For example, the recent closing of *Strategy and Management* for its critical article on Chinese policy toward North Korea underscores the sensitivity of discussing foreign policy issues. However, discussion and communication with those outside China continues apace.[4] With this in mind, we now turn our attention first to contextualizing the world in which China's dramatic rise takes place and then turn to the debate over a rising China.

CHINA AND THE WORLD IN THE 1990s

China began her dramatic entrance onto the world stage beginning with Deng Xiaoping's reform and opening in 1978. At that time, China's rise as a great power seemed far-fetched. By 2004 China was second only to the U.S. as a destination for foreign direct investment with an inflow of investment totaling $54.9 billion. Her GDP had risen from $444.6 billion in 1990 to $1,715.0 billion in 2004, and China had moved from the 4th largest to the 3rd largest economy in the world. Over the same period China increased her trade more than tenfold rising from the 6th largest trading nation to the 2nd largest with a trade volume of $US1,186.9 billion by 2004.[5] This phenomenal growth also brought new and intense challenges. These include an unprecedented need for strategic resources such as energy, raw materials, and water. Over the course of the decade China's energy consumption jumped from 27 quadrillion BTUs in 1990 to 59.6 quadrillion BTUs in 2004 moving it up to 2nd place just behind the U.S. in terms of energy consumption. Indeed, by 1993 China had become a net importer of oil. The International Energy Agency estimates that by 2030 oil imports will account for 80% of China's oil consumption.[6] Coupled with these statistics, China faces the continued problems of bringing its overall population out of poverty in light of limited resources. As Zheng Bijian points out, "China's per capita water resources are one-fourth of the amount of the world average, and its per capita area of cultivatable farmland is 40 percent of the world average. China's oil, natural gas, copper, and aluminum resources in per capita terms amount to 8.3 percent, 4.1 percent, 25.5 percent, and 9.7percent of the respective world averages."[7]

Second, the 1990s saw the development of China's military capability. Her defense budget has steadily increased jumping from $US25 billion in 2004 to US$29.5 billion in 2005 which compares to just $US11.3 billion in 1990. China has long been a member of the nuclear club, but the 1990s also saw an increase in long range missles and nuclear warheads. In 1990 China had 8 ICBMs which was increased to over 40 by 2005. She currently has 410 warheads. China's standing military contracted somewhat over the last decade and a half but her ranking moved from 2nd to 1st place as the world's largest army. As David M. Lampton succinctly notes in his testimony before the U.S. Congress in 2000 "the People's Republic of China (PRC) is the largest, most rapidly changing international actor on the world stage today. Never before has such a large economy moved so rapidly from a planned structure toward market operation; opened up so speedily to the world financial and trade system; changed so dramatically from a rural to increasingly urban society; switched from energy self-sufficiency to import-dependence so quickly; and, gone from an information-starved to information-rich status so abruptly, the many controls on the Internet notwithstanding. "[8]

Finally, the 1990s saw pivotal events for China's relations with the world. These include her changing relations with a newly disintegrated soviet block and restiveness on her western borders, the blossoming relationships with nations in Africa and Latin America as her oil needs increased, the first Gulf war in 1991, the 1995 Taiwan straits crisis, the return of Hong Kong to the mainland in 1997, the Asian financial crisis of 1998, the bombing of her embassy in Belgrade in 1999, the EP3 plane incident in 2000, entrance into WTO in early 2001, the bombing of the American World Trade Towers in September 2001, and the American entrance into Afghanistan with which China shares a small border. This period also included two leadership changes: the first from Deng Xiaoping to Jiang Zemin and then in 2002 the transition from Jiang Zemin to Hu Jintao. After emerging from the post-Tiananmen trauma, it is clear China had a very dynamic and busy 10 plus years. But they were not without increasing anxiety among some observing these events.

Although many Western business leaders welcomed the massive economic opportunities provided by China's development, other observers began to argue that China's growing economic and military power will make it a threat to Asian and global security. The concerns were driven primarily by concern over China's growing military capabilities in the absence of a clear threat. During this dramatic period articles, discussion, and even manuscripts addressed the question of China as a potential threat to the world. Implicit in this discussion was (and is) the notion that a rising China is dangerous.[9] The nature of the danger was centered on economic and military issues but it also focuses on uncertainty about what China's own ambitions are with regard to her increasing power. Militarily there is concern that China seeks to become a regional hegemon which might upset the military balance in the region and create further disharmony among her neighbors. There were also those who express concern about the values underlying the Chinese Communist Party (CCP) and their lack of democratic or transparent political processes which increases the potential for China to become an unstable power. And then there were the concerns over how a huge Chinese market would affect global trade. The connection between economic and military development was expressly made when, in July 2004 the politburo standing committee solidified the idea of economic development coupled with military strength with the slogan of 'prosperous nation, powerful military' (fuguo qiangbing).

Finally, nationalism as a variable in Chinese identity and foreign policy begins to emerge during this decade. The question of nationalism as it informs, impacts, or influences Chinese attitudes and foreign policy has been widely discussed by Chinese authors both in China and abroad.[10] Much of the discussion is centered on the role of nationalism in the Taiwan issue as well as being a variable in U.S.-China relations and foreign policy thinking more generally. Nationalism is a powerful, if delicate tool for the CCP to retain its legitimacy. As Wang Jisi points out, "(o)fficial speeches, reports, and domestic media are inundated with success stories suggesting the competence of the Communist Party and the correctness of its policies. These sources call too for Chinese people to unite and work together to realize the "great revival" of their nation by the middle of this century."[11]

The rise of nationalistic sentiment is not only causing a drastic shift of the popular feelings toward the western world, but it is also pushing China's foreign policy to swing hard-line in certain cases. Beijing needs internal cohesion, so sometimes its leaders use nationalism to forge unity at home. The rise of anti-American sentiment and intensification of anti-American activities by the mid-1990s marked a shift in the popular feelings toward the United States among the Chinese people, as well as marking the emergence of public opinion as a force shaping China's side in U.S.-China relations.[12] A similar situation also effects Sino-Japan relations. Although Beijing took steps to keep nationalistic sentiment in China under control, strong anti-Japanese feelings exist and have boiled over in the last few years demonstrating what Hays has argued is the delicacy and danger of spontaneous nationalism.

Conservatives in the leadership sense that China's reform and opening has given rise to the crisis of national identity, particularly since early 1990s. According to them, ideology is important to any Chinese regime as a means for unifying its huge population. Some of them turned first to fundamental Marxism and then to traditional culture in order to gauge performance of China's development. Although some believe that liberal democracy would be universalized as the final form of human government, they do not believe that the western prescription can work in the Chinese context. The success of the market- oriented reform has had a great impact on Chinese intellectuals and students. In their eyes, while China was moving toward a better society in the 1990s the United Stats model became more negative. This development led them to think that United States' really intended to maintain its international hegemony by democratization of other countries.

Related to the nationalist theme, another trend was a change in views toward the reform agenda itself. What has come to be called the 'new left' as mentioned above, began to emerge in earnest in the 1990s and by the middle of the 2000s they find themselves in conflict with the reform they had joined. Social justice, whether or not in terms of socialism, has become a fundamental principle for developing China's society. Indeed, with the ascendance of Hu to the positioin of General party secretary, there appears to be increased focus on the social impact of reform. But in terms of the debate over peaceful rise, the issues of domestic peace has become linked with the notion of equitable development as we discuss below.

The developments in the domestic and international setting had not been lost on China's international relations scholars. In the early 1990s they began to think about the perception of the international community as well as think more deeply about what China is doing, and what her goals are with regard to her rapidly rising status in the global community. IR scholars have since made significant contribution to considering the role of perception in Chinese foreign policy. Moreover, in the 1990's, China's scholars began to introduce research on the IR concept of a grand strategy to Chinese academic community. [13] It was in the midst of these changes that Zheng Bijian attempted to articulate a new strategy for development to the domestic audience and to signal foreign policy directions to the international community. It is to that attempt and the subsequent debates surrounding his formulation to which we now turn.

THE DEBATE

Zheng Bijian's Speech on China's Peaceful Rise

Zheng Bijian, executive vice president of Central Party School of the Communist party observed in his speech at the Boao conference that ambivalent feelings about China's rise were not only found in the United States and Europe, but also in China's neighboring countries. His speech included three questions of concern to Asians; how to understand Chinese development, the trajectory of

China's rise, and finally what this means for China's relations with her neighbors. This speech was aimed both at demonstrating China's confidence for the domestic audience as well as articulating foreign policy strategy. Interestingly, though Mr. Zheng used a new term, he stressed in his speech that it was not new. He argued that it was Deng Xiaoping, the chief architect of China's reform and opening-up who brought China onto such a road, and that it is under the leadership of Jiang Zemin, the core of China's third generation leadership, and Hu Jintao, the leader of the new generation that China will stride on this road into the 21st century.[14] Therefore, he suggested, it has already been a quarter of a century since China embarked on the road to engagement in globalization and a peaceful rise, and finally, this "peaceful rise" is China's future path. He would go on in the following several years to elaborate on this speech, and to consistently use it even after it was officially abandoned.

Following on Zheng's speech, the formal unveiling of this strategy came with Prime Minister Wen Jiabao's speech at Harvard University. For the first time China officially claimed confidence and determination in her rise stating that it is, at its core, peaceful.[15] Finally, China's new, and not yet consolidated leader Hu Jintao, using a politically powerful moment with his colleagues and politburo members gathered around for the 110th anniversary of the birth of Mao Zedong, on December 23rd reiterated that China would be guided by the concept of peaceful rise and must get along with other nations in the cause of development. Then on February 23rd Hu Jintao again stressed the issue at the Central Committee Politburo's 10th collective study session. Finally, Wen Jiabao elaborates on 5 points concerning peaceful rise at a press conference during the 2nd session of the 10th National People's Congress. Thus, the leadership in a few months sent a clear message that this ill-defined concept was the official Chinese position with regard to her foreign policy.[16]

With the slogan giving official sanction, the Chinese scholarly community responded immediately with conferences to explore what the concept of peaceful rise means. A conference on "The rise of China: International Environment and China's strategy" in Beijing was held on March 13th, 2004, jointly hosted by the editorial boards of the Journal of *Teaching and Research* and the School of International Studies, Renmin University of China with over 50 participants from similar institutes in attendance.[17] Lin Su, who attended the conference, notes that it was clear to those in attendance that the slogan itself was being used by the government for political and propaganda purposes. However, because of the presence of a large number of well-trained scholars including those returned from completing doctorates abroad, the discussion quickly turned into a far-ranging debate on international relations theories and the proposed peaceful alternative to a nation's rise. At this conference cadre from the CCPiInternational Liaison Department, the Ministry of Commerce, and the National Defense University were in attendance. While never published openly, it is common knowledge that reports of the discussion at the conference were passed up to the leadership since the written reports of the conference did not capture the full range of arguments presented.

Around the same time, serial discussions were organized in Shanghai by the Institute of World Economy and Politics, Shanghai Academic Social Science. They focused on "The Road Towards Great Power: An Historical Comparison"(March 27-28,2004); "Economic power and peaceful rise of China"(April 6); and "The role of China and strategy for peaceful rise"(April 12). [18] These three meetings covered comparative history, economics, and strategy. In the summary of this series of meetings, it becomes clear that there were a variety of opinions regarding multiple aspects of the idea of peaceful rise that had not been made clear by the leadership, but it also reveals, as discussed below, interesting national sentiments regarding China.

Another kind of symposium at this time included one where opinion pieces were submitted to an editorial board who then selected several to appear in a conference proceeding. It was entitled "The Rise of Great Powers and China's Options." It was mediated by the editorial boards of the Journal of Chinese Social Science and the Chinese Journal of International Social Science.[19] This publication provided further evidence of the variety of unofficial perspectives on a rising China. The debate about China's rise has, in addition to deepening discussion of IR theory, also provided the opportunity for the scholarly community to rethink Chinese development in light of incredible changes noted above. Moreover, ideas generated by these conferences have yielded an increase in literature addressing China's rise; including everything from masters' theses and dissertation topics to book length manuscripts.[20] Below we will disaggregate the variety of perspectives on the so-called national foreign policy strategy. But, as a way to proceed we begin with perhaps the most vexing part of the debate, how to define "peaceful" in the slogan "peaceful rise."

Defining "Peaceful Rise"

The first and most deeply discussed question is the meaning of peaceful rise. While much of the discussion centres on the current era, some like Hu Shaohua have taken the current literature on the nature of peace and war in the course of rising and investigates the idea of Chinese pacifism from an historical perspective, attempting, as he says "to salvage the thesis of Chinese pacifism." He concludes that regardless of whether "strong or weak, Imperial China seemed reluctant to initiate the use of force in its foreign relations for both moralistic and pragmatic reasons."[21] Much like the questions addressed in its definition and then below in terms of the possibility of a peaceful rise, Hu's historical investigation highlights both the conceptual and evidentiary problems raised in the concept.

In terms of the current debate, scholars wrestled with the idea of how to reconcile peace and the possibility of war with Taiwan or any other conflict that may emerge, and further, what must be the nature of the conflict to say that it either does or does not contradict the idea of peace. Or in other words, the study of "rise" and "peace" is not new; however, the leadership by putting the two ideas together created confusion over the meaning given that there is no empirical evidence to support the idea of the peaceful rise of a nation in world history, much less in China. Thus much debate took place about how one would need to define the terms such that they would make sense in the leadership's formulation.

The record of the Shanghai series of conferences provides an interesting optic for understanding the discussion of what peaceful means. For example, Huang Renwei, vice president of the Shanghai Academy of Social Sciences' Institute of World Economy and Politics suggests that peaceful should be understood as 'comparatively peaceful, not in absolute terms so that if it is necessary for China to attack Taiwan should Taiwan want to declare independence then one could still say that China is, in general, rising peacefully (WES p.4) Wang Xinkuai vice chairman of the Shanghai People's Political Consultative Conference provided the logic for this position. He states that it is impossible to avoid domestic and international conflicts in the process of rising peacefully but that since it isn't a major war it can still be considered peaceful. In this way, Wang allows for the possibility that China can still forcefully retake Taiwan (WES p.4). Similarly, in *Teaching and Research* Shi Yinghong, Professor of international relations at Remin University stresses that since China's rise is a long term process military conflict or the use of limited military forces for national defense or maintaining national unification is unavoidable. Thus, he argues that rising peacefully and limited military conflict is not contradictory (TAR p. 15-17). Pan Guang, Huang Renwei's colleague in Shanghai further notes that essentially peaceful rise means to use non-military means such as culture, economics, and legal approaches to solve problems in the international community. But, he continues one should not be indifferent to external threats to the national interests, and thus cannot rule out military action (WES, p.5-6). Shi Liangping, Professor of Huadong Technical University provided an interesting spin on the idea by arguing that peaceful rise does not include any form of military action, but developing defensive capability through the military is one approach to maintaining peace (WES p. 7).

In contrast to these positions, Zhang Youwen, the director of the Institute of World Economy and Politics argues that the core to the definition of peaceful is a nation's values. He argues that a "nation's value orientations will influence the standards and decisions surrounding her rise" (guojia jiazhi quxiang dui jueqi de biaozhun you juedingxing de yingxiang). Defining peace then is first an act of deciding on what a nation's values are. The crucial variable for peaceful rise is stable domestic development he continues, accordingly, all else flows from this variable (WES, p.7-8). If the domestic environment is not stable one can not speak of peaceful rise. Pang Zhongying argues similarly that to say one rises peacefully, one must have only peace, and the priority is domestic peace which includes stability, order, prosperity, unity and good governance.[22] Peace, he continues, can also be understood in its western framework such as 'pax' which suggests that peace is maintained under a hegemon as in pax Ecclesiastica, Pax Britannica etc. He goes on to say that in fact, the definition of "heping" in Chinese has a different connotation than the English word peace. It should be understood as harmony, and he notes that this usage goes back to Laozi and Confucius. At the Renmin University conference some articulated that trying to define peaceful rise is impossible and they early on argued that the terms should not be used together. Rather, it is better to speak of peace and development— and approach that would later be officially adopted but was only later written about.[23]

Finally, standing in further opposition to the definition of peace is the position of Yan Xuetong, a well known realist IR scholar. He argued that trying to define peace is not the main issue. Rather the fact that China is rising the most critical point. And within this fact what is important is that the Chinese government officially relates to the world from a confident position a rising power. In other words, it is a public acknowledgement that the gap between a rising power and other great powers has narrowed and will continue to narrow. Put another way, Yan says, it represents a significant change in the policy initiated by Deng Xiaoping. After the collapse of the Soviet Union, Deng urged his colleagues in 1991 to "hide our capabilities and bide our time; be good at maintaining a low profile; and never claim leadership" (Taoguang yanghui, juebu chutou).[24] No longer, argues Yan, should China hide her capabilities. This then leads to the second issue discussed which concerns the possibility that China can rise peacefully and if so, what conditions are necessary for her to do so.

The Possibility and Necessary Conditions for a Peaceful Rise

The related questions of the feasibility of China's rise and what conditions are necessary for her to continue rising have also been widely addressed by China's foreign policy scholarly community. There is a wide array of positions informed by international relations theories, history, and domestic politics. In contrast to the commentary in official media regarding the slogan which tended toward the simple and positive, the scholarly community writes with a deeper and to the extent possible, critical understanding of the constraints at both the international and national levels. Moreover, it is in tackling the questions about feasibility and priorities that we see the clearest contrast between those who focus on China's domestic problems and those who focus on China in the international community. And within the focus on the international community we can see both realist and constructivist approaches.

In thinking about conditions and feasibility some authors suggest that clarifying the means and ends is the first question to address. This idea is captured in the discussion over which part of the concept is the means to an end, and which is the goal. For example, is remaining peaceful the means to achieve the goal of rising to great power status, or is rising the means by which peace will be ensured? There are also those who argue that one can't separate peace and rise in light of China's goals for development. Pang Zhongying suggests that "(t)he purpose of rising is to attain peace. Peace is the means by which China should rise. And finally, the result of China's rise is peace" by which he means international peace (jueqi de mudi shi heping. Jueqi de shouduan shi heping. Jueqi de jieguo shi heping.).[25] For him, the definition and possibility are collapsed into one idea that centers on maintaining peace in the international and domestic environment.   Similarly, Zhang Minqian, a senior fellow at the Institute of Contemporary International Relations, in a somewhat elliptical fashion argues there will be no rise, peaceful or otherwise without maintaining peace.[26]

The theoretical considerations for the possibility of China's peaceful rise also characterize the discussion of whether or not, and under what conditions China would be successful. Every perspective in international relations theory was represented in these discussions. Ye Jiang, from the Shanghai Transportation University in his contribution to the symposium analyzed the feasibility of peaceful rise according to the realist, neo-institutionalist, and the constructivist positions. He argues, however, that "peaceful rise involves the dilemma of security."(WES. 18.)   He continues that it really doesn't matter whether you want to rise peacefully or not, rather it completely depends on the nature of the structure of the international order, and one's ability to operate effectively within it. Yan Xuetong, has often argued that first and most important one must understand the nature of 'rise' in the international arena. He argues that the question of peacefulness is tangential to the core discussion. Rather, by definition the idea of nations rising in an international framework is best understood as a 'zero-plus game' (linghexing).[27] Further, core to China's future is the dominance of the Sino-American relationship. Regardless of the steadily improving relations after 9/11, Yan, like many emerging elites remains suspicious that the United States will continue its pursuit of world domination under the new flag of anti-terrorism, thus the Chinese are less safe unless they also rise.[28] Moreover, Taiwan is the most "serious predicament for China's rise" (jueqi kunjing).[29]   Yan does argue, however, that maintaining a peaceful environment is critical to successfully rising to great power status.

Since the debate over peaceful rising Yan Xuetong has consistently argued that the term peaceful rising isn't useful but that the term rising is, even after the official slogan became peace and development. His argument is that the concept of development simply does not capture the reality of a China rising. Rather, development denotes progress in spheres such as economic and social, but does not include a notion of speed. His example is that if today one has US$1000 and tomorrow has US$1001 one can say this is development since the comparison is to oneself, rather than comparing against others. Moreover, it does not capture the idea of power. According to Yan, the term to rise is comparatively clear as a concept to denote power in terms of measuring a gap in power.[30] Yan focuses on China's rise which using realist perspectives of the international order is a term of increasing one's own power vis-a-vis the one with the most power. Yan, like Zheng Bijian in this respect, continues to defend the use of 'rising' though Zheng continues to argue at its core, China should continue to assert its rise is and will continue to be peaceful in nature. Yan argues that because of the fundamental changes in China, the Chinese must keep China's standing in the international arena firmly in mind as China's security issues with regard to her neighbors and the other major powers have and will continue to become more complicated.

In contrast to Yan Xuetong, Qin Yaqing, professor at the Foreign Affairs College has often argued from a constructivist position.[31] With regard to peaceful rising he suggests that if China plans to rise within the existing international structure and system, then it is a possible for her to do so. However, if China wishes to change the international order and international institutions, then it is likely she will not be able to rise peacefully. The logic here is that it is not possible to alter the international order without conflict because of its inherent anarchic tendencies. Consequently, it is clear that China's best chance of rising is to remain within the current international order. Indeed, he continues "(i)n the past twenty-five years Chinese strategic culture has become part of the mainstream cooperative culture" in the international arena.[32] In sum, he argues for a 'soft rise' (ruan jueqi) as opposed to 'forceful rise' (qiangxing jueqi) for peace to be maintained.

This notion is echoed by Huang Renwei who suggested during the Shanghai symposium that balanced development and domestic concerns should be China's top priority at present. And, if taken as a priority then it is possible for China to rise peacefully. He takes an historical perspective arguing first that late developers must rise within the context of a globalized economy, thus for China to rise peacefully she must depend on global markets for her resources, rather than take them through war. Second, he notes that Germany and Japan attempted to challenge British hegemony and failed. Thus, if China wants to rise peacefully, she must participate in the international system and only try gradually to change it. Third, China's rise depends on internal resources and whether she can achieve sustainable development in the long run. Fourth, rising also concerns the question of the strength of the nation's institutions and its soft power. Countries that failed in their attempt to rise, he notes, were all autocratic in nature, and indeed "non-democratic countries run a greater risk of going to war than do democratic nations." These four points, he concludes, all suggest that the most successful way to peacefully develop is through building economic relations with your neighbors and developing the market. His position reflects democratic peace theory and neo-liberalism which stresses that economic interdependence leads to peace. This argument follows on his earlier work where he articulates the reasons China needs to focus on development in service of her international standing.[33]

Close to this position is that outlined by Li Qiang, professor of political science at Peking University who bluntly states that "peaceful rise does not refer mainly to a change in foreign policy strategy, but rather to the unavoidable requirement to change one's domestic development strategy. Borrowing from Max Weber's concept to express this idea, (one can say) the essence of this change is to move from an economically oriented nation through to a political nation such that one can become politically mature."[34]

Hu Angang provides the most extensive elaboration of this perspective on what is required for China's peaceful rise, and the possibility of her rise in the current global order. Essentially he argues that the goal of China's strategy in the 21st Century centers on development with humanity as the foundation and the core (yi ren wei ben, yi ren wei zhongxin). In addition, he adds that "in promoting the development of humankind, one will realize sustainable development."[35] He boldly outlines six aims with regard to development as it concerns China's rise from the present to 2020.[36]

The first is economic growth. GDP should double so that China will be the largest economy in the world, in other words, China's share will comprise $1/5^{th}$ of the world's total GDP, and related, to this China's share of global trade should reach 10% of total trade. The second is to develop comprehensive forces (By this term it is commonly understood to include military, culture, economics, and science and technology etc.). The goal here is that by 2020 China's comprehensive power should have narrowed the gap with the United State's such that the U.S. will be is less than two times as large as China by 2020 (He places the gap at 5 times in 1980, and at 2.5 in 2000.) Though he does not specify how one measures the gap his point is that China's goal should be to significantly reduce it. The third goal is to raise the overall per capita income to insure balanced development. The fourth goal is to maintain national security and unification which includes military modernization. The fifth is to increase China's international competitiveness from a ranking of somewhere currently between 30 to 40 to being ranked among the top 10 most competitive nations. Finally, the sixth is to aim towards achieving sustainable development. Here he means to achieve a zero rate of growth within the population. This also includes reforming governance institutions including social security, and crisis management institutions as well as those designed to address natural disasters. In sum, Hu Angang argues it boils down to "zengzhang, qiangguo, fumin, guojia anquan, tigao guoji jingzhengli, kechixu fazhan" (growth, strong country, prosperous society, secure country, high level of international competitiveness, and sustainable development).

Sun Liping, though not directly discussing peaceful rise is nonetheless useful for our discussion because of his similarities and his differences with Hu Angang. Sun's central argument while, similar to Hu in his focus on development issues, differs in that he looks beyond the simple question of development to explore the fundamental changes in the social structure taking place within the context of development.[37] He believes that there is a fundamental shift from the social structure of the 1980s to a new social structure taking shape in the 1990s. This new social structure is characterized, unlike the 1980s where resources were distributed more equitably, by a re-concentration of resources that benefit fewer rather than greater numbers of citizens thus creating dangerous levels of social cleavages as GDP grows while unemployment, for example, also grows. Indeed, many scholars note that social imbalances, corruption and other social inequities could threaten the legitimacy of the government. The remedy for Sun requires a reworking of the social welfare system which will impact the pace of development. He also argues that the government's concentration at present should be on reestablishing social trust. Similarly, those authors associated with the 'new left' in China, while perhaps not directly addressing the issue of peaceful rise would nonetheless be considered to be part of the group of scholars who have been arguing for the last several years that China's focus must be on her domestic issues.[38] These authors would have China more closely approximate the other East Asian development experiences which strove to maintain a better balance in distributing the economic benefits of development.

These formulations of the domestic issues being critical for foreign policy goals is nicely underscored by David M. Lampton who argues that for China's current leaders these issues are linked to foreign policy : "(f)oreign policy is a means to essentially domestic ends."[39]   In other words, foreign policy surely must be designed with the domestic development agenda in mind.

CONCLUSION

As we mentioned at the beginning of this investigation, the explicit use of the term peaceful rise by the Chinese leadership was fairly short lived and characterized by controversy over its vagueness which naturally raises the question of why it emerged when it did and why it was suddenly dropped. There are at least two variables that emerge when we analyze the above arguments among both domestic and international scholars and when we consider the political environment. These variables, the political timing and the slogan itself go a long way to explaining the trajectory of the notion of the peaceful rise slogan.   They also help us frame the new slogan "peace and development" (heping fazhan) which is the current official Chinese statement on her foreign and domestic policy strategy.

The Politics of the Peaceful Rise Slogan

Scholars very early on in the process realized that not only was the slogan regarding China's growing strength unclear, but that the politics of the slogan also must be part of the dialogue on its meaning given the recent rise of Hu Jintao. Part of the reason it emerged when it did was simply as a response to the growing literature and concern about China as a potential threat to the regional and global security and economic order.

The idea that domestic politics played a key role has been suggested by others.[40] For example, Wang Jisi at the Renmin University conference suggested that "peaceful rise is a political set of questions, not an academic set of questions."[41] Others in conversation discussed the likelihood of the slogan being used for propaganda purposes.   Their arguments center on the leadership transition.

Hu Jintao officially became China's leader at the NPC meeting in early 2003, but only gained control of the all important Central Military Commission (CMC) upon Jiang Zemin's stepping down in 2004.   Thus in terms of the dynamics of politics it is important to remember that the Chinese leadership itself was in transition while attempting to address growing international concerns over China's rise.   One argument is that the politics of the slogan of peaceful rise lies in Hu Jintao's efforts to distinguish his leadership from that of

Jiang Zemin. While others argue that the slogan represents a compromise for the as yet to be solidified new leader of China.[42] While there is a small industry in speculating about the internal disputes and factions within China's leadership, it is not possible to say with certainty what the motivation of a Chinese leader is, but the political dynamics of a regime transition is core to understanding policy and policy changes regardless of the nature of the political system.

What is clear in the Chinese case, however, is that unlike the slow process of Jiang distinguishing himself from Deng Xiaoping's leadership, Hu Jintao has moved more quickly to assert his own ideas about China's future. Indeed he was kicked into action with the SARS outbreak where he presented an alert, populist face and even sacked cadre over the handling of the incident while Jiang appeared increasingly out of touch. Though giving a nod to Jiang Zemin's "three represents" (the CCP represents, advanced culture, advanced productive forces and the great majority of the Chinese people), Hu, within his first two years as China's leader articulated several distinctive slogans to accompany his ideas about China's future among which included 'peaceful rise.' Others include 'harmonious society' (hexie shehui), 'scientific concept of development' (kexue fazhanguan), and the people are the foundation (yiren weiben).[43] What this suggests is that the slogan 'peaceful rise' was an effort to use the Boao conference to further distinguish his new leadership that of Jiang Zemin and to directly assuage growing concerns among China's neighbors about her growing power.[44] So the next question begs to be answered: why was it dropped so quickly?

There are speculations that it was dropped because, as Wu Guoguang argues, Jiang Zemin didn't like the term "because of its foreign policy implication".[45] However, we argue that in thinking about new dimensions in Chinese foreign policy one must move beyond basic arguments about internal party struggles to include the influence of others. The chorus of those arguing that the terms is problematic for definitional reasons as well as its utility as we've discussed above, suggests that the reason it was dropped is more interesting than simply as an act of elite politics. This is not to suggest that politics no longer matters, but it is clear that under Hu Jintao policy directives and approaches are influenced by those outside the inner circle.

The Slogan Itself

Many have discussed the ways policy is influenced, and the study of the influence of intellectuals and specialists is rich with case studies. Early studies include Nina Halpern's work on economic specialists, Catherine Keyser's work on the System Reform Institute under Zhao Ziyang and professionaling the research community, David Shambaugh's work on national security research, Avery Goldstein's work on the influence of the science community and more recently the special *China Quarterly* issue devoted to the role of think tanks in Chinese politics.[46] But, for our purposes here, Zhao Chuansheng's outline of the multiple ways that intellectuals, think tanks and the scholarly community influence the leadership is useful because of his typography of the landscape of policy influence.[47]

Zhao, drawing on the work of Immanuel Wallerstein, moves away from the inner circle-outer circle description to talk about a center and periphery wherein there are various layers and channels through which policy influence travels from the periphery to the center. The forgoing debate accords with two of Zhao's seven channels. The first is channel 1: consultation with policymakers. In this channel a ministry, such as the foreign ministry will invite scholars to discuss policy issues with the leaders including the Politburo who also invite intellectuals and think-tank scholars to give lectures. As he notes, under Hu Jintao both Qin Yaqing professor at the College of Foreign Affairs, and Zhang Yuyan who is an economist at the Chinese academy of Social Sciences (CASS) have been invited to give lectures to the Politburo. Another channel through which scholars are thought to have some influence is his "Channel 3: Conferences and Public Policy Debates" where he notes some of the scholars we have discussed above appear at conferences, on television, and in commentary in newspapers regarding foreign policy. While not direct influence, the argument is that by having junior officials attending conferences, such as Yu Hongzhun from the CCP Liaison department attending the Renmin conference discussed above, the leadership gains insight and is provided feedback on what the scholarly community is saying. Moreover, it is a good opportunity for members of the politburo to learn about various areas and various approaches. This is clearly a channel that Hu Jintao appears ready to use more than his predecessors. Further, the TV and newspaper articles help influence public opinion which is another way scholars are able to attempt, within the confines of the publishing restrictions, to reach the leaders with alternative opinions. And as the above debate reflects, what the leadership is hearing is rich with diversity, and in the case of peaceful rise was clearly concerned with the vagueness and the policy contradictions inherent in the idea. The clearest problem lay in the definition, particularly as it laid bare an apparent contradiction with the leadership's current Taiwan policy. Further, it also opened up a more general debate over where China's priorities should be in the first part of the 21st Century.

A mere five months after it was first used, the term all but disappears from official language. It was replaced with a more benevolent sounding 'peace and development' which had originated with Deng Xiaoping and continued with Jiang Zemin. Given the recent speeches by Hu Jintao on the need to focus on China's 800 million peasants, his lack of patience with official malfeasance, and his consistent desire to make China a better place for her people it can be argued that he heard what scholars and intellectuals have been trying to tell him. He still refers to China's growing global presence but now he says that China is promoting the development of a 'harmonious world' (hexie shijie). Should the reader not make the connection, Hu Jintao has borrowed from his 'harmonious society' (hexie shehui) phrase he began to use a few years ago. It is clear he wants to make his mark on China's future with his own words, and presumably his own actions in both managing the rise and continued development of China.

Finally, the deep debate about the concepts of peace, rise, and the nature of development illustrate the growing diversity and complexity of opinion among Chinese scholars. The differentiation among starting points resemble well articulated theories of international relations. Those most clearly focused on the 'rise' in peaceful rise are best represented in the works of Yan Xuetong. Another group of scholars represented by Qin Yaqing, Pang Zhongyin Huang Renwei, Wang Jisi, and two authors cited in footnote 21, Ding Songquan and Liu Jie take what might generally be termed a constructivist approach when discussing 'rise.' They refer to themselves as neo-liberals. Moreover, we can also see the outlines of those scholars who draw a distinction between focusing on development, arguing that peaceful rise should be changed on either the grounds that the term is not usefully defined or on the grounds that the main focus should be on development and associated problems of internal peace and security and those, as mentioned above, who look at China first from the optic of the international arena.

The idea of peaceful rise is as deeply ambiguous as it is revealing of the growing breadth and depth of critical thinking among China's intellectuals and policymakers, and the short life of this debate provides an illuminating lens through which to more fully appreciate the intellectual foundations of new dimensions in Chinese foreign policy thinking in China.

Notes

[1] Wang Chaohua, "The Minds of the Ninties" in Wang Chaohua, ed., *One China: Many Paths* (London: Verso, 2003) pp. 9-45, p. 10 For a recent interview with one of China's better known "new leftists," see Panak Mishra "China's New Left," *New York Times,* Oct. 15, 2006 on-line edition. Accessed on Oct. 15, 2006.

[2] Wang, Ibid. p. 14.

[3] The Ford Foundation, in its review of past grant-making, studied the development of International Relations studies in China and noted steady development of theoretical and analytical research in IR. For the detailed analysis, see Wang Jisi "International Relations Studies in China Today: Achievements, Trends, and Conditions: A report to the Ford Foundation," 2003.

[4] Indeed, one of Wang's (2003) main arguments about the intellectual ferment of the 1990s is that the connection between universities in China with those abroad, as well as the relationships between Chinese scholars residing abroad and those who have returned has deeply enhanced the intellectual project in the cultural field. That same argument can be made with regard to politics and economics.

[5] All figures for China's economic development come from Tellis, Ashley J. and Michael Wills, *Strategic Asia: Trade, Interdependence, and Security* published by the National Bureau of Asian Research, 2006. The executive summary of the book as well as a data on Asian countries may be viewed online at www.nbr.org/pulications/book.aspx?ID=14.

[6] Pak K. Lee "China's Quest for Oil Security: Oil (wars) in the Pipeline?" *Pacific Review,* vol. 18 no. 2, June 2005, pp. 265-301 and 267. International Energy Agency data recounted in Lee, p. 267.

[7] See Zheng Bijian, "China's 'Peaceful Rise' to Great- Power Status" *Foreign Affairs*, Sept/Oct. 2005, p.19.

[8] David M. Lampton, "The Role of China in Latin America", testimony for Senate Foreign Relations Subcommittee on Western Hemisphere, Peace Corps and Narcotics Affairs, September 20, 2005. http://www.nixoncenter.org/index.cfm?action=showPage &page=lampton

[9] For a theoretical discussion about the China threat, see John J. Mearsheimer, *The Tragedy of Great Power Politics*, (W.W. Norton & Company, Inc., 2001); Zalamay khalizad et al., *The United States and a Rising China: Strategic and Military Implications*, Rand, 1999. Senate testimony by David M. Lampton, "What Growing Chinese Power Means for America", testimony for United States Senate Committee on Foreign Relations Hearing on "The Emergence of China Throughout Asia: Security and Economic Consequences for the U.S.," at the East Asian and Pacific Affairs Subcommittee, June 7, 2005. Robert D. Kaplan "How We Would Fight China" in *The Atlantic Monthly*, vol. 295, no. 5 June 2005 pp. 49-64. Popular books on the China threat include Ross Terrill, *The New Chinese Empire: What it Means for the U.S. (New York: Basic Books, 2003);* Bill Gertz, *China Threat: How the People's Republic of China Targets the U.S.* (Washington DC: Regnery Publishing, Inc. 2000); Herbert Yee, *China Threat; Perceptions, Myth and Reality* (New York: Routledge Curzon, 2002) and Gordon Chang, *The Coming Collapse of China* (New York: Random House, 2001).

[10] For a deep and systematic discussion on Chinese nationalism, see Zhao Shuisheng, *A Nation-State By Construction* (Stanford, Stanford University Press, 2004). For the role of nationalism in specific foreign policy arenas, see Zhidong Hao "Between War and Peace: The Role of Nationalism in China's U.S. Policy Making with Regard to Taiwan" in Yufan Hao and Lin Su, eds. *China's Foreign Policy Making* (Hampshire: Ashgate, 2005) pp. 139-168. For a focus on the spontaneous grass roots driven rise in nationalist sentiment, see Peter Hays Gries *China's New Nationalism: Pride, Politics, and Diplomacy* (Berkeley: University of California Press, 2004).

[11] Kokubun Ryosei and Wang Jisi, eds., *The Rise of China and a Changing East Asian Order* (Tokyo, Japan Center for International Exchange, 2004), pp. 3-4.

[12] For details on the rise of strong anti-American feelings which began in 1996, and culminated in mass demonstrations held in major cities after the bombing of the Chinese Embassy in Belgrade by the United States in May 1999, See Li Hongshan, "Recent Anti-Americanism in China: Historical Roots and Impact," in Yufan Hao & Lin Su, eds., *China's Foreign Policy Making: Societal Force and Chinese American Policy*, 2005, pp. 41-68.

[13] See Shi Yinghong, "The Regularity of International Politics and its Enlightenment to China" (Guojizhengzhi de shijixingguilu jiqi dui zhongguo de qishi), Strategy and Management, no. 4, 1995; Yan Xuetong, International Environment for China's Rise (Zhongguo jueqi—guojihuanjing pinggu), (Tianjing, China: Tianjing Renmin Press, 1998). This work represents one of the earliest uses of the term rise in discussing China's growing power.

[14] Zheng Bijian, "New Path for China's Peaceful Rise and the Future of Asia," Speech at the Bo'ao Forum for Asia 2003 (November 3, 2003), in Zheng Bijian, *Peaceful Rise – China's New Road to Development*, (Central Party School Publishing House, CPC, 2005), p33. See also the interview with Li Junru, Vce President of the Central Party School where he also notes that China's peaceful rise began in 1978, "Peaceful Rise," *Beijing Review*, April 22, 2004, vol. 47. no. 16, p. 19.

[15] Wen Jiabao, "Turn Your Gaze Upon China," Speech at Harvard University, Dec. 10, 2003. http://www.fmprc.gov.cn/chn/wjdt/zyjh/t56075.htm

[16] For an English version of the chronology, see *Beijing Review*, April 22, 2004. vol. 47, no. 16 p. 19.

[17] The Beijing conference is covered in "Review of the Symposium: China's Peaceful Rise: International Environment and Strategy," *Teaching and Research*, Vol. 4, April 2004, pp.5-20. (hereafter quotations taken from this review will be noted as TAR and page number)

[18] "Review of the Symposium: the Road to China's Peaceful Rise" (guanyu zhongguo heping jueqi daolu de tantao), *World Economic Study* (Shijie Jingji Yanjiu), Vol. 5, 2004, pp. 4-24. (hereafter all quotations taken from this review will be noted as WES and page number).

[19] "Collected Essays: The Rise of Great Power and China's Options" *Chinese Academic Social Science*, Vol. 5, 2004.

[20] A brief search at China's national library in Beijing revealed one Ph.D. dissertation, three maters' theses, and twelve books among which are: Peng Peng, ed., *Peaceful Rising Theory* (heping jueqi lun) (Guangzhou: Guangdong People's Press, 2005); Guo Wanchao, *Rise of China* (sic) (Zhongguo jueqi) (Nanchang:Jiangxi People's Press, 2004); Cao Yongxin, *Peace and Doctrine* (heping yu zhuyi) (Shanghai: Xuelin Press, 2005); Liu Jie, *Regimenazation (sic): The Strategic Choice in the Course of China's Peaceful Rise* (jizhihua sheng cun) (Beijing: Shishi Press, 2004); Ding Songchuan, *China's Rising and Sino-American Relations* (zhongguo jueqi yu zhongmei guanxi) (Beijing: Chinese Social Science Press, 2005). In English, see the newly released edited volume, Sujian Guo, ed., *China's 'Peaceful Rise' in the 21st Century* (London: Ashgate, 2006).

[21] See Shaohua Hu, "Revisiting Chinese Pacifism" in *Asian Affairs: An American Review*, vol. 32, no. 4 (Winter) 2006, pp. 256-278. Quotations taken from pages 258 and 275 respectively.

[22] Pang Zhongying, "The Core of Peaceful Rising is Peace" (heping jueqi guanjian zai heping), See the Forum of Public Diplomacy in *Southern Weekend* (nanfang zhoumuo), March 25, 2004.

[23] But, as Quansheng Zhao notes, it is important to remember that "a scholar who is allowed to discuss foreign policy issues in public is expected to explain and validate only the official party lines." See Quansheng Zhao, "Impact of Intellectuals and Think Tanks on Chinese Foreign Policy," in Yufan Hao and Lin Su eds., *China's Foreign Policy Making*, pp. 123-138; p. 125.

[24] Yan Xuetong and Sun Xuefeng, eds., *The Rise of China and its Strategy* (Beijing: Peking University Press, 2005), p. 2.

[25] "Deng Initiates New Policy 'Guiding Principle'," *Hong Kong Ching Pao*, Translated in FBIS HK061100091, November 5, 1991.

[26] Zhang Minqian, "Peaceful Rise: the Aim at Peace," (Hepingjueqi de mubiao zaiyu heping), *Teaching and Research*, Vol. 4, April 2004, pp.5-20

[27] A zero sum game, a common concept in IR theory is a "game" in which one nation's win is another's loss. Moreover, in the arena of security, if one country strengthens their security it automatically means another country is less secure.

[28] For survey research on the emerging attitudes of elites toward the U.S., see Hao YuFan and Lin Su "Contending Views: Emerging Chinese Elite's Perception of America" in Hao and Lin, eds. *China's Foreign Policy Making*, pp. 19-40.

[29] Sun Xuefeng, "Strategic Options and Rise of Great Power," in Yan Xuetong and Sun Xuefeng, eds., *The Rise of China and its Strategy*, 2005, pp. 27-30.

[30] Yan Xuetong, "Preface" in Yan Xuetong and Sun Xuefeng, eds., *The Rise of China and Its Strategy*, p. 2.

[31] Yaqing Qin "A Response to Yong Deng: Power, Perception and the Cultural Lens," *Asian Affairs: An American Review*, Fall 2001, Vol. 28, Issue 3, pp. 155-159.

[32] Qin Yaqing "Anarchic Culture and International Violence" in Collected Essays: The Rise of Great Power and China's Options" *Chinese Academic Social Science*, Vol. 5, 2004; pp. 53-56; p. 54.
[33] For Huang Renwei's statements in Shanghai, see *Shanghai Review*, pp. 11-12. For his earlier formulation, see Huang Renwei, *Zhongguo jueqi de shijian he kongjian* (Time and Space in China's Rising) (Shanghai: Shanghai Academy of Social Science Press, 2002).
[34] Li Qiang "heping queqi zaiyu heping" (Peaceful Rise Lies within Peace) in Yan Xuetong and Sun Xuefeng, eds., *The Rise of China and Its Strategy*, pp. 216-219, p. 216.
[35] See Hu Angang "How to View China's Rise-Preface" (ruhe kandai zhongguo jueqi-dai xuyan) in Men Honghua, ed., *Zhongguo: Daguo Jueqi* (The Rise of Modern China) (Hangzhou: Zhejiang Renmin Chubanshe, 2004), pp. 1-17; p. 8.
[36] The following discussion of Hu's six points draws on his chapter as noted above.
[37] See Sun Liping, *Cleavage: Chinese Society since the 1990s* (duanlie: 20shiji 90 niandai yilai de zhongguo shehui) (Beijing: Social Science Documentation Publishing House, 2003).
[38] For writings from the new left perspective see Gong Yang, ed., *Trends of Thought* (sichao) (Beijing: Chinese Social Sciences Press, 2003).
[39] David M. Lampton, "The Role of China in Latin America", testimony for Senate Foreign Relations Subcommittee on Western Hemisphere, Peace Corps, and Narcotics Affairs. September 20, 2005, http://www.nixoncenter.org/index.cfm?action=showPage &page=lampton
[40] See, for example, Wu Guoguang, "The Peaceful Emergence of a Great Power?" *Social Research*, Vol. 73, No. 1, Spring 2006, pp. 317-344, especially page 321-322.
[41] Wang Jisi "The Significance of Peaceful Rise" (heping jueqi tichu de yiyi) in Yan Xuetong and Sun Xuefeng, eds., *The Rise of China and Its Strategy* (Beijing: Peking University Press, 2005), pp. 215-216 and p. 215.
[42] For an argument on Jiang's "hawks" versus Hu's "doves," see Abanti Bhattacharya, "Revisitng Chna's "Peaceful Rise:" Implications for India" in *East Asia* Vol. 22. No. 4 (Winter). pp. 59-80 and p. 63.
[43] Indeed, in the lead up to the 6th plenum of the 16th Communist Party Congress, party bosses were arrested, and then at the Congress, Hu Jintao clearly and forcefully articulated the need for China to focus on balanced development. Some have argued that this is the strongest statement by a Chinese leader in many years. For a review of the meeting in English, see Li Li "In Pursuit of Social Harmony," *Beijing Review*, Vol. 49, No. 42, October 19, 2006.
[44] Yiwei Wang, On the Rise, *Asia Times Online* (atimes.com), 2004. Elizabeth Economy, "China's Rise in Southeast Asia: Implications for Japan and the United States," *Journal of Contemporary China*, August 2005; also published in *Japan Focus* on October 6, 2005; Nam Young-sook, "China's Industrial Rise and the Challenges Facing Korea," *East Asian Review*, Vol. 16, No.2, Summer 2004, pp.43-64; Nicholas R. Lardy, "The Economic Rise of China: Threat or Opportunity?" August 1, 2003, http://www.clevelandfed.org/Research/Com2003/0801.pdf
[45] Wu Guoguang "The Peaceful Emergence of a Great Power?" p.324.
[46] See Nina Halpern "Economic Specialists and the Making of Chinese Economic Policy, 1955-1985 (University of Michigan, PhD dissertation, 1985); David L. Shambaugh, "China's National Security Research Bureaucracy." *China Quarterly*, No, 110 (June) 1987, pp. 276 – 304; Carol Lee Hamrin and Timothy Cheek, eds. *China's Establishment Intellectuals* (Armonk: ME Sharpe, 1986). Nina Halpern, "Scientific Decision Making: The Organization of Expert Advice in Post - Mao China." In Denis Fred Simon and Merle Goldman, eds., *Science and Technology in Post-Mao China* (*Cambridge: Harvard University Press,* 1989), pp. 157-174; Nina Halpern, "Social Scientist as Policy Advisors in Post-Mao China: Explaining the Pattern of Advice." *The Australian Journal of*

Chinese Affairs, Issue 19/20, 1988, pp. 215-240; Timothy Cheek, "From Priest to Professionals: Intellectuals and the State Under the CCP" in Jeffrey N. Wasserstrom and Elizabeth J. Perry, eds., *Popular Protest and Political Culture* (Bolder, Co: Westview, 1992); Merle Goldman, "Hu Yaobang's Intellectual Network and the Theory Conference of 1979," *China Quarterly,* No. 126 (June) 2001, pp. 219-242; Catherine Keyser, *Professionalizing Research in Post-Mao China: The System Reform Institute and Policy Making* (Armonk, M.E. Sharpe, 2002). See also, the special issue of *China Quarterly* 171 (September 2002) which includes several articles discussing the influence of various think tanks and research organizations in a variety of fields including foreign policy.

[47] Chuansheng Zhao "Impact of Intellectuals and Think Tanks on Chinese Foreign Policy" in *China's Foreign Policy Making,* pp. 123-138. The following paragraph draws heavily from this chapter.

Chapter 3

China Rising and its Foreign Policy Orientations: Perspectives from China's Emerging Elites

Xiaoyu Pu and Guang Zhang

Since the 1990s, the prospect of China's rise to prominence has been subject to endless speculation and debate within the international community, the crucial questions being whether China's emergence will destabilize the international order and whether the established powers will be able to incorporate China peacefully.[1] Most previous studies on this topic are based on deductions from international relations theories and/or empirical observation of Chinese foreign policy behavior. In addition, although some evaluations indicate that China has a status quo orientation, this still leaves open a more crucial question about China's strategic intentions in the future: Will China shift its currently moderate foreign policy to a more assertive approach as its power status changes in the international system? To investigate this question, evaluation of China's material capabilities is far from enough: it is equally important to systematically analyze the ideational factors of Chinese foreign policy. This chapter draws on Q methodology for a study of opinions about Chinese foreign policy among China's emerging elites.[2] The "emerging elites" in this study refer to those individuals who have current or potential influence on public policy in Chinese society, including middle-level elites (such as bureaucrats and scholars) and those who have the potential to influence Chinese policy process in the future (such as university students). The study will focus on participants' perspectives on current Chinese foreign policy and their appraisal concerning what Chinese foreign policy should be in the next two decades.

The first and the second sections introduce the debate on the rise of China from a variety of theoretical perspectives. The third section introduces Q methodology. The fourth section discusses research design and data collections. The fifth section presents the analysis of the findings. In the conclusion, theoretical and policy implications of this study are discussed.

THE DEBATE ON THE RISE OF CHINA

In the international community, the prospect of an ascendant China has been a source of endless speculation and debate. Realist scholars have focused on the growth of China's material capabilities and its implications for power politics in the international system. According to realist theory, an emerging great power often challenges the *status quo* of the international system and thus leads to international instability.[3] From the standpoint of the realist approach, there are different understandings of great power politics. Offensive realists such as Mearsheimer argue that great powers will always maximize their relative power with hegemony as their ultimate goal.[4] In particular, Mearsheimer argues that "a wealthy China thus would not be a *status quo* power but an aggressive state determined to achieve regional hegemony."[5] Defensive realism assumes that nation-states are security-seekers in an anarchic international system.[6] Following the framework of defensive realism, China's foreign policy behavior is understood as a search for security in international relations.[7] For instance, according to Nathan and Ross, "China has been a reactive power, striving not to alter but to maintain regional patterns of power."[8] Power transition theory proposes that wars among great powers are most likely when a power transition occurs between the dominant state and a dissatisfied challenger.[9] According to this approach, China is seen as a potential future contender for global leadership, but a war is not an inevitable certainty.[10] According to this approach, the key issue is whether China could be persuaded by the Western powers to join the *status quo* of the international order.[11]

Liberal scholars emphasize that China rises within the new context of economic globalization and interdependence.[12] Economic interdependence will make it unprofitable to fight wars for territories and natural resources, and even very strong countries will be partly dependent on industries headquartered somewhere else.[13] Liberal scholars also believe that its increasing participation in international institutions should give China a growing stake in the stability and continuity of the current international order, and that China has become more cooperative within international institutions.[14]

From a constructivist perspective, Chinese foreign policy is largely shaped by social and subjective factors such as ideas, identities and norms.[15] According to Johnston, there are ideational roots to Chinese strategic behaviors,[16] and Callahan states that understanding the rise of China is a matter of interpretation.[17] Thus it is important to interpret the discourse and texts of the Chinese discussion on the rise of China.[18]

Since not all rising powers are dissatisfied with the *status quo* of international order, the established great powers should evaluate the intentions of a rising power before they decide what types of responses are appropriate to deal with it.[19] Having evaluated the pattern of Chinese foreign policy behaviors, Johnston argues that China has been more cooperative and more integrated into the current international order.[20] However, foreign policy behaviors do not necessarily indicate the strategic intentions of a rising great power, because even states with *revisionist* intentions do not necessarily exhibit *revisionist* behaviors.[21] Thus, even though evaluations of current Chinese foreign policy indicate that China has adopted a *status quo* orientation in the short term,[22] this still leaves open a more crucial question about China's strategic intentions in the future: Will China shift its currently moderate foreign policy to a more assertive approach as its power status changes in the international system?[23]

IDEAS AND CHINESE FOREIGN POLICY

To investigate China's strategic intentions, it is important to systematically analyze the ideational factors in Chinese foreign policy. The crucial question is: How do the Chinese understand the rise of China and its foreign policy implications?

There is a growing literature on Chinese worldviews of international affairs. Based on survey data obtained in Beijing, Johnston reports that the Chinese middle class exhibits a more liberal attitude towards international affairs.[24] Also through the analysis of survey data, Jie Chen has examined urban Chinese perceptions of threats from the United States and Japan.[25] In addition, Hao and Lin have identified contending views about the United States among China's emerging elites.[26] Drawing on in-depth interviews of Chinese officials and strategic analysts, Goldstein argues that China's grand strategy is to promote the growth of its power while avoiding other countries perceiving its rise as a threat.[27] Through analyzing the literature by Chinese strategists and IR scholars, Pillsbury argues that Chinese analysts believe in geopolitics and perceive an "inevitable" multipolar future.[28] A more recent study provides a different picture—of mainstream Chinese analysts generally perceiving the United States as the only superpower in the foreseeable future.[29] Combining the analysis of Chinese strategic literature with elite interviews, Mumin Chen identifies three points of view concerning China's strategic choices: a "globalist" view, an "autonomist" view, and an "economic nationalist" view.[30]

Some scholars turn to the literature of strategic culture in order to predict the long-term pattern of Chinese strategic intentions. However, recent studies of Chinese strategic culture provide inconsistent answers. By taking two forms of content analysis (cognitive mapping and symbolic analysis), Johnston argues that China has a *parabellum* culture of offensive realism that leads to a pattern of aggressive behavior.[31] Following Johnston's argument, Goldstein predicts that it is highly likely that China will shift its current moderate foreign policy to an assertive one when its power is stronger.[32] By taking another form of content analysis (operational code analysis), Feng indicates that Johnston's cultural realist argument is only partially correct and needs to be qualified in important respects.[33] Furthermore, by examining the operational code of four top Chinese leaders (Mao Zedong, Deng Xiaoping, Jiang Zemin and Hu Jintao), Feng argues that Chinese leaders' cultural underpinnings are defensive, and that China may not initiate conflicts under most conditions despite its power changes.[34] The literature on Chinese strategic culture has shed new light on China's long-term pattern of foreign policy behaviors. However, as answers to questions about

China's strategic intentions, the strategic culture studies by Johnston and Feng have limitations. Both scholars have taken historical materials as the main evidence, and whereas history always matters in shaping Chinese foreign policy, we are not sure to what extent the historical pattern is relevant to current and future orientations of Chinese foreign policy.

If we conceive of China's international relations in personal terms, its intention is neither dispositionally defensive nor dispositionally offensive.[35] Rather, its foreign policy orientation is shaped by the strategic context that China faces as well as the ideas of its elites. By taking an empirical approach, this study seeks to problematize the notion of a coherent "Chinese worldview."[36] As some prominent China experts emphasize, "China is also arguably much more pluralistic in its views on the outside world, with important, wide-ranging debates within the country and within the government about how Beijing should address the world. This means China's future is far from determined."[37] More specifically, the purpose of this study is to investigate what kinds of ideas the emerging Chinese elites entertain in the context of the present and of the strategic future. Furthermore, in the literature on Chinese views of international affairs, a variety of methodologies have been applied, including survey research, elite interviewing, and content analysis. This study adds to this literature by employing Q methodology in the study of the subjective opinions of China's emerging elites. Thus, this study serves two purposes: first, to reveal alternative perspectives on the current Chinese foreign policy orientation; and second, to provide a window into the pattern of possible future Chinese policy orientations.

Q METHODOLOGY

This chapter draws on Q methodology for a study of opinions on Chinese foreign policy orientations among China's emerging elites. Invented by psychologist William Stephenson, Q methodology is a unique conceptual framework and accompanying social-scientific method (Q technique) that provides the basis for a systematic examination of human subjectivity.[38] Q methodology has been widely used in a variety of disciplines such as psychology, mass communication, public administration and advertising. Within political science, Q methodology has recently been applied to a variety of topics, such as identity politics, democracy and comparative democratization, and environmental politics.[39]

Procedurally, Q methodology can be divided into the following steps. First, the *concourse* (population of statements) for a topic of discussion is defined and a representative set of statements (Q sample) is selected, typically on the basis of experimental design principles. Second, an equally representative set of participants is selected, often on the basis of theoretical dimensions related to the study. Third, the statements in the Q sample are rank-ordered by participants in an array that reflects each participant's overall perspective on the topic. Finally, the rank-orderings (Q sorts) are statistically analyzed through correlation and factor analysis.[40] Q methodology therefore provides an intensive and statistically relevant analysis for gaining a deeper understanding of participants' subjective points of view.[41]

Compared to conventional quantitative methods (collectively referred to as R methodology) such as survey research, Q methodology is unique in combing intensive depth with quantitative rigor, thus providing a bridge between qualitative and quantitative traditions.[42] There are several differences between Q methodology and conventional quantitative methods. First, whereas R methodology is primarily concerned with correlating opinions with objective traits such as age, gender and socio-economic status, Q methodology is concerned with patterns of subjective views *within* persons, i.e., from the standpoint of the political actor.[43] For example, Johnston's survey study endeavors to show how the foreign policy attitudes of the Chinese middle class are different from those of other social groups.[44] By way of contrast, the purpose of a Q-methodological project such as in this paper is to study people's subjective attitudes themselves as a whole—i.e., directly and for themselves, and not as they correlate with objective traits. Second, whereas the population in survey research refers to all participants within a respondent domain, the population in Q methodology refers to all statements within a domain of discourse.[45] Thus, whereas survey research examines the distribution of opinions within a population of persons, Q methodology focuses intensively on the subjective patterns and structures within a universe of communicability. For this reason, whereas the participants in survey research are usually randomly selected so as to ensure external validity, the selection of participants in Q study is usually theory-driven, and a relatively small number of participants are generally sufficient.[46] Third, whereas in survey research participants' responses take on meaning in relation to the prior meanings and constructs of researchers, in Q methodology participants are given the opportunity to speak for themselves and to reveal their own individual standpoints.[47]

The relationship between Q and R as methodologies can be complementary.[48] In particular, Q methodology can help identify patterns of subjectivity that survey research might not find. For instance, although survey research often assumes the "unification/status quo/independence" trifurcation in Taiwanese opinion on national identity, Wong and Sun's Q study identified five discourses: Chinese nationalism, status-quoism, confused identity, Taiwan-prioritism and Taiwanese nationalism.[49]

RESEARCH DESIGN AND DATA COLLECTION

In Q methodology, the *concourse* represents all the statements related to a topic of discussion, such as China's foreign policy orientation, which are innumerable and in principle infinite. The statements in the concourse were collected from a variety of sources, including books, journals and newspapers. By constructing a Q sample, the statements are reduced to a manageable number that is theoretically representative of all the opinions on the topic. Based on a theoretical framework for the study of Chinese foreign policy, the universe of statements was reduced to a Q sample of 27 statements (see Table 4, statements 1-27).

A theoretical framework was adopted to help achieve representativeness in the Q-sample statements. Initially, the statements from the concourse were divided into three categories: The first included statements on the philosophy and guiding principles, drawn mainly from some comprehensive studies of Chinese strategic culture and grand strategy;[50] the second included statements on patterns of foreign policy behaviors, adopting Johnston's criteria for evaluating Chinese foreign policy behaviors;[51] and the third included statements on various important policy issue areas, including China's U.S. policy, Japan policy, Asian regional policy, Taiwan policy, and policy toward other great powers. Within each of these categories, statements were included that related to different theoretical perspectives, including realism, liberalism and social constructivism.

Participants selected to provide their viewpoints were purposely drawn from a variety of backgrounds. In Q methodology, the goal is not to generalize based on demographic or other characteristics, nor in terms of the proportion of the respondent population belonging in one factor rather than another; rather, all that is required are enough participants "to establish the existence of a factor for purposes of comparing one factor with another."[52] The selection of participants in Q methodology is therefore theoretically-driven and the goal is representativeness, but not in a random-sampling sense.[53] The P-set structure helps us identify the participants that can be theoretically relevant to the topic of discussion (see Table 1). A variety of issues were considered to assist in achieving diversity and representativeness in the participant sample—e.g., different career backgrounds that might influence people's opinions on foreign policy,[54] or gender and age in so far as these might also influence people's points of view.[55]

Theoretically, the P-set structure represents an ideal-type combination designed to maximize the breadth and comprehensiveness of participants.[56] In practice, this study includes 24 participants from various backgrounds, including diplomats and other Chinese officials, businessmen, journalists, scholars and students. The participants come from a variety of institutions and agencies: officials from China's Ministry of Foreign Affairs, Ministry of Commerce, National Auditing Office, and Tianjin Municipal Government; journalists from *Metro Express* (Tianjin); business managers from China Unicom and Shandong International Trust & Investment Corporation (SITIC); and scholars and students (including overseas Chinese students) from Nankai University, Stanford University, Ohio State University, Kent State University, and Purdue University.[57] The ages of these participants range from early 20s to 60s, and there are both male and female participants.

The data were collected from December, 2005 to January, 2006, and Q sorts were obtained under two conditions of instruction: (1) First, participants rank-ordered the 27 statements according to their own individual understandings of *current* Chinese foreign policy. (2) Under the second condition of instruction, participants were asked to predict and evaluate Chinese foreign policy as they expected that it would be in 2020, i.e., to predict *future* Chinese foreign policy. A total of 42 Q sorts were obtained.[58]

FINDINGS

The 42 Q sorts were analyzed through factor analysis with the aid of the PQMethod software.[59] The participants' factor loadings and their demographic backgrounds are presented in Table 2, and the factor arrays of each statement are presented in Table 4. The interpretation of each factor takes into account both the relative magnitude of the factor scores as well as the theoretical meaning of statements.

Four different perspectives (factors A, B, C, D) are identified among the participants; i.e., four different orientations toward Chinese foreign policy. This suggests that the Chinese foreign policy audience is segmented into four significantly different groupings, or discourses, relative to the foreign policy discussion represented in the sample of statements.

Factor A: "Orthodox Globalist"

As indicated in the pattern of scores associated with the statements (Table 4), factor A is comparable to an orthodox version of the "peaceful development" (or "peaceful rise") proposition promoted by Chinese government and China's top leaders.[60] The factor supports the "peaceful development" position advanced by the Chinese government (statement no. 6), and proposes that China actively participate in the current international orders and norms (statement no. 12). On grand strategy, this factor emphasizes that China should foster favorable conditions for its modernization and increase its international status while reducing the risk that others will feel threatened by a rising China (statement no. 1). This factor also emphasizes that China should appreciate international norms and the soft powers (statement no. 23). However, this factor also argues that China should stand firm in some historical and political disputes with other Western countries (statement no. 25). In particular, this factor disagrees with the "new thinking" proposition toward Japan (statement no. 20).

The most typical participant that belongs to this factor—i.e., the person with the highest and purest factor loading—is a senior diplomat in China's Ministry of Foreign Affairs (participant 016a, b, Table 2). Other participants belonging to this factor include officials of other central government agencies, journalists, academics, and overseas Chinese students (see Table 2).

Factor B: "New Thinking Globalist"

As examination of the scores in Table 4 also reveals, factor B largely shares the same proposition on China's "peaceful development," and largely agrees that

China should actively participate in the current international orders. But this factor is different from the orthodox version of China's "peaceful development." First of all, this factor proposes that China should adopt some "new thinking" toward Japan and other Western powers. For instance, this factor indicates that China should put historical issues out of diplomatic agenda toward Japan (statement no. 20). It also emphasizes that China will not exclude the U.S. from Asia (statement no. 21). However, this factor still emphasizes China's bottom-line position concerning the Taiwan issue (statement no. 25).

The most typical participant in this factor is a younger-generation diplomat in China's Ministry of Foreign Affairs (participant 017a, b, Table 2). The other participant with membership in this factor is an official in Nankai University (participant 020a).

Factor C: "Economic Nationalist"

This factor represents a nationalistic stance relative to Chinese foreign policy. This factor emphasizes that China should focus for now on economic development, but that when its power is strong enough, it should challenge the United States (statement no. 4). On the traditional disputes (such as those involving Taiwan and Japan), this factor is even more nationalistic. For instance, this factor strongly disagrees with any new thinking concerning historical issues regarding Japan (statement no. 20), and this factor emphasizes China's willingness to use military force were Taiwan to declare independence (statement no. 25).

The participants that belong to this factor include a businessman (participant 007a, Table 2), a journalist (participant 009a, b), a computer scientist (participant 012a, b), and an official of economic affairs (014b).

Factor D: "Pacifist"

With regard to many policy issues, factor D largely agrees with the "peaceful development" proposition of the Chinese government (e.g., statement no. 6), but what makes the factor unique is that it takes peace as the ultimate means and purpose of foreign policy regardless of policy issue, while other factors might agree that China should use military force in specific situations.

First of all, with respect to the principle of foreign policy, factor D strongly supports the argument that war should be avoided and the military should be the last resort (statement no. 3). This factor also strongly opposes the notion that China should use military force in dealing with the core issues of its rise (statement no. 5), and disagrees with the idea of translating economic strengths into military power in order to challenge the U.S. in the future (statement no. 4). Even though this factor worries about potential security threats from Western powers (statement no. 17), it does not support an active strategic and military balance against those powers (statement no. 15). Furthermore, while factors A,

B, and C largely agree that China should use military force if Taiwan declares independence (statement no. 25, scores +2, +4, and +4, respectively), factor D has reservations (score 0).

The participants that belong to this factor include two officials of economic affairs (013a, b, 015b, Table 2) and an overseas Chinese PhD student (001b).

The above findings reveal that there are at least four possible groupings among China's emerging elites regarding Chinese foreign policy. Both factor A ("orthodox globalist") and factor B ("new thinking globalist") generally agree with the "peaceful development" proposition promoted by the Chinese government, but factor B has more innovative ideas that are different from the orthodox version of China's current foreign policy. Factor C ("economic nationalists") has a strong nationalistic point of view on various issues of Chinese foreign policy. What makes factor D ("pacifist") different from other factors is that this factor emphasizes peace as the ultimate goal regardless policy issue, while other factors might support possible Chinese military actions under some specific circumstances, such as containing Taiwan independence.

We did an analysis of variance (ANOVA) on the factor loadings (in table 2) to determine whether there was any significant current/future difference in any of the four factors. And we find that there is no statistically significant difference (see Table 3). This indicates that, as a whole group, Chinese emerging elites who participated in this project do not demonstrate any significant difference when they evaluate current and future Chinese foreign policy. However, this does not mean that there is no individual different opinion. For instance, a Chinese PhD student (participant 001a, b) shifted his opinion from factor A ("orthodox globalist") to factor D ("pacifist") when he evaluated current and future Chinese foreign policy (see Table 2).

CONCLUSION

Many previous studies on the topic of the rise of China have been based on deductions from international relations theories and/or empirical observation of Chinese foreign policy behavior. While many realist scholars are concerned about China's growing material power, scholars from other theoretical perspectives pay more attention to the intentions of Chinese foreign policy makers.[61] The crucial issue is that although some evaluations of current Chinese foreign policy indicate that China has a status quo orientation, there will still be endless speculation about China's future strategic orientation: Will China shift its currently moderate foreign policy to a more assertive approach as its power status changes within the international system?

To investigate China's strategic intentions, it is important to systematically analyze the ideational factors in Chinese foreign policy. The debate about defensive vs. offensive strategic culture in Chinese foreign policy does not provide us with consistent indicators about China's future strategic intentions. This study assumes that China's intention is neither dispositionally defensive nor dispositionally offensive; rather, that its foreign policy orientation is shaped by the strategic context that China faces as well as the ideas of Chinese elites.

By taking an empirical approach to open the "black box" of Chinese foreign policy, this chapter rejects the notion of a coherent and singular "Chinese worldview." This study has examined the ideas that emerging Chinese elites have adopted in the context of current and future strategic frames of reference, and four types of foreign policy idea systems have been identified: "orthodox globalist," "new thinking globalist," "economic nationalist," and "pacifist."

This study has taken a functional rather than a social-structural approach for the grouping of opinions.[62] Different from the grouping of opinions by social categories, this chapter demonstrates that objective traits (such as career backgrounds and social-economic status) do not determine people's subjective opinions on foreign policy.[63] Among those people with the same social-economic status (such as several diplomats), there are diverse opinions on Chinese foreign policy. Furthermore, although the "peace development" proposition has become a dominant discourse within discussions about Chinese foreign policy, this study has demonstrated the existence of multiple points of view regarding orientations of Chinese foreign policy among China's emerging elites.

The purpose of this Q-methodological study has been to investigate the structure of people's subjective opinions, but it does not address the question about the proportion of emerging Chinese elites that belongs to each type of opinion. In order to predict future Chinese foreign policy, studies need to be undertaken to determine which of the idea types will play a dominant role in Chinese policy decision making. To answer this question, further studies (involving surveys and in-depth interviews) will be needed to find how each type of ideas is distributed in the Chinese foreign policy decision-making community.

Appendix

Table 3.1 P-set Structure: Backgrounds of Participants

Main Effects	Levels			N
A. Professions	(a) government (c) business	(b) media (d) academia		4
B. Gender	(e) male	(f) female		2
C. Age	(g) young	(h) middle	(i) old	3

Note: *ABC=(4)(2)(3)=24 combinations*

Table 3.2 Factor Matrix
(Significant loadings in boldface)

Participants		A	B	C	D	Occupation	Age
		Factor Loadings					

Current Chinese Foreign Policy

	Participants	A	B	C	D	Occupation	Age
1	001a	**41**	31	09	07	Student (KSU)	30-50
2	002a	**55**	21	26	18	Student (KSU)	<30
3	003a	13	58	45	20	Student (Stanford)	<30
4	004a	39	30	66	16	Student (Purdue)	<30
5	005a	62	03	42	-16	Official (Commerce)	<30
6	006a	66	41	15	-09	Business (China Unicom)	<30
7	007a	23	25	**56**	-10	Business (SITIC)	<30
8	008a	**45**	14	**-52**	-01	Journalist	30-50
9	009a	32	-08	**78**	01	Journalist	30-50
10	010a	67	38	32	-14	Journalist	30-50
11	011a	**73**	25	01	29	Journalist	30-50
12	012a	33	-09	**65**	-03	Computer Scientist	<30
13	013a	29	-14	33	**68**	Senior Official (Auditing)	30-50
14	014a	59	-04	27	36	Official (Auditing)	<30
15	015a	37	40	25	33	Official (Auditing)	30-50
16	016a	**84**	19	05	-01	Senior diplomat	50-60
17	017a	18	**53**	-12	17	Diplomat	30-50
18	018a	**66**	20	19	13	Diplomat	30-50
19	019a	56	47	15	23	Student (Nankai)	<30
20	020a	28	**51**	31	-21	Official (Nankai)	<30
21	021a	72	21	09	35	Official(Tianjin)	50-60
22	022a	**82**	21	21	03	Student (KSU)	<30
23	023a	50	68	26	-06	Student (KSU)	<30
24	024a	42	-04	15	-40	Student (OSU)	<30

Future Chinese Foreign Policy

		A	B	C	D	Occupation	Age
25	001b	22	08	27	**51**	Student (KSU)	30-50
26	002b	15	29	15	05	Student (KSU)	<30
27	003b	26	44	37	19	Student (Stanford)	<30
28	004b	50	30	40	40	Student (Purdue)	<30
29	006b	**44**	29	24	-21	Business (China Unicom)	<30
30	007b	**58**	20	31	-18	Business (SITIC)	<30
31	008b	**71**	07	26	-16	Journalist	30-50
32	009b	32	-08	**78**	01	Journalist	30-50
33	010b	67	38	32	-14	Journalist	30-50
34	011b	**61**	28	12	18	Journalist	30-50

35	012b	16	-32	**61**	-14	Computer Scientist	<30
36	013b	19	02	11	**68**	Senior Official (Auditing)	30-50
37	014b	24	-26	**44**	27	Official (Auditing)	<30
38	015b	30	15	23	**73**	Official (Auditing)	30-50
39	016b	**81**	-02	12	01	Senior diplomat	50-60
40	017b	14	**59**	08	20	Diplomat	30-50
41	018b	57	-11	22	40	Diplomat	30-50
42	019b	59	38	09	28	Student (Nankai)	<30

1. Significant loadings ($p<.01$) in boldface; decimals to two places omitted.
2. Six participants declined to evaluate future Chinese foreign policy and we excluded those invalid Q-sorts

Table 3.3 ANOVA

		Sum of Squares	Df	Mean Square	F	Sig.
Factor A	Between Groups	84.028	1	84.028	.170	.682
	Within Groups	16772.944	34	493.322		
	Total	16856.972	35			
Factor B	Between Groups	702.250	1	702.250	1.315	.259
	Within Groups	18155.389	34	533.982		
	Total	18857.639	35			
Factor C	Between Groups	96.694	1	96.694	.148	.703
	Within Groups	22238.944	34	654.087		
	Total	22335.639	35			
Factor D	Between Groups	117.361	1	117.361	.186	.669
	Within Groups	21496.278	34	632.243		
	Total	21613.639	35			

Table 4 Factor Q-Sort Values for Each Statement

		Factor Arrays			
		A	B	C	D
1.	A rising China's grand strategy is to foster favorable conditions for continuing China's	4	1	3	3

modernization and increasing China's
international status while reducing the risk
that others will feel a threat from a rising
China

2. War and conflict are constant features of   -3   -4   -1   -2
international politics, the conflict between
adversaries is a zero-sum game, and military
is a highly efficacious means for dealing with
conflict.

3. War is inauspicious and should be avoided;   -1   2   4   4
even the enemy is not necessarily a
dispositional demon; military must be a last
resort.

4. China should concentrate on economic   -2   -1   3   -4
development now, and when Chinese
economy is bigger than the U.S. economy,
China would translate economic strength into
military might and challenge the U.S.
dominance in Asia.

5. China should have the determination to use   -2   -3   1   -4
military force in dealing with the core issues
related to its rise.

6. China will not rise through military conquest   4   0   2   4
as other previous great powers did. Instead,
China should rise peacefully through trade
and integration into economic globalization

7. Chinese intentions remain fluid and that   -1   -1   2   -3
premature adaptation of belligerent policies risks
creating a self-fulfilling prophecy – treat China
as an enemy and it will be one.

8. China's strategic orientation and Sino-   1   1   1   1
American relations in the 21st century would
be highly contingent, depending on the
ideational interactions between China and the
world

9. Through its participation in multilateral   -1   0   1   2
institutions, China would seek to prevent the
strengthening of U.S. capabilities and
alliances in the Asia-Pacific. China seizes the
opportunities to counter American primacy.

10. China joins multilateral international   -1   -2   -1   -1
organizations to avoid losing face and
influence. Chinese government does not
allow these organizations to prevent it from
pursuing its own economic and security
interests

11.	China has become more integrated into and more cooperative within international institutions than ever before.	1	-1	0	2
12.	China does not believe that its future depends on overturning the fundamental order of the international system. In fact, Chinese success depends on being networked with the modern world.	2	0	0	1
13.	As a great power, China has some vital interests unresolved. China resents the role of the United States in the Asia-Pacific region, which means that China is not a "status quo" power but one that would alter Asia's balance of power.	0	-3	2	1
14.	China has to be cautious in the short run in challenging U.S. power, but that the long-term goal should be to develop the strategic and diplomatic alliance to do so.	0	0	-1	1
15.	China is not trying as hard as it might to construct anti-U.S. alliances nor undermine U.S. alliances globally or regionally.	0	-2	0	2
16.	At least for the next several years, the United States will not regard China as its main security threat, and China will avoid antagonizing the United States	1	-1	-3	-1
17.	The United States is a major threat to Chinese national security and domestic stability	0	2	0	3
18.	China and the United States are economic competitors, that we may become to a degree geopolitical or diplomatic competitors, but we should not become strategic(security) competitors	1	0	-3	0
19.	Japanese power would be more threatening than American power and the status quo in the U.S.-Japan security arrangement can constrain Japan and thus is desirable for China.	-2	-4	-2	0
20.	To ease the tension in Sino-Japanese relations, China could temporarily put "historical issues" out of diplomatic agenda toward Japan.	-4	1	-4	-3
21.	China will put the United States out of Asia.	-3	-2	-2	0
22.	China should not try to exclude the United States from Asia. The U.S. has a long-standing influence here and should contribute to regional security, stability, and development.	0	2	-2	-1

23.	China's Asian regional policy reflects an increased appreciation by the Chinese government of the importance of international norms and "soft power" in diplomacy.	3 3 0 -1		
24.	To contain the "Taiwan independence" by military force, the sooner the better.	-4 1 -4 0		
25.	If Taiwan were to declare independence, China would intervene with armed force, regardless of the perceived economic or military costs.	2 4 4 0		
26.	Growing trade and economic links between Taiwan and the mainland will foster a comfortable environment for peaceful resolution of the Taiwan issue.	2 4 1 -2		
27.	China should pursue a strategic partnership with other great powers, which is a middle ground between allies and adversaries	3 3 -1 -2		

Notes

[1] For the discussion of the management of a rising power, see Randall L. Schweller, "Managing the Rise of Great Powers: History and Theory," In Alastair Iain Johnston and Robert S. Ross, eds., *Engaging China: the Management of an Emerging Power* (New York: Routledge, 1999), pp. 1-31.

[2] The opinions of Chinese foreign policy can be divided into different levels, such as elites (top leadership), subelites (bureaucrats and public intellectuals), and popular. For the discussion of different levels of opinion in Chinese foreign policy, see Joseph Fewsmith and Stanley Rosen, "The Domestic Context of Chinese Foreign Policy: Does 'Public Opinion' Matter?" In David M. Lampton, ed., *The Making of Chinese Foreign Policy and Security Policy in the Era of Reform, 1978-2000* (Stanford, CA: Stanford University Press 2001), pp. 151-187.

[3] Within the literature on realism and great power politics, see Robert Gilpin, *War and Change in World Politics* (New York: Cambridge University Press, 1981); John J. Mearsheimer, *The Tragedy of Great Power Politics* (New York: W.W. Norton, 2001).

[4] Mearsheimer, *The Tragedy of Great Power Politics*, pp. 1-29.

[5] Ibid, pp. 402.

[6] For the classic book on defensive realism , see Kenneth N. Waltz, *Theory of International Politics* (Reading, MA: Addison-Wesley, 1979).

[7] Andrew J. Nathan and Robert S. Ross, *The Great Wall and the Empty Fortress: China's Search for Security* (New York: W.W. Norton, 1997).

[8] Ibid, p. 230.

[9] A.F. K. Organski and Jacek Kugler, *The War Ledger* (Chicago: University of Chicago Press, 1980).

[10] Power transition theory is not deterministic on the case of China, see Jacek Kugler, 'The Asian Ascent: Opportunity for Peace or Precondition for War?" *International Studies Perspectives* 7, no. 1 (February 2006), pp. 36-42.

[11] Ibid, p. 41.

[12] Richard Rosecrance, "Power and International Relations: The Rise of China and Its Effects," *International Studies Perspectives* 7, no. 1 (February 2006), pp. 31-35. For an overview of liberal international theory, see Michael W. Doyle, "Liberalism and World Politics Revisited," In Charles W. Kegley, Jr., ed., *Controversies in International Relations Theory: Realism and the Neoliberal Challenge* (New York: St. Martins Press, 1995), pp. 83-106.

[13] Rosecrance, "Power and International Relations: The Rise of China and Its Effects," pp. 31-35.

[14] For an overview of China and international institutions, see Elizabeth Economy and Michel Oksenberg, eds., *China Joins the World: Progress and Prospect* (New York: Council on Foreign Relations Press, 1999). For an evaluation of China's behaviors in international institutions, see Alastair Iain Johnston, "Is China a Status Quo Power?" *International Security* 27, no. 4 (Spring 2003), pp. 12-14.

[15] For a constructivist interpretation of Chinese foreign policy, see Alastair Iain Johnston, *Cultural Realism: Strategic Culture and Grand Strategy in Chinese History* (Princeton, NJ: Princeton University Press, 1995); William A. Callahan, *Contingent States: Greater China and Transnational Relations* (Minneapolis: University of Minnesota Press, 2004).

[16] Johnston, *Cultural Realism: Strategic Culture and Grand Strategy in Chinese History,* pp..248-266; also see Alastair Iain Johnston, "Cultural Realism and Strategy in Maoist China," In Peter J. Katzenstein, ed., *The Culture of National Security: Norms and Identity in World Politics* (New York: Columbia University Press, 1996), pp. 216-268.

[17] William A. Callahan, "How to Understand China: The Dangers and Opportunities of Being a Rising Power," *Review of International Studies* 31, no. 4 (October 2005), pp. 701-714.

[18] Chih-yu Shih, "Breeding a Reluctant Dragon: Can China Rise into Partnership and Away from Antagonism?" *Review of International Studies* 31, no. 4 (October 2005), pp. 755-774.

[19] Randall L. Schweller, *Unanswered Threats: Political Constraints on the Balance of Power* (Princeton, NJ: Princeton University Press, 2006), pp. 22-45.

[20] Johnston, "Is China a Status Quo Power?" pp. 5-56.

[21] Yuan-kang Wang, "Offensive Realism and the Rise of China," *Issues & Studies* 40, no.1 (March 2004), p. 174.

[22] Johnston, "Is China a Status Quo Power?" pp..5-56; also see Steve Chan, "Realism, Revisionism, and the Great Powers," *Issues &Studies* 40, no. 1 (March 2004), pp. 135-172; Avery Goldstein, *Rising to the Challenge: China's Grand Strategy and International Security* (Stanford, CA: Stanford University Press, 2005).

[23] Ibid, pp..210-212.

[24] Alastair Iain Johnston, "Chinese Middle Class Attitudes towards International Affairs: Nascent Liberalization?" *The China Quarterly* 179 (September 2004), pp. 603-628; Alastair Iain Johnston, "The Correlates of Beijing Public Opinion Toward the United States, 1998-2004, " In Alastair Iain Johnston and Robert S. Ross, eds., *New Directions in the Study of China's Foreign Policy* (Stanford, CA: Stanford University Press, 2006), pp. 340-377.

[25] Jie Chen, "Urban Chinese Perceptions of Threats From the United States and Japan," *Public Opinion Quarterly* 65, no. 2 (Summer 2001), pp..254-266.

[26] Yufan Hao and Lin Su, "Contending Views: Emerging Elites's Perception of America," In Yufan Hao and Lin Su, eds., China's Foreign Policy Making: Societal Force and Chinese American Policy (Burlington, VT: Ashgate 2005), pp. 19-40.

[27] See Goldstein, *Rising to the Challenge: China's Grand Strategy and International Security.* For another important study of elite worldviews, see Jianwei Wang, *Limited Adversaries: Post-Cold War Sino-American Mutual Images* (Hong Kong: Oxford University Press, 2000).

[28] Michael Pillsbury, *China Debates the Future Security Environment* (Washington, DC: National Defense University Press, 2000).

[29] Biwu Zhang, "Chinese Perceptions of American Power, 1991-2004," *Asian Survey* 45, no..5 (September/October 2005), pp. 667-686.

[30] Mumin Chen, "Going Global: The Chinese Elite's Views of Security Strategy in the 1990s," *Asian Perspective* 29, no.2 (2005), pp. 133-177.

[31] See Johnston, *Cultural Realism: Strategic Culture and Grand Strategy in Chinese History*; also see Johnston, "Cultural Realism and Strategy in Maoist China," pp. 216-256.

[32] Goldstein, *Rising to the Challenge: China's Grand Strategy and International Security*, pp. 210-211.

[33] Huiyun Feng, "The Operational Code of Mao Zedong: Defensive or Offensive Realist?" *Security Studies* 14, no. 4 (October/December 2005), pp. 637-662.

[34] Huiyun Feng, "The Operational Code of Four Generations of Chinese Leaders: Is China a Revisionist Power?" paper presented at the American Political Science Association Annual Meeting, Washington, DC, September 1-4, 2005.

[35] For the discussion of personhood of states in international relations, see Alexander Wendt, "The State as Person in International Theory," *Review of International Studies* 30, no..2 (2004), pp..289-316; this idea is also attributed to professor Philip Zimbardo's lecture on human nature at 2005 Summer Institute in Political Psychology, Stanford University.

[36] See, for instance, Xuetong Yan, "The Rise of China in Chinese Eyes," *Journal of Contemporary China* 10, no. 26 (February 2001), pp. 33-39; Yiwei Wang, "Seeking China's New Identity: The Myth of Chinese Nationalism," paper presented at International Studies Association Annual Meeting, San Diego, March 24, 2006.

[37] Thomas J. Christensen, Alastair Iain Johnston, and Robert Ross, "Conclusions and Future Directions, " in Alastair Iain Johnston and Robert Ross, eds., New Directions in the Study of China's Foreign Policy (Stanford, CA: Stanford University Press, 2006), p. 380.

[38] William Stephenson, *The Study of Behavior: Q-technique and Its Methodology* (University of Chicago Press, 1953); Steven R. Brown, *Political Subjectivity: Applications of Q Methodology in Political Science* (New Haven, CT: Yale University Press, 1980); Bruce McKeown and Dan Thomas, *Q Methodology* (Newbury Park, CA: Sage Publications, 1988).

[39] See for instance, Richard Robyn, ed., *The Changing Face of European Identity* (New York: Routledge, 2005); John S. Dryzek and Jeffrey Berejikian, "Reconstructive Democratic Theory," *American Political Science Review* 87, no. 1 (May 1993), pp. 48-60; John S. Dryzek and Leslie Holmes, eds., *Post-Communist Democratization: Political Discourses Across Thirteen Countries* (Cambridge, UK: Cambridge University Press, 2002); Timothy Ka-ying Wong and Milan Tung-wen Sun, "Democratic Theorizing in Taiwan: A Reconstruction," *Democratization* 7, no.2 (Summer 2000), pp. 90-112; N. Patrick Peritore, "Environmental Attitudes of Indian Elites: Challenging Western Postmodernist Models," *Asian Survey* 33, no. 8 (1993), pp. 804-818.

[40] For an introduction to procedures in Q methodology, see Brown, *Political Subjectivity: Applications of Q Methodology in Political Science*, pp. 259-263.

[41] Ibid, pp. 112-115.

[42] For a discussion of Q methodology as a bridge between quantitative and qualitative methods, see Simon Watts and Paul Stenner, "Doing Q Methodology: Theory, Method and Interpretation," *Qualitative Research in Psychology,* 2 (2005), pp. 67-91; Steven R. Brown, "Q Methodology and Qualitative Research," *Qualitative Health Research* 6, no. 4 (September 1996), pp. 561-567.

[43] Brown, *Political Subjectivity: Applications of Q Methodology in Political Science*, p..19.

[44] For instance, see Johnston, "Chinese Middle Class Attitudes towards International Affairs: Nascent Liberalization?" pp. 603-628.

[45] Brown, *Political Subjectivity: Applications of Q Methodology in Political Science*, p. 28; See also John S. Dryzek, *Discursive Democracy* (New York: Cambridge University Press, 1990), pp. 173-189.

[46] Brown, *Political Subjectivity: Applications of Q Methodology in Political Science*, pp. 191-192.

[47] Ibid, pp. 1-5.

[48] An example of using both Q methodology and survey research in the same project, see John L. Sullivan, Army Fried, and Mary G. Dietz, "Patriotism, Politics, and the Presidential Election of 1988," *American Journal of Political Science* 36, no. 1 (February 1992), pp. 200-234. For a discussion of complementary relationship, also see Milan Tung-wen Sun and Timothy Ka-ying Wong, "Taiwan's National Identity Revisited: A Dialogue between R and Q" (Occasional Paper no. 142), Hong Kong Institute of Asia-Pacific Studies (January 2004), Chinese University of Hong Kong.

[49] Timothy Ka-ying Wong and Milan Tung-wen Sun, "Dissolution and Reconstruction of National Identity: The Experience of Subjectivity in Taiwan," *Nations and Nationalism* 4, no. 2 (1998), pp. 247-272.

[50] For instance, see Johnston, *Cultural Realism: Strategic Culture and Grand Strategy in Chinese History*; Goldstein, *Rising to the Challenge: China's Grand Strategy and International Security*.

[51] Johnston, "Is China a Status Quo Power?"

[52] Brown, *Political Subjectivity: Applications of Q Methodology in Political Science*, p. 192.

[53] Ibid., p. 19.

[54] [54] For instance, Minmin Chen argues that there are different type of worldviews among Chinese elites largely because of their different economic interests in Chinese foreign policy; see Chen, "Going Global: The Chinese Elite's Views of Security Strategy in the 1990s," pp. 133-177.

[55] Within the huge literature on gender and world politics, see J. Ann Tickner, *Gendering World Politics: Issues and Approaches in the Post-Cold War World* (New York: Columbia University Press, 2001).

[56] Brown, *Political Subjectivity: Applications of Q Methodology in Political Science*, p. 194.

[57] Several Chinese students overseas are selected as the participants because returnees have played an increasing role in China's political, economic and academic circles; see Cheng Li, ed., *Bridging Minds Across the Pacific: U.S.-China Educational Exchanges, 1978-2003* (New York: Lexington Books, 2005).

[58] For various reasons, six participants declined to evaluate future Chinese foreign policy and we excluded those invalid Q-sorts in the final analysis. Q-sorts coded as 001a to 024a are participants' opinion on current Chinese foreign policy; Q-sorts coded as 001b to 019b are participants' opinion on future Chinese foreign policy

[59] The PQMethod software is available for free download, http://www.lrz-muenchen.de/~schmolck/qmethod/

[60] Zheng Bijian, a leading Chinese thinker and political advisor, is the primary initiator of the concept "peaceful rise " for China's foreign policy, see Zheng Bijian, *China's Peaceful Rise: Speeches of Zheng Bijian, 1997-2005* (Washington, DC: Brookings Institutions, 2005).

[61] This does not mean that no realist scholars pay attention to the intentions of nation-states. Some neoclassical realists emphasize the importance of evaluating intentions of

great powers, for instance, see Randall Schweller, *Deadly Imbalances: Tripolarity and Hitler's Strategy of World Conquest* (New York: Columbia University Press, 1998); Jason W. Davidson, *The Origins of Revisionist and Status-quo States* (New York: Palgrave Macmillan, 2006).

[62] For discussion of differences between structural and functional information, see Steven R. Brown, "Structural and Functional Information," *Policy Sciences* 35 (2002), pp. 285-304.

[63] This is different from those studies that correlate people's opinions with their social/economic backgrounds. See for instance, Chen, "Going Global: The Chinese Elite's Views of Security Strategy in the 1990s," pp. 133-177.

Chapter 4

China's Contested Rise: Sino-U.S. Relations and the Social Construction of Great Power Status

Michael Alan Brittingham

The impending rise of China as a great power has become a popular topic of discussion among academics, policy-makers, and the media, as evidenced by the recent flurry of books and China-related cover stories in major media outlets. Titles like *China Rising* and *China Shakes the World* have become familiar additions to bookstore shelves,[1] and "China Rising" was also the theme of the journal *Foreign Affairs* in September 2005. In addition, *Newsweek*, *U.S. News & World Report*, and *Time* magazines all had cover stories within weeks of each other in 2005 touting China's booming economy as a sign of its growing importance in international affairs (May 9 – "China's Century," June 20 – "The China Challenge," and June 27 – "China's New Revolution," respectively). Such attention represents the widely accepted wisdom that China has become, or is on the cusp of becoming, a major power in the world, not just economically, but politically and even (perhaps) militarily. As Fareed Zakaria put it, "China's rise is no longer a prediction. It is a fact."[2]

Yet the "fact" of China's rise is neither as unproblematic nor as unambiguous as many observers would seem to suggest. While its continuing economic growth and the implications this may have for its ascendance on the world stage cannot be easily ignored, discussion of China's potential to impact world affairs is nothing new. The current selection of books touting its rise was preceded a decade ago by similar titles such as *China Wakes* and *The Rise of China*,[3] many of which were just as convinced that China was about to take center stage in a new 'Pacific Century.' Indeed, predictions and warnings of the consequences of China's 'rise' or 'awakening' go back at least as far as Napoleon Bonaparte's famous statement: "Let China sleep. For when China wakes, it will shake the world." Recent discussion about China's rise thus does not represent a revelation about new and dramatic developments, much less an unassailable 'fact.' It simply represents the latest incarnation of a discourse that has ebbed and flowed with the times and changing circumstances. This discourse seems to have an almost cyclical quality – China jumps to the forefront of public attention and debate when some otherwise minor event touches a chord with the public (e.g., the attempted purchase of the American energy company Unocal by the China North Offshore Oil Corporation (CNOCC)), only to recede again as the question of its role in the world gets lost in a sea of other issues. While one could easily dismiss this as simply the result of the short attention span of the American media and public, it is symptomatic of a much deeper phenomenon – the contested nature of China's status as a great power.

At first glance, China's claim to great power status would seem secure. It has the largest military in the world, a booming economy, a more than ample population, nuclear weapons, and a permanent seat on the UN Security Council. While it may not (yet) be able to match the power of the United States, it appears to have the military, economic, and political capabilities necessary to be considered a great power. Yet this has not stopped debate on the subject.[4] In a somewhat controversial article entitled, "Does China Matter?," Gerald Segal argued that China "is overrated as a market, a power, and a source of ideas. At best, China is a second-rank middle power that has mastered the art of diplomatic theater: it has us willingly suspending our disbelief in its strength. In fact, China is better understood as a theoretical power – a country that has promised to deliver for much of the last 150 years but has consistently disappointed."[5]   While few China-watchers would be as blunt in their assessment, the very fact that the theme of the discourse on China's rise always seems to be 'China rising' rather than 'China risen' is indicative of the fact that its status remains contested. Indeed, it seems that the only real 'fact' regarding China's rise is that the idea itself has become crystallized in the public imagination.

Why is China's status as a great power so contested? One explanation is that China's long struggle to modernize has only begun to produce results relatively recently. Prior to the beginning of economic reforms in the late-1970s China had been wracked by a nearly continuous series of wars, rebellions, and revolutions, as well as general social and political upheaval, that undermined its vast potential to play an important role in world affairs. Only after a quarter century of relative stability is it finally in a position to tap that potential. Such an explanation might be satisfactory if China was just now beginning to step onto the world stage. However, China has had one foot on that stage for decades despite its numerous problems. It was effectively recognized as a great power in the 1940s, long before its capabilities warranted it. Yet some 60 years later, despite enormous material progress, China's status remains in question. In essence, there appears to be a fundamental disconnect between its material capabilities and its social acceptance as a great power. The time it has taken for China to successfully modernize is not enough to explain this. An alternative explanation is required.

Such an alternative can be found in the nature of great power status itself. While it certainly also has a material dimension, great power status is, like many political phenomena, socially constructed. In other words, it is at least partly dependent on the existence of shared ideas and social norms. States do not simply become great powers once they reach a particular level of development or military prowess. Being a great power is an identity that must be enacted by a state, and recognized and reinforced by its peers. In the case of China, that social recognition came as a result of U.S. actions during WWII to treat it as a great power in order to create a more stable post-war international order in East Asia. However, China's acceptance was based on beliefs about its future potential, not its actual capabilities, which made its identity as a great power highly vulnerable. Despite concrete advances in its position vis-à-vis other actors over the last quarter century, this vulnerability has continued. Using a synthesis of realist and constructivist interpretations of great power status, this chapter will examine how China's identity as a great power has been socially constructed through its relations with other actors, specifically the United States, and how that process has left its status contested. It will be argued that improvements in China's material capabilities may not be enough to force a reevaluation in the near future, partly because of U.S. attempts to 'raise the bar' for entry into the club of great powers by changing the necessary criteria. This could have serious repercussions for Sino-U.S. relations and China's acceptance of the current international order.

POWER, IDENTITY, & GREAT POWER STATUS

Any analysis of how or when China could achieve great power status must begin with the question of what a great power is. This might seem unnecessary given the prevalence of the term in studies of international politics. Its usage dates back centuries and has been formalized in international conferences and organizations since the Congress of Vienna (1815).[6] As such, the importance of great powers in world affairs is generally taken for granted. However, as Jack Levy once pointed out, "the widespread recognition of the importance of the Great Powers is not matched by analytical precision in the use of the concept."[7] Perhaps because its meaning seems self-evident, many scholars have "duck[ed] the task of defining" the term.[8] Instead of developing theoretically-informed criteria for what makes a state a great power, they have preferred to simply identify them empirically. Martin Wight once wrote that this was far easier since there has generally been agreement on which states count as great powers in any particular period.[9] Indeed, he suggested that "the truest definition of a great power must be a historical one, which lays down that a great power is a power which has done such and such. A scientific definition, laying down the attributes that a great power may be supposed to possess, will be an abstraction in some degree removed from our complicated and unmanageable political experience."[10]
　　While identifying great powers empirically is a tempting strategy, such temptation should be avoided. Not only does it complicate discussion of ambiguous cases, like China, it also makes for sloppy analysis and risks obscuring important contradictions. Barry Buzan has suggested that when one 'digs deeper' into the literature on great powers, "one finds two clear threads in

the attempts to formulate the criteria by which to distinguish great powers from other states in the system: material capabilities and social role."[11] The former requires that a state possess material capabilities, particularly military capabilities, greater than those of most other states. The latter requires that a state seek to take on the responsibilities associated with being a great power and be recognized as one by its peers. While both make intuitive sense from the standpoint of identifying great powers empirically, they represent somewhat of a theoretical challenge. In contemporary IR theory, material capabilities and social roles (i.e., identity) remain the focal points of debate between two theoretical perspectives – realism and constructivism – that are generally viewed as incompatible. Thus, in order to understand what makes a state a great power, one must first reconcile competing claims regarding the importance of power and identity in international politics. This section will attempt to do so by examining both realism and constructivism, as well as the prospects for a synthesis of the two, and evaluating their strengths and weaknesses for understanding great power status. It will be argued that a synthetic approach – realist constructivism – holds the best opportunity for developing a better theoretical understanding of great power status.

Realism, Constructivism, & the Need for Synthesis

The debate between realism and constructivism is simply the latest round of a long series of theoretical debates that have divided the field of IR almost since its beginning as an academic discipline.[12] Indeed, it is actually the more active part of a broader debate between *rationalism* (which includes modern versions of both realism and liberalism) and constructivism.[13] Neither realism nor constructivism is a single theory, but instead represents a broad approach to the study of international politics based on a few basic assumptions. Realism, which is the oldest, and arguably still the dominant, approach in the discipline, is based on four such assumptions: 1) states are the most important actors in international politics and should therefore be the primary units of analysis; 2) states can be treated, for purposes of theory, as rational actors that seek to pursue their interests so as to maximize their gains; 3) the successful pursuit of these interests necessarily requires the accumulation and utilization of power; and 4) the use of power in pursuit of frequently conflicting interests makes international politics highly competitive and prone to interstate conflict. In essence, realists see international politics as a struggle between states for power, either as a means to an end or the end itself. While various kinds of power may be recognized as important, most realists place special emphasis on military power.

Despite a resurgence of interest in domestic politics by some scholars (neoclassical realism),[14] most modern realists remain focused on the structure of the international system (neorealism). Neorealists are primarily concerned with the constraints placed on states by the structure of the international system that predispose them toward certain behaviors. This is an essentially rationalist model of international politics that involves a three-step analysis. "First, there is the specification of a set of constraints. Then comes the stipulation of a set of actors who are assumed to have certain kinds of interests. Finally, the behavior of the actors is observed, and that behavior is related to the constraining conditions in which these actors, with their assumed interests, find themselves."[15] The most important constraint posited by neorealists is anarchy – i.e., the absence of a central political authority. In a system characterized by anarchy, states are responsible for their own security. This requires them to seek to balance the power of other states in order to survive, by increasing their own capabilities or engaging in strategic alliances. Thus, the distribution of capabilities (i.e., the balance of power) is a key factor in explaining state behavior.[16] Taken together, the anarchical nature of the international system and the distribution of material capabilities represent the structure of threats and opportunities to which states must respond in order to safeguard their own security.

Constructivism is a far newer theoretical approach and has arguably become the predominant critique of more traditional ones such as realism and liberalism (broadly defined). In contrast to realism, it is rooted in "the assumption that the human world is not simply given and/or natural but that on the contrary, the human world is one of artifice; that it is 'constructed' through the actions of the actors themselves."[17] As J. Samuel Barkin succinctly puts it, "constructivists see the facts of international politics as not reflective of an objective, material reality but an intersubjective, or social reality."[18] The interests and beliefs of states cannot be assumed, nor can the impact that seemingly 'objective' constraints like power and anarchy have on the way states pursue them. Such assumptions fail to take into account the social dimension or structure of the international system, which "consists of the stock of interlocking beliefs, ideas, understandings, perceptions, identities, or what [Alexander Wendt] would call 'knowledge' held by members of the system."[19] For instance, "what a 'state' is, what 'sovereignty' implies, what 'international law' requires, what 'regimes' are, how a 'balance of power' works, how to engage in 'diplomacy,' what constitutes 'war,' what an 'ultimatum' is, and so on"[20] represent knowledge shared by international actors. For constructivists, this shared knowledge – what one might call the distribution of ideas in the system – provides the necessary social context in which actors interact by giving meaning to those interactions, and to the material structure of the system itself. Thus, the international system does not simply *cause* preexisting actors to behave in particular ways; it *constitutes* them with certain identities and interests that inform their actions.

While realism focuses on power, constructivism focuses on identity. Identity can be defined as "the state of being similar to some actors and different from others in a particular circumstance. Identity involves the creation of boundaries that separate self from other."[21] Such boundaries may exist on a number of levels. Some elements of identity may be material – e.g., physical characteristics that aid in distinguishing one actor from another. However, such material factors may have little meaning in and of themselves; their salience may depend on the circumstances of a given social interaction. As such, identity has a strong sociological component that is likely to be far more important than any material differences, particularly for collective actors like states. Thus, in contrast to realists, constructivists argue that "material capabilities as such explain nothing; their effects presuppose structures of shared knowledge."[22] For example, Wendt suggests that the U.S. perception of North Korean nuclear capabilities as threatening and British nuclear capabilities as non-threatening, despite the relative superiority of the latter, can only be understood in terms of shared understandings of amity and enmity, not by referencing the capabilities themselves.[23] In essence, material capabilities simply represent physical characteristics whose salience will depend on the circumstances of a given social interaction.

One form of identity relevant to this discussion that is particularly dependent on social structure is what Wendt refers to as role identity. A role can be thought of as "identity mobilized in a specific situation."[24] According to Philippe Le Prestre, "the articulation of a national role betrays preferences, operationalizes an image of the world, triggers expectations, and influences the definition of the situation and of the available options. It imposes obligations and affects the definition of risks."[25] In essence, roles provide guidance for state behavior in specific situations. While other forms of identity may be at least partially dependent on material factors, "role identities are not based on intrinsic properties and as such exist *only* in relation to Others. There is no preexisting property in virtue of which a student becomes a student or a master a master; one can have these identities only by occupying a position in a social structure and following behavioral norms toward Others possessing relevant *counter-identities*. One cannot enact role identities by oneself."[26] For instance, "Smith can stipulate her identity as 'the President' any time she likes, but unless others share this idea she cannot *be* the President, and her ideas about herself will be meaningless."[27]

Realism and constructivism thus represent radically different approaches to the study of international politics. Realism focuses on material factors (e.g., capabilities) that make it more or less costly for states to pursue particular courses of action. As such, it views state behavior as driven by a logic of consequences – i.e., states make decisions based on the relative costs and benefits associated with the consequences of that decision. Thus, while states may be influenced by social norms, such norms are only likely to be followed if they provide some utility to the state. This form of analysis generally requires assumptions about the interests and preferences of the states in question. On the other hand, constructivism focuses on ideational factors (e.g., identity) that give meaning to state actions. As such, it views state behavior as driven by a logic of appropriateness – i.e., states make decisions based on their beliefs about what is appropriate in a given situation. Social norms are thus followed not because they are necessarily useful, but because they are deemed right. This form of analysis is usually highly interpretive and generally requires careful examination of how and from where a state's interests and preferences are derived.[28] These differences are stark enough that realism and constructivism are commonly seen as incompatible.

However, there is a growing sense among some IR scholars that the debate between rationalism and constructivism in general, and between realism and constructivism more specifically, is counterproductive and may overlook "substantial areas of agreement."[29] According to Henry Nau, "the history of the modern state system suggests that both material (realist) and social (constructivist) factors have always combined at the structural level to determine the character of state behavior."[30] As such, neither power nor identity alone can adequately address many of the important issues in IR, including, as will be discussed below, great power status. Although the discussion is still in its infancy, it has been suggested that realist concerns for power and constructivist concerns for identity should be synthesized into a new approach – realist constructivism. In essence, Barkin suggests that, just as rationalism has both a realist and liberal variant, constructivism too can have both a realist and liberal variant. The former "would look at the way in which power structures affect patterns of normative change in international relations and, conversely, the way in which a particular set of norms affect power structures."[31] While an in-depth discussion of the theoretical merits of such an approach are beyond the scope of this chapter, a brief reappraisal of the seeming incompatibility between material and ideational factors is necessary for understanding great power status.

The author would contend, not uncontroversially, that material capabilities are far from inconsequential to constructivist theory. Although the constructivist view of international politics is often seen as being "ideas all the way down,"[32] Wendt and others do not fully discount the importance of material power. As he puts it, "the claim is *not* that ideas are more important than power and interest, or that they are autonomous from power and interest....The claim is rather that power and interest have the effects they do in virtue of the ideas that make them up."[33] In essence, while physical reality and material constraints may set the parameters for what is possible, ideas determine how states will act within those parameters. As such, Wendt suggests that this rump materialism is simply "less important and interesting than the contexts of meaning that human beings construct around them."[34] For example, "the material fact that Germany has more military power than Denmark imposes physical limits on Danish foreign policy toward Germany, but those limits will be irrelevant to their interaction if neither could contemplate war with the other."[35]

Yet this seems overly restrictive. There are a number of circumstances in which material power could be critical to understanding the development and/or operation of socially constructed identities and norms. For instance, they could significantly influence the outcome of social learning. Wendt points out that "where there is an imbalance of relevant material capability social acts will tend to evolve in the direction favored by the more powerful."[36] In other words, less powerful states may be forced to adopt new identities and interests in order to subscribe to the social norms of stronger states. In addition, material capabilities could be important indicators of who can or cannot assume a particular identity and play a particular role. Thus, the ability or inability of a state to successfully do so may depend on whether or not that role is complemented by the state's material capabilities. As will be discussed below, this is certainly the case with great power status. Indeed, a realist-constructivist approach that analyzes the interaction of the material and social dimensions of international politics would be well suited to the task of developing a more theoretically grounded understanding of great power status.

A Realist-Constructivist Interpretation of Great Power Status

As already mentioned, the literature on great powers has commonly recognized both material capabilities and social roles as important criteria for which states properly deserve the label. However, the emphasis on one or the other varies considerably depending on the scholar. Some take a realist perspective by defining great powers primarily, if not exclusively, in terms of material capabilities possessed. Others take an essentially constructivist perspective (though they would not in most cases be considered constructivists per se) by focusing more on social roles – i.e., acceptance of certain rights and responsibilities, and recognition by others. Given the tendency to treat the issue empirically rather than theoretically, these differences are usually not treated as a major problem. However, if we are to clarify the status of ambiguous cases such as China, it is important to reconcile the material and social dimensions of great power status. Since it recognizes the importance of both material capabilities and identity, realist constructivism can provide a useful theoretical framework for doing so. Before applying such a framework, however, it is first necessary to examine the material and social dimensions of great power status individually, along with their shortcomings.

The material dimension of great power status is certainly the most commonly recognized and most straightforward criterion for identifying great powers. From this perspective, a state is a great power if it possesses the requisite material capabilities relative to other states. According to Kenneth Waltz, the rank of states in the system "depends on how they score on *all* of the following items: size of population and territory, resource endowment, economic capability, military strength, political stability and competence."[37] Similarly, Raymond Aron points out that "the political units considered to be great powers were defined, above all, by the volume of their resources (territory and populations) and their military strength."[38] Although the importance of such material capabilities in defining great power status is universally recognized even among scholars who prefer to focus on its social dimension, this is an essentially realist perspective on great power status. Indeed, given its focus on power, it is not surprising that the great powers – conceived of in primarily material terms – have a particularly prominent place in realist theory. As Waltz asserts, "the theory, like the story, of international politics is written in terms of the great powers of an era."[39]

Of the material capabilities considered important for identifying great powers, military capabilities are generally presented as the most critical. For instance, Levy argued that "a Great Power must possess both relative self-sufficiency with respect to security, including invulnerability against secondary states, and the ability to project military power beyond its borders in pursuit of its interests."[40] Similarly, John Mearsheimer suggests that "to qualify as a great power, a state must have sufficient military assets to put up a serious fight in an all-out conventional war against the most powerful state in the world."[41] Economic factors might also be considered important, particularly in the event that economic weakness undermines military power (e.g., the Soviet Union). However, military factors tend to override such considerations, as seen in debates over whether Japan can be a proper great power without effectively translating its economic weight into military muscle. The same could be said of other factors, such as population, territory, or resources. Their value as determinants of great power status generally depends on whether or how they can be translated into military power. They might best be considered as secondary capabilities that enable states to pursue the primary military capabilities than are necessary to achieve great power status.

One of the main advantages generally associated with using military capabilities, or material capabilities more generally, as criteria for great power status is that they allow one to objectively determine with a reasonable degree of accuracy whether or not a state ranks as a great power since the size and disposition of a state's armed forces, as well as its wealth, population, natural resources, etc., can be readily quantified. Perhaps because of this, Waltz suggests that identifying great powers is essentially a matter of "common sense."[42] However, while material capabilities provide a useful shorthand for measuring it, power involves an inherently psychological relationship. This makes exact measurement problematic since it is essentially relational in nature. As such, merely possessing ample capabilities is no guarantee of success in international competition (e.g., US defeat in the Vietnam War). A state may fail to properly employ its capabilities, either out of a lack of knowledge and planning, or simply out of an unwillingness to spend resources that could be needed elsewhere. Thus, an alternative is to look at actual success in war, which can demonstrate a state's skill in employing its capabilities. As Wight suggested, "the self-revelation of a great power is completed by war... as the head-hunters of Borneo entered into manhood by taking their first head, so a power becomes a great power by a successful war against another great power."[43] For instance, Prussia and Japan both achieved great power status through victory in war. In addition, Wight suggests that great power status can be just as easily lost, either temporarily or permanently, through defeat in war.[44] As a result, he notes that "at any time there are likely to be some powers climbing into [the class of great powers] and others declining from it, and in a time of revolutionary changes, formal recognition will lag behind the growth or decay of power."[45]

Unfortunately, while material capabilities provide a useful criterion for identifying great powers, whether measured directly or implied through successful utilization, they are inadequate. Buzan argues that "by itself, the materialist definition is clearly unsustainable. It is impossible to define levels of relative power with anything like the precision and consistency necessary for positivist science."[46] Despite his obvious preference for the material dimension,

Wight makes a similar observation, suggesting that "it may be obvious that a great power is stronger than the average state in respect of some at least of the components of power – in population, extent of territory, industrial resources, social organization, historical tradition and will to greatness. But in respect of some of them, or most or all? And how much stronger? And what is the average state?"[47]   Indeed, it is these questions that lead him to prefer an empirical approach to identifying great powers.   More importantly, Wight's observation about the possibility of lag between a great power's rise (i.e., its acquisition of the necessary capabilities) and its formal recognition opens up an important question – namely, how important is recognition to defining great power status?

Levy argues that recognition of one's status, both by other powers and by international organizations, is an important part of being a great power.[48]   This introduces a key social element into the discussion.   Just as the norm of sovereignty involves mutual recognition of which actors have legal standing as states in the international system, great power status involves mutual recognition of which states are the most important in the system.   As Hedley Bull argued,

> great powers are powers recognised by others to have, and conceived by their own leaders and peoples to have, certain special rights and duties.   Great powers, for example, assert the right, and are accorded the right, to play a part in determining issues that affect the peace and security of the international system as a whole.   They accept the duty, and are thought by others to have the duty, of modifying their policies in the light of the managerial responsibilities they bear.[49]

Thus, from a constructivist perspective, great power status (like sovereignty) is part of the system's social structure or shared knowledge.   Being a great power means that a state seeks to enact that identity (i.e., it claims the rights and responsibilities associated with it) *and* that it is accepted as one by others in the system.   As such, great power status may be "in a continuous state of flux."[50]   Although great power identity may remain stable over time if a state continues to act like a great power and is accepted as one by others, it may also become contested if the state no longer takes up the responsibilities associated with a great power *or* it is no longer clear that the state in question can live up to the role.

However, to suggest that a state is a great power if others accept it as one begs the question of what criterion other states use to determine who is and who is not a great power.   This inevitably leads back to the issue of material capabilities, since these are invariably what states use to judge which of them counts as one.   After all, if great power status carries with it certain social responsibilities, a state must possess the capacity to carry them out.   Thus, even scholars who focus on the social dimension of great power status generally include "a materialist benchmark"[51] – i.e., states must still possess significant military capabilities in order to be ranked as great powers.   For many this represents a critical flaw in using recognition as a criterion for great power status.   As Wight rightly points out, "such recognition may contain an element of the wishful or the conventional."[52] As a result, he argued in favor of the material dimension, saying that "the existence of what is recognized determines the act of recognition, and not the other way round."[53] While Buzan seems more favorably disposed to the social dimension, he also notes its inherent limitations. He argues that "the recognition approach is not workable by itself either, because there are too many situations when some great powers politically promote to formal great power status states lacking first-class capabilities. They do this to gain an ally, frustrate a rival or help the power in question manage a difficult transition downward or upward in status."[54] Thus, both Wight and Buzan recognize the potential disconnect between the material and social dimensions of great power status.

Dealing with such a disconnect requires examining the interplay of both dimensions, a task for which realist constructivism is well suited. Doing so yields several intriguing possibilities. First, it is possible for a state to possess the capabilities necessary for it to be a great power, but fail to fully enact a great power identity. For instance, it is a common view that after WWI the United States declined to play a role in world affairs commensurate with its power. Secondly, among those states that seek to enact a great power identity, the social dimension of great power status helps to explain the mismatch that periodically occurs between a state's level of capabilities and its acceptance as a great power. Declining powers have often continued to be recognized as great powers long after their capabilities no longer warrant it. For instance, Hans Morgenthau suggested that after the Napoleonic Wars, Portugal, Spain, and Sweden continued to be granted recognition as great powers, temporarily at least, "out of traditional courtesy."[55] France was afforded the same courtesy after WWII. On the other hand, a rising power whose capabilities have dramatically increased could be denied recognition as a great power because others do not yet realize that its capabilities have reached the necessary level. As in the cases mentioned earlier of Prussia and Japan, social acceptance may only come through demonstrations of military prowess. Alternatively, a state may be granted great power status prematurely based on an incorrect assumption of its existing capabilities, or on expectations of its future capabilities. In this latter case, recognition will likely remain only provisional until the state can demonstrate that it can live up to its potential. This will make the state's position highly vulnerable and contested. As will be discussed in the next section, this seems to be the case for China.

SINO-U.S. RELATIONS & CHINA'S CONTESTED STATUS

As with most states, one can identify many role conceptions that China has sought to enact at various times.[56] Yet one particular role has arguably been by far the most important – the role of great power. Despite a continuing sense of victimization at the hands of foreign powers, many Chinese believe that "the rise of China is granted by nature....They believe China's decline is a historical mistake which they should correct."[57] In the days of Mao, this confidence manifested itself as a fervent belief in China's ability to be a leader in the international communist movement, a bulwark against imperialism and superpower hegemony, and a model for the developing world. As economic reform has brought unprecedented prosperity, China has come to define its role in far less ideological terms. Thus, while Samuel Kim has suggested that "the People's Republic... has succumbed to wild swings of national identity projection over the years, mutating through a series of varying global roles,"[58] the role of "great power" has remained a cornerstone of Chinese foreign policy, one that has only been strengthened in recent years. "Of all of the contenders in the [Chinese] quest for national identity in the 1990s," Gilbert Rozman argues, "the notion of China as a great power (*daguo*) has gained a clear-cut victory."[59]

As already noted, however, one cannot enact a role by oneself; successful role enactment requires validation from others. In order for China to *be* a great power, it must be accepted as one by other great powers, particularly the United States. However, this acceptance has remained ambivalent because of the terms under which it was granted. One might best think of China as a 'provisional great power' – a state granted conditional acceptance as a great power based not on its actual capabilities, but on expectations (real or rhetorical) of its future potential, and thus dependent on its ability to live up to that potential in the future. It was precisely under these conditions that China was granted preliminary status as a great power in the 1940s. Yet continued gaps between capabilities and expectations have left China on rather shaky ground. It exists in a sort of limbo between expectations and fulfillment – powerful enough to elicit concerns from the United States and its neighbors, but not powerful enough to dispel questions about its status or for others to fully accept its membership in the club of great powers. It is for this reason that China seems to be always on the rise but never risen. This becomes evident when one looks at the circumstances behind China's conditional acceptance, and how Sino-U.S. relations have continued to create problems for its enactment of great power identity.

China Becomes a "Provisional Great Power"

For a century after its first clash with the West, China had remained the veritable 'sick man of Asia' – in decline, struggling to modernize, and narrowly avoiding outright colonization. It was not until WWII that it began to take its first real steps toward becoming a great power, and this was the direct result of U.S. actions to *make* it a great power. At the beginning of the war, the United States was focused on the European theater and concentrated its resources on defeating Germany. As such, China remained, in the words of Warren Cohen, "an honored ally, but alas, a second-class ally" relegated to keeping Japan divided in a two-front war.[60] Yet as the conflict wore on, the United States decided to officially include China among the ranks of the other major Allied powers by allowing it to participate in the Washington and Quebec Conferences (May and August 1943, respectively). Indeed, according to Secretary of State Cordell

Hull, "the recognition and building up of China as a major power entitled to equal rank with the three big Western Allies, Russia, Britain, and the United States" became a main policy objective.[61] Along with largely symbolic acts such as the relinquishing of American claims of extraterritoriality,[62] China was formally acknowledged as one of the Big Four in the Declaration of the Moscow Conference (October 1943).[63] At the end of the war, it was also given a prominent place in the newly created United Nations as one of the five permanent members of the Security Council.

Given the sorry state of China's position vis-à-vis the Western powers just a few years before, this "transition from pupil to power"[64] was nothing short of remarkable, all the more so because it occurred despite China's continued relative weakness. There was early optimism on the part of at least some American decision-makers that China could provide a valuable contribution to the war effort through the provision of air bases and manpower, as well as by keeping Japan's attention divided.[65] Fear of losing it as an ally gave China the leverage it needed to force the United States to recognize it, at least officially, as an equal. However, China never managed to live up to the high expectations of American optimists. As the military and political realities of the situation set in, it became increasingly clear that keeping the Japanese pinned down was the most that could be hoped for. Its material capabilities were simply not on par with its allies and large amounts of military and financial aid were required from the United States just to keep it afloat. As such, numerous U.S. officials warned of "the dubious military value of China in the current war effort."[66] Nor did the Nationalist government of Chiang Kai-shek demonstrate the desire to use what capabilities it had to fight the Japanese, preferring instead to prepare for the inevitable showdown with the Chinese Communist Party (CCP). Indeed, it has been suggested that China's inadequacy as a major wartime ally was a primary reason for the perceived necessity of getting the Soviet Union involved in the Pacific War after the defeat of Germany.[67]

The fact that it was recognized as a great power without having the requisite capabilities makes China an excellent case for examining the importance of both the material and social dimensions of great power status. The explanation for how such a disconnect could occur depends on how one interprets the Roosevelt administration's reason for pursuing the policy of making China a great power. Doing so is not easy; as one contemporary observer noted, "at the White House...the making of FDR's China policy was almost as great a secret as the atom bomb."[68] However, three possible explanations present themselves. The first is that, despite its political inadequacies, Roosevelt believed that China's sheer size and population gave it enormous potential as a great power.[69] As Winston Churchill would later write, Roosevelt countered his skepticism about China's ability to contribute to the war effort by pointing out to him that "there were five hundred million people in China. What would happen if this enormous population developed in the same way as Japan had done in the last century and got hold of modern weapons?"[70] The view that China would inevitably play a vital role in the postwar order was echoed by Hull, who asserted his belief that "if there was ever to be stability in the Far East, it had to be assured with China at the center of any arrangement that was made."[71] Whatever political mismanagement it might suffer from, the importance of China "was a geopolitical fact"[72] that had to be dealt with.

It should be pointed out of course that China's membership in the club of great powers was not universally welcomed. Neither Winston Churchill nor Joseph Stalin shared Roosevelt's belief in its inevitable importance. Churchill referred to China as the "Great American Illusion"[73] and considered the idea that proper arms and equipment would allow China to exercise substantial military power as "exaggerated."[74] Of his discussions with FDR, he later wrote:

> At Washington I had found the extraordinary significance of China in American minds, even at the top, strangely out of proportion. I was conscious of a standard of values which accorded China almost an equal fighting power with the British Empire, and rated the Chinese armies as a factor to be mentioned in the same breath as the armies of Russia. I told the President...that he must not expect me to adopt what I felt was a wholly unreal standard of values.[75]

Churchill was far more blunt in his private correspondence, suggesting that "the idea that China...should be rated...above France or Poland or whatever takes the place of Austria-Hungary, or above even smaller but ancient historic and glorious states like Holland, Belgium, Greece and Yugoslavia – has only to be stated to be dismissed" and "that China is one of the world's four great Powers is an absolute farce."[76] Stalin also seemed skeptical of China's worthiness as a great power.[77] It was only Roosevelt's stubborn insistence on its inclusion that allowed China to gain official, if grudging, recognition of its status from Britain and the Soviet Union.

That stubbornness has led to the common assessment that Roosevelt had an "infatuation with the image of China as a great power."[78] However, while he worked hard to overcome Allied resistance to China's recognition, he was not as 'infatuated' with this image as has often been suggested. Indeed, it has been argued that he acted largely out of political calculation. Roosevelt was under tremendous political pressure from the pro-China lobby even before the war began to do more to aid China.[79] Treating it as a valued partner could help to alleviate this pressure. In addition, including China as a permanent member of the UN Security Council would help to demonstrate to the American public that it "was not...an exclusively European club and...would be a truly international body worthy of American participation."[80] He might thus avoid the same pressures for renewed isolationism that doomed Woodrow Wilson's efforts to gain U.S. entry into the League of Nations. It has also been suggested that "Roosevelt and his advisors...acted on the assumption of a China grateful to the United State, *dependent* on the United States – as Churchill suspected, 'a faggot vote' on the side of the United States."[81] From this perspective, the recognition of China as a great power was more form than substance, which helps explain why, despite the official rhetoric, "Roosevelt, no less than Churchill or Stalin, denied Chiang an equal role in the process of making strategic or logistical decisions."[82]

The first explanation tends to portray Roosevelt as overly idealistic about China's ability to play an important role on the world stage, while the second portrays him in a far more cynical light. Although both contain elements of truth, there is an alternative – namely, that the policy of making China a great power was initiated by strategic considerations and continued due to inertia. The elevating of China's status was initially predicated on a genuine belief that it could play a vital role in the war effort and in the establishment of a post-war order. However, U.S. wartime strategy placed concrete limits on its potential contribution. China's subordinate position with respect to high-level decision-making was, at least in part, the logical outcome of the decision to focus on defeating Germany first. Furthermore, China's utility in fighting even the secondary war against Japan deteriorated over time, not just because it had proven itself unable or unwilling to fight effectively, but because the United States shifted its plans away from pursuing a major campaign on the Chinese mainland in order to speed the end of the war and avoid a negotiated settlement.[83] Thus, U.S. perceptions of China's value as an ally quickly changed as its own strategy and China's weakness undermined the original rationale for treating it as a great power. As a result, by the time of Roosevelt's death, Akira Iriye suggests that "peace, order, and stability in postwar Asia depended...on the new balance of power being established among the Big Three, not among the mythical 'four policemen.'"[84]

Yet the myth remained. While American perceptions of Chinese capabilities became more realistic, the policy of treating it as a great power was little changed. Thus, at the end of the war China retained its official seat at the table of great powers (literally, given its seat on the Security Council) despite its relative weakness. This demonstrates the critical importance of the social dimension of great power status. Social acceptance – the newly shared (and still vulnerable) belief that 'China mattered' – was enough to make China a great power. From a purely constructivist perspective this makes perfect sense. Social structures are products of social practice. China could therefore be a great power so long as others were willing to treat it as one. However, because they only exist through practice, social structures are never static, even if they remain unchanged. They are always subject to the possibility that new ideas or beliefs might alter their character, and even when this possibility is not realized the lack of change is the product not of constancy, but of a process of reinforcement and reproduction. Realist constructivism would add another element of potential change. While the international system may be socially constructed based on shared knowledge, social structures that deviate significantly from material bases of power may be unsustainable in the long run. Just as many declining great powers may eventually be denied the title as it becomes evident that they no longer deserve it, a provisional great power whose capabilities do not yet match the presumption of others may be particularly vulnerable to having its status contested. This has certainly been the case for China.

China's Contested Status – Cold War to Post-Cold War

After attaining at least provisional status as a great power during WWII, China was faced with a long struggle to maintain its position. Throughout the Cold War, its capabilities were well behind those of the two dominant superpowers, or even those of Britain and France. Its weight could be felt close to its borders (as it was during the Korean War), but its ability to project power much beyond them remained severely limited. Indeed, the bloody nose it received while trying to 'teach a lesson' to Vietnam in 1979 demonstrated the difficulty China has often had exercising military power. Although China became a nuclear power in 1964, its nuclear capabilities remained moderate relative to other nuclear powers. Thus, in many ways China failed the most basic material criteria for great power status. At best, it seemed to be a regional power, always fearful of its own security with respect to the superpowers. Its interests were largely regional in character (e.g., territorial claims, the regional balance of power),[85] and its foreign relations correspondingly centered on the Asia-Pacific.[86] As a result, Avery Goldstein suggests that "until the last decade of the Cold War China remained only a 'candidate' great power...[Its] limitations kept it in the group of second-ranked powers, and among them perhaps the least capable."[87]

This did not stop China from trying to play the role of great power by defining its largely regional interests in global terms. This led Steven Levine to describe China in the 1980s as "a regional power without a regional policy."[88] As he observed:

> China has regarded its conflict with Vietnam as a microcosm of a global struggle against Soviet expansionism. It sees its support of Malaysia's and Indonesia's claims to the Straits of Malacca as part of a broader pattern of Third World opposition to the maritime hegemony of the superpowers. It portrays its policies toward Taiwan and South Korea as examples of a worldwide resistance against American imperialism. It depicts its trade with ASEAN as an instance of South-South economic cooperation.[89]

Kim makes a similar point, arguing that China's continued lack of a regional policy is a result of the fact that "during the Cold War years, none of China's multiple identity enactments and role playing had much to do with Asian regionalism."[90] In essence, "without first having acquired the reach of a global power, China act[ed] as if it [had] already become a global power."[91] In other words, it sought to enact a great power identity without possessing the necessary capabilities.

During the Cold War, China's ability to do so successfully depended on the willingness of the superpowers to play along. However, given their preoccupation with each other, such willingness was not always forthcoming. Like Britain and France in the Western bloc, China found itself playing the role of junior partner to a superpower in the 1950s. Although efforts at rallying the developing world provided "a way of...enhancing China's stature,"[92] its ability to be a major player in the global balance of power was severely limited. It was even further hampered by its break with the Soviet Union in 1959 and the decade-long isolation China experienced afterward. It could not even fall back on its official 'seat at the table' – the UN Security Council – which was being held with even less justification by the Nationalist government-in-exile on Taiwan. Had this situation continued indefinitely, it is entirely possible that the idea of China as a great power might have faded into history. While it would no doubt have continued to be an important factor in Asia, its brief time on the world stage might have come to an end.

However, after years of international isolation, the United States once again began actively courting China, this time as a potential counterweight to the Soviet Union. In doing so, it helped to reinvigorate China's identity as a great power.[93] The emergence by the early-1970s of the strategic triangle thus became the key to China's great power role enactment; it provided necessary external validation. Indeed, Rozman suggests that "even more than Moscow or Washington, Beijing became enamored of the strategic triangle...Increasingly, it measured its importance as one of three global powers capable of shifting the balance of world power."[94] While the international system might have technically remained bipolar, China's position between the two camps introduced a degree of tripolarity that proved extremely useful to it, "enabling Beijing to exploit superpower rivalry to gain its own strategic leverage, economic and trade benefits, and global weight."[95] Kim suggests that "the structural reality of [this system] is an answer to the puzzle of how a regional power managed to be treated as a global power without first having acquired the reach or the requisite normative and material resources of a global power."[96]

However, the fact that China's role as a great power continued to depend more on the willingness of others to treat it as such than on its own capabilities meant that its status remained highly vulnerable. The end of the Cold War and the collapse of the Soviet Union meant an end to the strategic triangle, requiring China to make major adjustments in its strategic outlook. On the one hand, these events represented a dramatic improvement in China's security environment. Yet at the same time, Kim notes that China's security policies – e.g., accelerated military modernization, increased defense spending, continued nuclear testing – have been indicative of a certain level of insecurity that seems paradoxical to its professed satisfaction with the end of Cold War tensions. While he suggests that such insecurities may simply be a result of uncertainty due to dramatic changes in the international system, he notes that "part of the problem also has to do with the wrenching national identity difficulties that practically all major powers encounter in trying to adjust to a world in which conflict no longer takes place along an East-West divide."[97]

For China, such difficulties were particularly serious. Although some Chinese observers had begun predicting the movement of the international system to multipolarity as early as the mid-1980s,[98] the suddenness with which the Cold War came to an end risked undermining China's role as a great power. Support for the concept of 'multipolarization' (*duojihua*) was strong in some policy circles, leading it to be adopted as the CCPs official characterization of the international system at the 14th Party Congress in October 1992. However, others remained hesitant. Kim points out that "a multipolarizing world was seen by many Chinese strategic analysts as bereft of the much-coveted balancing third force – the vaunted China card – in global triangular geopolitics."[99] Similarly, Jing-dong Yuan argues that "the end of the Cold War has to some degree created an identity crisis for China. The decline and demise of the Soviet Union, the collapse of communism in Eastern Europe, the U.S.-led victory in the Gulf War, and the appearance if not the reality of a 'unipolar moment' have spelled an end to the relevance of China in the superpower balancing game."[100] Yong Deng has also suggested that "the end of the Cold War brought about a peculiar status crisis."[101] Thus, even if China were one of many major powers, its overall importance in global affairs seemed arguably diminished.

On the other hand, China recognized the possibility of a far worse alternative – a unipolar world led by the United States. Such a possibility was already being suggested as early as 1990.[102] By the late-1990s, this interpretation was becoming widely accepted. As Stephen Brooks and William Wohlforth point out, American capabilities are so far beyond those of any potential competitor, according to every measure, that "if today's American primacy does not constitute unipolarity, then nothing ever will."[103] This has been of great concern to Chinese leaders. As many neorealists would argue, the rise of a single, dominant power should be seen by others as a potential threat to their interests, and this is certainly true of China. Yet beyond the possibility that an unrestrained United States could threaten Chinese interests (e.g., by preventing reunification with Taiwan), unipolarity would also seriously threaten China's identity as a great power. After all, if a shift from de facto tripolarity to multipolarity required a certain degree of adjustment to maintain China's status and relevance in the post-Cold War world, then a shift to unipolarity would be far more problematic.

This may help to explain China's eventual whole-hearted embrace of multipolarity, not just as a description of the system as it is, but as a goal to be pursued by the international community. While China has come to recognize the position of the United States as the world's preeminent power,[104] Chinese analysts continue to describe the international system in largely multipolar terms, frequently using the term *yi chao duo qiang* – "one superpower and four big powers"[105] – to imply a rough equivalence within the context of an asymmetric distribution of power.[106] The desire to promote its idea of multipolarity has been a major impetus behind China's pursuit of partnerships with other important states, including the EU, Japan, and Russia. Their purpose, according to Joseph Cheng and Zhang Wankun, has been "to redefine its position" in the international system.[107] More specifically, "Chinese leaders wanted to promote global multipolarization and seek due recognition of China's status as an important pole in a multipolar world."[108] In essence, China has sought to replace the strategic triangle with a multipolar alternative that allows it to maintain its identity as a great power in the face of vastly superior U.S. capabilities. This continued insecurity about its status attests to the fact that China's role as a great power remains contested.

Raising the Bar

Given China's concrete advances in recent years, and U.S. concerns (at least in some quarters) that these advances may constitute a 'China Threat,' Chinese worries about their own irrelevance in a unipolar world dominated by the United States might seem paradoxical. After all, if China's role as a great power is partly (and arguably primarily) constructed through its relations with the United States, and it sees China's growing material capabilities (economic and military) as a potential threat, then China can remain secure in the knowledge that it is as important as it thinks. Why would its role as a great power still be contested? The answer is that great power status involves more than just having an ability to threaten; it involves a certain measure of respect from other great powers, even it is only the grudging respect of one adversary for another. After its troubled entrance into the family of nations, it is precisely this kind of respect that China wants most, and feels is owed it. While China may initially have been given its (provisional) seat at the table of great powers based on expectations of its future importance, most Chinese believe that such expectations have now been fulfilled. As such, "the new leadership has identified pursuing international respect for China as a major theme of China's foreign relations."[109] Whatever the significance of China's material capabilities, without this respect its identity as a great power will remain contested.

Yet respect is precisely what the Chinese feel is most lacking in their relationship with the United States. For China, it was a cruel irony that just as its reform efforts were fulfilling the promise of great power status by putting it on track to become one of the world's largest, most dynamic economies, the United States began a wholesale reorientation of its policy toward it as a result of Tiananmen Square. The Chinese government's crackdown against student demonstrators in 1989 shattered what has been called the 'liberal China myth' that modernization and economic reform would inevitably lead to the acceptance of Western (i.e., American) political norms.[110] It was replaced by what Rey Chow has referred to as the 'King Kong syndrome' – a "structure of cross-cultural, cross-racial representation aimed at producing 'China' as a spectacular monster whose despotism necessitates the salvation of its people by outsiders."[111] That salvation was to come through economic sanctions and political pressure aimed at forcing China to improve its record on human rights, and was accompanied by a vigorous debate about whether it constituted a new threat. Thus, instead of accepting China's growing importance in international politics and treating it as an equal, the United States after 1989 began to treat it as a near-pariah, little better than the rogue states it sought to contain through diplomatic isolation, economic sanctions, and occasional military chastisement.

Although Sino-U.S. relations have improved considerably since the days of confrontation over human rights and MFN status, and since 9/11 has involved various levels of cooperation, Deng suggests that "China is not yet fully accepted as a legitimate member of the U.S.-centered great power club, defined by shared in-group collective identity and a strong sense of security community."[112] In 2002, the White House explicitly identified China as one of three "*potential* great powers" in its official National Security Strategy (NSS).[113] The reason for China's continued 'outlier' status (to use Deng's term) becomes clear when one examines how the NSS characterized Sino-U.S. relations and the developments it sees as being necessary for China to be accepted as a great power.

> The United States relationship with China is an important part of our strategy to promote a stable, peaceful, and prosperous Asia-Pacific region. We welcome the emergence of a strong, peaceful, and prosperous China. *The democratic development of China is crucial to that future.* Yet, a quarter century after beginning the process of shedding the worst features of the Communist legacy, China's leaders have not yet made the next series of fundamental choices about the character of their state. *In pursuing advanced military capabilities that can threaten its neighbors in the Asia-Pacific region, China is following an outdated path that, in the end, will hamper its own pursuit of national greatness. In time, China will find that social and political freedom is the only source of that greatness.*[114]

In essence, the United States does not view economic and military capabilities as sufficient for China to be accepted as a great power. Indeed, it seems to suggest (perhaps self-servingly) that the development of improved military capabilities could actually hamper its rise as a great power. What matters are not material capabilities, but the achievement of normative standards set largely by the United States. To put it simply, the United States has attempted to raise the bar for acceptance as a great power.

To some extent, China seems to have taken this change to heart. While it seems unlikely that it will pursue Western-style democracy simply to be accepted by the international community, Deng suggests that "Chinese political and intellectual elite[s] have come to realize that material power alone cannot catapult China to its great power status."[115] As a result, 'responsibility' has become the key watchword in Chinese foreign policy in order to enhance its legitimacy in the eyes of others.[116] However, he also points out that "the lack of social standing as a legitimate great power candidate may be more difficult to overcome than the materialist obstacles."[117] If the United States continues to treat China as an outlier because of its lack of democratic values, then only a radical restructuring of the Chinese political system is likely to substantially influence U.S. acceptance. This is likely to continue to produce tensions in Sino-U.S. relations as China grows increasingly frustrated with its lack of acceptance. While definitive predictions about China's future behavior are always risky, one might suggest two possible directions that this could go. Continued 'responsible' behavior on the part of China (combined with continued material progress) could eventually force other powers, including the United States, to once again redefine the standards for being a great power so as to include it in the 'club' without requiring major political reforms. Or continued resistance from the United States and others could lead China to become a more explicitly revisionist state and challenge the existing rules of the system.

Evidence of the former may already be found in the Bush administration's most recent NSS, published in March 2006. While it still maintains that

"China's transition remains incomplete,"[118] its tone is noticeably softer. Gone are explicit references to China as a potential power and the necessity for it to embrace democracy to fulfill that potential. Instead, it asserts that

> As China becomes a global player, it must act as a responsible stakeholder that fulfills its obligations and works with the United States and others to advance the international system that has enabled its success: enforcing the international rules that have helped China lift itself out of a century of economic deprivation, embracing the economic and political standards that go along with that system of rules, and contributing to international stability and security by working with the United States and other major powers.[119]

In essence, the United States seems willing to accept 'responsible' behavior in the international arena, along with vague references to acceptance of 'political standards,' as sufficient to treat China as a great power. Compared to the explicit expectations of democratic development stated in 2002, this seems to provide a more manageable way to settle the disconnect between China's growing material capabilities and social acceptance of its status on the part of the United States in a way that does not lead to tension and conflict.

CHINA'S FUTURE AS A GREAT POWER

The above analysis of the social construction of China's identity as a great power yields three important conclusions. First, neither realist nor constructivist interpretations of great power status are adequate by themselves. A strictly realist interpretation cannot explain why China was initially, if tentatively, accepted as a great power despite significant deficiencies in its material capabilities. With the exception of manpower, it was ranked well behind even many medium powers according to virtually any measure until quite recently. At the same time, a strictly constructivist interpretation cannot explain why, after being granted recognition as a great power, its role became so contested. A lack of material capabilities remained a serious impediment to China's ability to maintain its relevance on the world stage. The disconnect between the material and social dimensions of China's status as a great power can only be fully understood through a synthesis of realist and constructivist theory that takes *both* power and identity seriously. Being a great power is a socially constructed identity dependent on shared knowledge and social norms, but it also requires a 'materialist benchmark' in order for it to be enacted successfully.

Second, because great power status is socially constructed, the criteria for what makes a state a great power may change as ideas regarding what makes a state important change. Such changes might come in two conceivable forms. On the one hand, the kinds of material capabilities that are necessary for a state to be considered a great power may change. Although realists could explain this simply by noting that innovations in weaponry may render states that fail to adapt obsolete, one could also suggest a social component to this. For instance, acquisition of nuclear weapons often seems to be as much about improving one's status – i.e., joining the nuclear club – as it is about obtaining a deterrent. On the other hand, U.S. attempts to make democracy a criterion for great power status (whether or not such attempts would necessarily be successful) demonstrate the possibility of adding (or perhaps changing) normative requirements. This warrants further examination.

Finally, while China's final transition to becoming a fully-accepted great power may be underway, the potentially fluid meaning of what a great power is means that the outcome can never be guaranteed. After all, it is due to changes in the beliefs and perceptions surrounding great power status that China's rise has been so contested for so long. While its relative lack of capabilities certainly opened the door for its status to be questioned, it was a change in beliefs regarding its potential to play a major role in world affairs that first put China in the inherently vulnerable position of a power always on the rise, but never risen. The more recent attempt to change the normative standards for being a great power has presented China with an additional challenge just as the first was being met. As such, the potential for conflicts over normative standards (e.g., discrepancies between conceptions of 'responsible' behavior), as well as the potential for the meaning of great power status to continue to evolve, mean that China's status could remain contested for some time. Predictions regarding its eventual rise must therefore be tempered with the recognition that any success will be dependent, not just on continued economic growth or military modernization, but on prevailing social norms. The 'fact' of China's rise is thus far from being established.

Notes

[1] Yong Deng and Fei-Ling Wang, eds., *China Rising: Power and Motivation in Chinese Foreign Policy* (Lanham: Rowman & Littlefield Publishers, Inc., 2005); and James Kynge, *China Shakes the World: A Titan's Rise and Troubled Future – and the Challenge for America* (New York: Houghton Mifflin Company, 2006).
[2] Fareed Zakaria, "Does the Future Belong to China?," *Newsweek*, 9 May 2005, p. 29.
[3] Nicholas D. Kristof and Sheryl Wudunn, *China Wakes: The Struggle for the Soul of a Rising Power* (New York: Random House, Inc., 1994); and William H. Overholt, *The Rise of China: How Economic Reform is Creating a New Superpower* (New York: W. W. Norton & Company, 1993).
[4] For instance, see Barry Buzan and Rosemary Foot, eds., *Does China Matter? A Reassessment: Essays in Memory of Gerald Segal* (London: Routledge, 2004).
[5] Gerald Segal, "Does China Matter?," *Foreign Affairs*, vol. 78, no. 5, September/October 1999, p. 24.
[6] Martin Wight, *Power Politics*, Edited by Hedley Bull and Carsten Holbraad. (New York: Holmes & Meier Publishers, Inc., 1978), p. 41.
[7] Jack S. Levy, *War in the Modern Great Power System, 1495-1975* (Lexington: The University Press of Kentucky, 1983), p. 10.
[8] Barry Buzan, *The United States and the Great Powers: World Politics in the Twenty-First Century* (Malden: Polity Press, 2004), p. 58. See also Levy, *War in the Modern Great Power System*, pp. 10-1.
[9] Wight, *Power Politics*, p. 41.
[10] Ibid., p. 48.

[11] Buzan, *The United States and the Great Powers*, p. 59.

[12] For a basic overview of the evolution of these debates, see Steve Smith, "The Self-Images of a Discipline: A Genealogy of International Relations Theory," in Ken Booth and Steve Smith, eds., *International Relations Theory Today* (University Park: The Pennsylvania State University Press, 1995); and Yosef Lapid, "Sculpting the Academic Identity: Disciplinary Reflections at the Dawn of a New Millenium," in Donald J. Puchala, ed., *Visions of International Relations: Assessing an Academic Field* (Columbia: University of South Carolina Press, 2002).

[13] Both realism and liberalism, at least in their 'neo' forms, are often seen as competing schools of thought within a broader rationalist paradigm. See Ole Wæver, "The Rise and Fall of the Inter-Paradigm Debate," in Steve Smith, Ken Booth, and Marysia Zalewski, eds., *International Theory: Positivism and Beyond* (Cambridge: Cambridge University Press, 1996).

[14] See James E. Dougherty and Robert L. Pfaltzgraff, Jr., *Contending Theories of International Relations: A Comprehensive Survey*, 5th ed. (New York: Addison Wesley Longman, Inc., 2001), pp. 88-9.

[15] Peter J. Katzenstein, "Introduction: Alternative Perspectives on National Security," in Peter J. Katzenstein, ed., *The Culture of National Security: Norms and Identity in World Politics* (New York: Columbia University Press, 1996), p. 14.

[16] See Kenneth N. Waltz, *Theory of International Politics* (New York: McGraw-Hill, Inc., 1979.

[17] Friedrich V. Kratochwil, "Constructivism as an Approach to Interdisciplinary Study," in Karin M. Fierke and Knud Erik Jørgensen, eds., *Constructing International Relations: The Next Generation* (Armonk: M. E. Sharpe, 2001), pp. 16-7.

[18] J. Samuel Barkin, "Realist Constructivism," *International Studies Review*, vol. 5, September 2003, p. 326.

[19] Alexander Wendt, "Identity and Structural Change in International Politics," in Yosef Lapid and Friedrich Kratochwil, eds., *The Return of Culture and Identity in IR Theory* (Boulder: Lynne Rienner Publishers, 1996), p. 49.

[20] Alexander Wendt, *Social Theory of International Politics* (Cambridge: Cambridge University Press, 1999), p. 158.

[21] Glenn Chafetz, Benjamin Frankel, and Michael Spirtas, "Introduction: Tracing the Influence of Identity on Foreign Policy," in Glenn Chafetz, Michael Spirtas, and Benjamin Frankel, eds., *The Origins of National Interests* (London: Frank Cass, 1999), p. viii.

[22] Alexander Wendt, "Constructing International Politics," *International Security*, vol. 20, no. 1, Summer 1995, p. 73.

[23] Ibid., p. 73.

[24] Peter du Preez, cited in Michael Ng-Quinn, "National Identity in Premodern China: Formation and Role Enactment," in Lowell Dittmer and Samuel S. Kim, eds., *China's Quest for National Identity* (Ithaca: Cornell University Press, 1993), p. 33.

[25] Philippe G. Le Prestre, "Author! Author! Defining Foreign Policy Roles after the Cold War," in Philippe G. Le Prestre, ed., *Role Quests in the Post-Cold War Era: Foreign Policies in Transition* (Montreal: McGill-Queen's University Press, 1997), p. 5.

[26] Wendt, *Social Theory of International Politics*, p. 227.

[27] Ibid., p. 335.

[28] James Fearon and Alexander Wendt, "Rationalism *v.* Constructivism: A Skeptical View," in Walter Carlsnaes, Thomas Risse, and Beth A. Simmons, eds., *Handbook of International Relations* (London: SAGE Publications, 2002), pp. 58-65.

[29] Ibid., p. 52.

[30] Henry R. Nau, "Identity and the Balance of Power in Asia," in G. John Ikenberry and Michael Mastanduno, eds., *International Relations Theory and the Asia-Pacific* (New York: Columbia University Press, 2003), p. 217.

[31] Barkin, "Realist Constructivism," p. 337.

[32] Wendt, "Constructing International Politics," p. 74.

[33] Wendt, *Social Theory of International Politics*, p. 135.

[34] Ibid., p. 136.

[35] Ibid., p. 112.

[36] Ibid., p. 331.

[37] Waltz, *Theory of International Politics*, p. 131.

[38] Raymond Aron, *Peace and War: A Theory of International Relations*, translated from the French by Richard Howard and Annette Baker Fox (New York: Frederick A. Praeger, Publishers, 1967), pp. 57-8.

[39] Waltz, *Theory of International Politics*, p. 72.

[40] Levy, *War in the Modern Great Power System*, p. 14.

[41] John J. Mearsheimer, *The Tragedy of Great Power Politics* (New York: W. W. Norton & Company, 2001), p. 5.

[42] Waltz, *Theory of International Politics*, p. 131.

[43] Wight, *Power Politics*, p. 46.

[44] Ibid., p. 48.

[45] Ibid., p. 46.

[46] Buzan, *The United States and the Great Powers*, p. 63.

[47] Wight, *Power Politics*, pp. 48-9.

[48] Levy, *War in the Modern Great Power System*, pp. 17-8.

[49] Hedley Bull, *The Anarchical Society: A Study of Order in World Politics*, 2d ed., (New York: Columbia University Press, 1977), p. 196.

[50] Buzan, *The United States and the Great Powers*, p. 61.

[51] Ibid., p. 60.

[52] Wight, *Power Politics*, p. 45.

[53] Ibid., p. 46.

[54] Buzan, *The United States and the Great Powers*, p. 63.

[55] Hans J. Morgenthau, *Politics Among Nations: The Struggle for Power and Peace*, 6th Ed., Revised by Kenneth W. Thompson (New York: Alfred A. Knopf, 1985), p. 361.

[56] See Onnig Beylerian with Christophe Canivet, "China: Role Conceptions after the Cold War," in Philippe G. Le Prestre, ed., *Role Quests in the Post-Cold War Era: Foreign Policies in Transition* (Montreal: McGill-Queen's University Press, 1997).

[57] Yan Xuetong, "The Rise of China in Chinese Eyes," *Journal of Contemporary China*, vol. 10, February 2001, p. 33.

[58] Samuel S. Kim, "China and the World in Theory and Practice," in Samuel S. Kim, ed., *China and the World: Chinese Foreign Relations in the Post-Cold War Era*, 3d ed. (Boulder: Westview Press, 1994), p. 3.

[59] Gilbert Rozman, "China's Quest for Great Power Identity," *Orbis*, vol. 43, Summer 1999, p. 385.

[60] Warren I. Cohen, *America's Response to China: An Interpretive History of Sino-American Relations* (New York: John Wiley & Sons, Inc., 1971), p. 153.

[61] *The Memoirs of Cordell Hull*, vol. 2 (New York: The Macmillan Company, 1948), p. 1583.

[62] Ibid., p. 1583.

[63] John W. Garver, *Chinese-Soviet Relations 1937-1945: The Diplomacy of Chinese Nationalism* (New York: Oxford University Press, 1988), pp. 193-94.

[64] William C. Kirby, "The Internationalization of China: Foreign Relations at Home and Abroad in the Republican Era," *The China Quarterly*, vol. 150, June 1997, p. 433.

[65] Tang Tsou, *America's Failure in China, 1941-50* (Chicago: The University of Chicago Press, 1963), pp. 41-3.

[66] Michael Schaller, *The U.S. Crusade in China, 1938-1945* (New York: Columbia University Press, 1979), pp. 89-90. While the same could be said of France at the time, the French could at least benefit from their past history as a great power.

[67] Akira Iriye, "The United States as an Asian-Pacific Power," in Gene T. Hsiao, ed., *Sino-American Détente and Its Policy Implications* (New York: Praeger Publishers, Inc., 1974), p. 8.

[68] Cited in Barbara W. Tuchman, *Stilwell and the American Experience in China, 1911-45* (New York: The Macmillan Company, 1971), p. 239.

[69] Robert Dallek, *Franklin D. Roosevelt and American Foreign Policy, 1932-1945* (New York: Oxford University Press, 1979), p. 328.

[70] Winston S. Churchill, *The Hinge of Fate* (Boston: Houghton Mifflin Company, 1950), p. 133.

[71] *The Memoirs of Cordell Hull*, p. 1587.

[72] Tuchman, *Stilwell and the American Experience in China*, p. 239.

[73] Edward R. Stettinius, Jr., *Roosevelt and the Russians: The Yalta Conference* (Garden City: Doubleday & Company, Inc., 1949), p. 71.

[74] Churchill, *The Hinge of Fate*, p. 785.

[75] Ibid., p. 133.

[76] Cited in Iriye, "The United States as an Asian-Pacific Power," p. 12.

[77] Tsou, *America's Failure in China*, p. 59.

[78] Iriye, "The United States as an Asian-Pacific Power," p. 11.

[79] Dallek, *Franklin D. Roosevelt and American Foreign*, p. 329.

[80] Iriye, "The United States as an Asian-Pacific Power," p. 11.

[81] Cohen, *America's Response to China*, p. 162.

[82] Ibid., p. 153.

[83] Tsou, *America's Failure in China*, pp. 68-73.

[84] Iriye, "The United States as an Asian-Pacific Power," p. 11.

[85] Steven I. Levine, "China in Asia: The PRC as a Regional Power," in Harry Harding, ed., *China's Foreign Relations in the 1980s* (New Haven: Yale University Press, 1984), p. 110.

[86] Ibid., p. 107; and Samuel S. Kim, "China's Pacific Policy: Reconciling the Irreconcilable," *International Journal*, vol. 50, Summer 1995, p. 464.

[87] Goldstein, *Rising to the Challenge*, p. 50.

[88] Levine, "China in Asia," p. 107.

[89] Ibid., pp. 110-11.

[90] Kim, "China's Pacific Policy," p. 464.

[91] Samuel S. Kim, "China's International Organizational Behaviour," in Thomas W. Robinson and David Shambaugh, eds., *Chinese Foreign Policy: Theory and Practice* (Oxford: Clarendon Press, 1995), p. 417.

[92] John W. Garver, *Foreign Relations of the People's Republic of China* (Englewood Cliffs: Prentice Hall, 1993), p. 49.

[93] Rozman, "China's Quest for Great Power Identity," p. 388.

[94] Ibid., pp. 388-89.

[95] Kim, "China's Pacific Policy," p. 466.

[96] Ibid., p. 466.

[97] Ibid., p. 463.

[98] For a detailed discussion of this issue, see Michael Pillsbury, *China Debates the Future Security Environment* (Honolulu: University Press of the Pacific, 2005).

[99] Kim, "China's Pacific Policy," p. 466.

[100] Jing-dong Yuan, "Threat Perception and Chinese Security Policy after the Cold War," *Pacific Focus*, vol. 8, no. 1, Spring 1998, p. 56.

[101] Yong Deng, "Better Than Power: 'International Status' in Chinese Foreign Policy," in Yong Deng and Fei-Ling Wang, eds., *China Rising: Power and Motivation in Chinese Foreign Policy* (Lanham: Rowman & Littlefield Publishers, Inc., 2005), p. 51.

[102] See Charles Krauthammer, "The Unipolar Moment," *Foreign Affairs*, vo. 70, no. 1, 1990/1991, pp. 23-33.

[103] Stephen Brooks and William Wohlforth, "American Primacy in Perspective," *Foreign Affairs*, vol. 81, no. 4, July/August 2002, p. 21.

[104] For a discussion of China's reaction to the United States as a unipolar power, see Denny Roy, "China's Reaction to American Predominance," *Survival*, vol. 45, no. 3, Autumn 2003, pp. 57-78.

[105] The four big powers generally refer to the European Union, Japan, Russia, and China. See Suisheng Zhao, "Chinese Foreign Policy: Pragmatism and Strategic Behavior," in Suisheng Zhao, ed., *Chinese Foreign Policy: Pragmatism and Strategic Behavior* (Armonk: M. E. Sharpe, 2004), p. 13.

[106] Similar formulations have been suggested in the Western international relations literature. For instance, see Aaron L. Friedberg, "Ripe for Rivalry: Prospects for Peace in a Multipolar Asia," in Michael E. Brown, Sean M. Lynn-Jones, and Steven E. Miller, eds., *East Asian Security* (Cambridge: The MIT Press, 1998), p. 4; and Richard K. Betts, "Wealth, Power, and Instability: East Asia and the United States after the Cold War," in Michael E. Brown, Sean M. Lynn-Jones, and Steven E. Miller, eds., *East Asian Security* (Cambridge: The MIT Press, 1998), p. 39.

[107] Joseph Y. S. Cheng and Zhang Wankun, "Patterns and Dynamics of China's International Strategic Behavior," in Suisheng Zhao, ed., *Chinese Foreign Policy: Pragmatism and Strategic Behavior* (Armonk: M. E. Sharpe, 2004), p. 180.

[108] Ibid., p. 196.

[109] Yongnian Zheng, *Discovering Chinese Nationalism in China: Modernization, Identity, and International Relations* (Cambridge: Cambridge University Press, 1999), p. 125.

[110] See Richard Madsen, *China and the American Dream: A Moral Inquiry* (Berkeley: University of California Press, 1995), pp. 28-29; and Thomas Laszlo Dorogi, *Tainted Perceptions: Liberal-Democracy and American Popular Images of China* (Lanham: University Press of America, Inc., 2001), p. 18.

[111] Rey Chow, "King Kong in Hong Kong: Watching the 'Handover' from the U.S.A.," *Social Text*, vol. 16, no. 2, Summer 1998, p. 94

[112] Deng, "Better Than Power," p. 54.

[113] The White House, *The National Security Strategy of the United States of America* (Washington, 2002), p. 26; emphasis added.

[114] Ibid., p. 27; emphasis added.

[115] Deng, "Better Than Power," p. 62

[116] For a detailed discussion of this issue, see Yongjin Zhang and Greg Austin, eds., *Power and Responsibility in Chinese Foreign Policy* (Canberra: Asia Pacific Press, 2001).

[117] Deng, "Better Than Power," p. 62.

[118] The White House, *The National Security Strategy of the United States of America* (Washington, 2006), p. 41

[119] Ibid., p. 41.

Chapter 5

Tapping Soft Power: Managing China's "Peaceful Rise" and the Implications for the World

Wanfa Zhang[*]

INTRODUCTION

China's "rise" in the past quarter century has precipitated widespread reactions. These reactions include not only praises and admirations for China's great economic achievement, but also suspicion and fear about its rapidly growing power and intention to project that power in the future. A significant number of scholars postulate, in accord with the realist literature about international politics, that countries undergoing economic transition tend to pursue "assertive and expansionist" foreign policies.[1] China will be no exception.

However, since the mid-1990s, there has been more and more evidence indicating a clear shift in the path of China's domestic and foreign policies contrary to most predictions of realist scholarship.[2] Beijing has been pursuing a more liberal policy characterized by exercising self-restraint, and promoting trade and interdependence in foreign policy, that centers on cultivating and managing soft power.[3] This seemingly paradoxical situation, however, presents a positive indication regarding what road this awakening giant shall take and how it is going to flex its muscles in the years to come.

Because of the dramatic growth of China's hard power and its potential impact upon the world, this policy change has profound implications for China itself as well as for the world. For China, the new goal to tap soft power symbolized by promoting attractiveness may well imply an earnest drive toward building the country into a modern, democratic and "harmonious society."[4] For other countries, it means that this potential superpower is planning to play a facilitative rather than a disruptive role in world affairs. China's motivation to develop soft power, rather than obsess itself with hard power will help it become a "responsible stakeholder" that will project its rapidly expanding strength in a benevolent way.[5]

This chapter is a study of these issues. The first section will be a discussion of the conceptualization of soft power and the implications of soft power tapping. The second will be devoted to the background, purpose and logic of China's attempt to cultivate this power. The third section is a study of the strategy, measures and policies adopted by China for the realization of the goal. Section four will explore the resources China may have for cultivating soft power and the barriers it will confront. Finally, I will present the implications of China's soft power tapping for the world and some policy suggestions on increasing the mutual benefits between China and the world resulted from Beijing's new orientation of policy.

SOFT POWER AND BEYOND

Joseph Nye introduced the term *soft power* into international relations literature in *Bound to Lead* (1990).[6] Soft power is also the central theme of two other books by Nye, *The Paradox of American Power—Why the World's Only Superpower Can't Go It Alone* and *Soft Power—the Means to Success in World Politics*, that are widely read and discussed. Soft power, according to Nye, is a state's ability to "shape the preferences of others" and the ability to induce international compliance without resorting to coercive means. In other words, it "is the ability to get what you want through attraction rather than coercion or payments."[7] Following Nye's logic, we can reason that soft power lies in a comprehensive and positive image a country presents or communicates to other countries or peoples. Such a positive image can help justify a behavior even it is selfishly motivated.

Nye's arguments in these books are built on the central theme of how to make use of soft power to serve U.S. national interests. These discussions are innovative; however, he fails to point out, and does not attempt to explore, the other side of the coin. Soft power, especially the tapping and management by a country, can benefit other countries as well. First, soft power stems from a state's positive image in the eyes of others expressed in the attractiveness of its political ideas, culture and foreign policies.[8] Therefore, it entails a soft power tapping state to present a positive image of itself and behave in a way other countries deem benevolent. Second, this factor will preclude this country from neglecting the views, interests and welfare of other states and "go it alone."[9] On the contrary, it will become more considerate of other states' interests and exercise restraint in actions that would potentially harm its own image. Third, the country may have strong incentives to adopt policies that have a strong mutually beneficial or even altruistic nature, such as providing foreign aid, cultivating and developing international cooperation programs, and expanding cultural and economic ties with other countries. These combined features will make soft power tapping and management especially implicative.

Growing evidence since the 1990s has shown that China's domestic and foreign policies are following a strategy that prioritizes the tapping and management of soft power. Those features pertaining to the power render

China's effort significant and to have far-reaching implications due to its correlation with Beijing's intention to project its dramatically growing hard power.

CHINA'S SOFT POWER TAPPING: BACKGROUND, PURPOSE AND LOGIC

As an old country that has been heavily influenced by Confucianism, cultivating and managing soft power is not a novel topic for China. Throughout China's millennia-long history, there has been a litany of works addressing the essence and utilities of soft power in domestic and international politics.[10] It is not difficult to find in its history the periods when the projection of soft power, rather than hard power, was adopted as dominant state policy.[11] Nevertheless, the revitalization of Chinese interest in cultivating soft power is relatively recent, resulting from a variety of domestic and international forces in the 1990s.

By the mid-1990s, China's continuous economic growth for more than a decade had drawn wide attention from across the world.[12] As a communist giant that had embraced the free-market economic system, China reemerged on the world stage in a new manner that was not encountered before. Politically, the Beijing regime was still adhering to its socialist ideology, if not communism. Yet economically, it had integrated into the world capitalist system on such a scale and to such an extent that even the oldest and most developed capitalist countries could not match.[13] In an international system that is still dominated by *realpolitik* and egoist, self-help politics, the rapid rise of a new power with such a complex hybrid of socialist ideological doctrines and a capitalist economic system is destined to worry the existing global order. Because almost all international relations theories in the past that discuss rising power painted a pessimistic picture.[14] The rise of Germany and Japan and the subsequent aftermath seemed to be an illustration of this pattern.

Such anxiety out of international relations theories and dire consequences in the past quickly surfaced when China's rise turned into a reality beyond academic discussions and theoretical speculation. A China threat theory that argues for the potential danger posed by China out of an entrenched Chinese revisionist intention and a growing capability materialized. Whether the China threat theory emerged out of unsound speculation or reasonable concerns, their negative impact upon the world's perspective of China can not be underestimated.

By the end of the 1990s and early 2000s, these potential negative impacts had started to manifest themselves. The argument about China's threat has spilled over from worries over security issues into a broad range of speculations over problems China might cause in international politics, economy, environmental protection, and even energy and food consumption.[15] Moreover, the chorus of the China threat has developed from theoretical argument into actions against China. Some even trumpeted a new "containment" policy toward China like that against the former Soviet Union.[16] In the security field, the U.S.

and Japan have intensified their military alliance as well as their efforts to persuade Brussels to hold on to its anti-China arms embargo.[17] The most prominent case in economy is the U.S. congress's intervention to prevent China's state-owned CNOOC Ltd. from buying the American company Unocal in 2005. The U.S. has also repeatedly warned China's neighbors of the danger from an emerging dragon, exerting pressure on Israel to cancel early-warning plane transactions with China. Obviously, "The security dilemma confronting Beijing will gain momentum if its threat image worsens and material capabilities grow simultaneously."[18] These reactions are only the tip of the iceberg.

Without a proper response, the proliferation of the China threat theory and those anti-China rhetoric callings will degenerate, and eventually ruin a congenial international environment China desperately needs for its development.[19] They will also cause unnecessary difficulties for China in its political reform, diplomacy, economic development, and even national security. Among Beijing's responses, two were especially worth deliberation. The first was Beijing's direct rebuttal of the China threat theory; the second was its design to mold a benign image by tapping soft power.

The intuitive reaction to address the "China threat" syndrome gradually evolved into a more widely accepted strategy that has long-term goals. Among China's top state leaders, policy-makers and academics, a growing consensus has been reached that Beijing should put more emphasis on presenting the world with an amicable image so as to reduce stereotypes of China and the misunderstanding from the outside world.[20] Only by doing this, could China be regarded as a positive and constructive force that will be welcomed into the world community.

In the end, it is expected that China will gain a congenial rather than a hostile environment for its further development. With growing interactions with other countries and deepening integration into the world community, a favorable image is ever more important. Strong soft power will help serve its national goals, as is the case with other great powers in the past. This passive response to negative international repercussions eventually became the inner drive for the country to ameliorate itself and adjust its foreign policy.

Meeting the Needs of Domestic Politics

Although cultivating soft power is considered largely an extroversive enterprise, it is no less significant for China's domestic politics. A high international prestige is able to raise people's confidence in the Communist Party of China (CPC), and, therefore, legitimize its rule. A good reputation is also able to increase Beijing's attractiveness to Taiwanese and overseas Chinese communities and improve their attitude toward Beijing. A positive international image is pertinent to the Beijing regime since it is one of the few governments ruled by a Communist Party presently, which is seemingly going against the world trend of democratization. Under such circumstance, the Party has to make even harder efforts to establish and prove its legitimacy.

Two decades' reform has brought tremendous economic benefits to China and opportunity and prosperity for hundreds of millions of its people. However, the continuous buildup of social maladies stemming from the rapid political, economic and social transformation is increasingly endangering the domestic stability and the CPC's rule.[21] These maladies, more specifically the widening gap between the rich and poor, uneven economic development among the coastal and interior provinces, widespread corruption in government, flagging public services and serious environment pollution, have spelled serious political discontent and any worsening of conditions may trigger serious social upheaval. The successful establishment of an honorable image in the world will win the CPC domestic support, and extra time to find solutions to these social problems. Beijing's initiative to improve its image has implications for the cross-Strait relations between the mainland and Taiwan as well. A positive view of the mainland government may help dampen Taiwanese interest and determination for independence and facilitate the building of political trust. The willingness of the Taiwanese people to maintain a closer political relationship, even a possible reunification with the mainland, has much to do with their views of the Beijing regime and the circumstances on the other side of the Taiwan Strait.[22]

The growing number of Chinese citizens studying, working or living abroad have strong sensitivities to the image of their country in the world. Frequent criticism of China's corruption and poor human rights record by foreign state leaders and international media can become a source of dissatisfaction with the Beijing regime. Due to their role as an important bridge that helps to link China and the world, their investments for China's economic growth and their character as the most reliable ally of Beijing in its fight against Taiwan separatists overseas, they form a special force whose demands and needs can not be neglected by Beijing's policy-makers.[23] Similarly, the prestige of the mainland government is important for the stabilization of the returned colonies of Hong Kong and Macao. The image of the central government in the world and its credibility to provide needed help for the people of these former foreign colonies is highly correlated with their acceptance and recognition of the new government in their minds and hearts.

In short, the CPC's legitimacy depends on its strategy and capability to address the serious problems, and its continuous delivery of political, economic and social benefits to the Chinese people. Tapping soft power abroad will have a reactive influence upon the solution to these problems since recognition and the reputation earned from abroad will in turn boost its image and help to strengthen its position at home. To some extent, its success in achieving the above goals is associated with its effective presentation of itself as a peace-loving, cooperative and trustworthy partner in the world. This reality will give the Beijing regime strong incentive and sufficient rationale to improve domestic conditions and satisfy the demands and needs of the people. Beijing also has good reasons to act in accordance with international norms and widely accepted rules and values concerning democracy, the rule of law and human rights, hence its endeavor to tap soft power has deep implications for domestic politics as well.

Rejuvenating China and Driving for Great Power

To rejuvenate China has always been an ideal used by the CPC to rally support of the Chinese people in the past. With the collapse of Communism and its failure as a political appeal to win support, the CPC has to resort to other ideals. To lead the country to great power status is not just a political slogan; it is also a necessity as "soft sources of power ... are part of what makes a great power."[24] On different occasions, generations of China's state leaders have expressed their enthusiasm for such goals.

Historically, China was not a country with just hard power, but one with great soft power as well. China's political, economic and cultural systems were the models neighboring nations Japan, Korea, Vietnam and other minority ethnic regimes eagerly copied and borrowed. China also had considerable influence on the written system, social structure, customs and habits, educational system, family relationship and social organization in these countries.[25] China's mighty soft power also helped to sinicize China's conquerors, like the Xianbei, the Mongols and the Manchus. These peoples who inhabited on the periphery of China in ancient times once ruled part or all of China; however, they were eventually sinified by their subjects. In contrast with ancient times, today's China does not seem to have many things to offer to the world. Rejuvenating China does not simply mean the growth of its hard power, but also the building and expansion of its soft power. With the rise of China's capability, comes along with the success in its economic construction, it is natural for Beijing to incorporate cultivating soft power into its agenda.

A brief review of other countries will present evidence that all great powers in history are those which possessed both hard and soft power. The U.S. and the Soviet Union, the two Cold-War adversaries with conflicting political ideologies and oppositional economic systems, are exemplary models for case study. The U.S. demonstrated its unusual attractiveness that is expressed by its political ideals and values like democracy, freedom and human rights, social conditions like a high level of economic development and standard of living, widely-loved popular culture highlighted by Hollywood movies and music, and admirably high level of advanced science and technology. Although the Soviet Union was quite different from the U.S. in its politics and economy, it also radiated its great appeal with its successful experiences of rapid industrialization and development under socialism, Marxist-Leninist ideals of building an equalitarian society without exploiting the working class and other social underdogs, foreign policies marked by supporting decolonization and promoting national liberation movements from old colonial and imperialist rule in the third world countries. Despite the vastly different natures of their soft power, each of the superpowers successfully rallied respective followers. This provided the foundation and extra strength for a Cold War confrontation between the two camps. Without their respective soft power, it is questionable if they were able to build up their own camps, even by coercive means.

These historical and contemporary cases provide concrete evidence manifesting the great importance and implications of soft power for great powers. China's drastic growth in hard power has greatly raised the country's influence and status in the world. Beijing clearly knows that without soft power, the country will never restore its historical place and ascend to great power status in our time. China has to tap this "third dimension of power" if it aspires to recover its historical grandeur in East Asia and even play a new leadership role in the world. Its development of soft power has to move in line with the pace of its hard power growth on its way toward great powerdom; thus, its reorientation of foreign policy on soft power tapping is a logical step that has to be taken on its long march toward those ambitions.

Tapping Soft Power: Strategy, Measures and Policies

Ever since the debut of the Jiang Zemin-Zhu Rongji administration in early 1990s, Beijing has stepped up endeavors in constructing and raising its international image.[26] Beijing's grand strategy has three tactics that cover foreign affairs, domestic politics and international publicity respectively. The first tactic is aimed at building trust with other countries and establishing a benign image of a responsible power that abides by the established rules of the international organizations and regimes. The second tactic is directed at solving domestic problems and building a *hexie shehui* (harmonious society), and the last one launches a series of initiatives aimed at expanding its "soft" influences based on a favorable image.

Building Confidence and Enhancing the Image of a Responsible Power
The tactic is composed of two complementary measures. The first is aimed at explicit reiteration of its policies of peaceful intention on different occasions by state leaders and China's no interest to "seek hegemony."[27] The second measure targets concrete policies and actions to substantiate the policy renunciation in the first measure. By doing the former, Beijing hopes that it will lucidly communicate to the international community its benevolent intentions and foreign policies to prevent misunderstandings and reduce their skepticism and anxieties. Beijing then tries to corroborate those claims by adopting actual policies. Beijing hopes that, when combined, these measures will address the legitimate concerns of its Asian neighbors and concerned powers in the region, stabilize relations with these countries and advance its international image, and eventually invite reciprocal actions from other states.

The declaration and reiteration of the "peaceful rise" policy is an important instance of the tactic. In this policy statement, Beijing assured other states that a peaceful, rather than unstable, international environment is the best guarantee for China's development and its own interests; therefore, China has no intention to challenge the current world order. China's economic growth is so deeply embedded in the context of the current world order that it is in China's interest to preserve this status quo.[28] When some scholars correlated China's use of "rise" to the rise of Germany and Japan in the first half of the 20th century, Beijing quickly replaced the term with "peaceful development".[29] This change of phrasing also portrays Beijing's acute sensitivity and awareness to outside views of its policy renunciation.

Beijing has also invested great efforts into proving its sincerity, especially towards its neighbors in Southeast Asia. The 1997 financial crisis is a striking example of these efforts. During the crisis, Beijing stuck to its currency values and tolerated huge economic losses when almost all countries in the region were devaluating their currencies. Beijing did so in an attempt to show its neighbors and the world that China is not explicitly a self-interested power on the rise, but rather a flourishing great power capable of playing a constructive role, not only in the region, but also in the world. This effort "established new credibility for Beijing."[30] Moreover, in the disaster relief activities for the region - the tsunami disaster relief in 2005 and the Indonesian earthquake assistance in 2006 - China made disproportionately large donations to the involved countries relative to its own economic capability.[31] In all these cases, Beijing was devoted to present an image that it is willing and also has the capability to help its neighbors when they are in trouble. Furthermore, to enhance greater trust, Beijing expanded cooperation with these countries by sending its state leaders to participate in China-ASEAN summit regularly, pushing for ASEAN Plus Three forum, promoting the establishment of the China-ASEAN free trade zone and joining in multilateral talks with ASEAN countries about the territorial conflict in the South China Sea. By doing so, Beijing expects to convince its neighbors that its good-neighbourhood policy is earnest because "China needs a long-term peaceful international environment and a good neighbourly environment in particular to realize its modernization programme" and "the establishment and development of the good-neighbourly partnership of mutual trust oriented to the 21st century between China and ASEAN" will benefit all sides.[32]

In addition to these measures related to Southeast Asian countries, Beijing has also invested heavily to expand and stabilize relations with other countries, such as the U.S. and Japan, in order to increase their mutual trust. For example, China actively participates in a series of multilateral actions aimed at maintaining international security, notably its push for the six-party talks in solving the nuclear weapons predicament of North Korea and commitment of forces for UN peacekeeping operations in different parts of the world, such as Cambodia, Liberia and Haiti. It also has opened Chinese military exercises to foreign military attaché, held joint military exercises in non-traditional security areas with the former foes of PLA, including the U.S., Russia and India. Most strikingly, Beijing even allowed the U.S. Defense Secretary Donald H. Rumsfeld as the first foreigner to visit the headquarters of China's Second Artillery, the country's major nuclear missile forces in October 2005, which was unimaginable a few years back.

All these measures have an explicit goal of establishing an affable image and they are believed to have achieved certain success so far.[33] Although the China threat theory is stirred up repeatedly and still cast some negative impact, an anti-China encirclement has never taken form as many realists expected.

Tackling Domestic Problems, Building a hexie shehui

To cultivate soft power, solid domestic bases are vital. For the outside world, how Beijing ends up handling its own people might have much to do with how a strong China ends up handling the world.

Even during the period of the Jiang-Zhu administration, domestic problems like social inequality and corruption had become rampant. The Jiang administration vowed to fight against these social vices; however, "the single-minded focus on coastal development at the expense of the vast inland region and from the obsession with GDP growth without regard for social issues" actually left these problems unsolved.[34] The transition of the leadership started at the 16th National Congress of the CPC in November 2002 from the third to the fourth generation, i.e. from the Jiang-Zhu administration to the Hu Jingtao-Wen Jiabao government, has given hope for a solution. The new Hu-Wen leadership's initiatives contain the following measures:[35]

A. Raising government efficiency and accountability, and fighting government corruption. The most prominent cases include firing the minister of health, Zhang Wenkang, and the mayor of Beijing, Meng Xuenong, who mishandled the SARS epidemic in 2003, and the most recent dismissal and investigation of the Party secretary, Chen Liangyu, of Shanghai for corruption in September 2006.

B. Constantly pushing for economic development and financial stability. Like their predecessors Jiang and Zhu, current president Hu and premier Wen also believe that economic development remains the key to China's future, and problems that arise in this process can not be barriers to this vital plan.

C. Continuously promoting piecemeal advances in political reform, such as pushing for inner-Party democracy, allowing more openness at the grassroots level, adjusting Party-state and Party-local relations,[36] and improving a law-governed political order.[37]

D. Strengthening stability of the cross-Strait relations and preventing Taiwan from going to *de jure* independence. Hu's measures are especially striking in a combination of soft and hard approaches, apparent in making and passing the Anti-Secession Law in March 2005 on the one hand while holding an unprecedented meeting with Kuomintang leader Lien Chan in April 2005 on the other hand.

E. Building a *hexie shehui* (harmonious society). This is thought to be the chief guideline of the Hu-Wen government and the most important goal they want to achieve during their administration.

Among these measures, the most prominent is building a "harmonious society," which means the establishment of a society featured with "democracy, the rule of law, equity, justice, sincerity, amity and vitality."[38] This is not just a symbol of the Beijing regime's change and drive towards building a more open and civilized society; it is the most concrete evidence revealing Beijing's determination to solve those social problems. To be specific, it not only means a shift from the elitist approach of the earlier administration, but it also symbolizes the "softness" of the new administration aims to help the lower class of society and reconcile the growing tension between social groups in China. This policy is designed to address the social inequality created over the course of the reform and distribute the social wealth and benefits of the reform to every class of the society, especially those who are left behind such as farmers, migrant workers, the urban unemployed and poor.

Beijing is certain that the CPC will legitimize its rule at home and abroad if these goals can be reached. The achievement of success will be able to raise the prestige of the government and the Party, and will eventually enhance the image of the country as a whole. Because of the interlaced nature of international politics and domestic politics, domestic policies have great significance as well since any of China's soft power has to be built on the basis of good domestic politics and a harmonious society in which its citizens can enjoy democracy, freedom and prosperity.

Enhancing Public Relations and Expanding Cultural Influence

Some of these measures seem to be purely domestic; however, they have a strong extroversive feature and are actually targeted at the outside world with an ultimate goal of raising the image of China.

A. Build/expand the agencies for international publicity

These measures include creating and expanding the departments of publicity so that they can do a more effective job presenting China to the world. For example, as early as 1990, the CPC established an Overseas Publicity Department under the Party Central Committee. In the following year, the central government established a new Information Office under the State Council. China's state-sponsored China Central Television Station and China Radio International also increased their overseas programming and hours of broadcast in foreign languages. A system of public relations spokesman was instituted for all major ministries and commissions. Beijing hopes that the improvement in public relations will be able to lift its voice about the positive things of China.

B. Increase government transparency

Beijing has also strived hard to increase the transparency of public policy-making in order to allay criticisms of China's illiberal nature, though the efforts by Beijing have been considered insufficient by Western observers. Since 1991, the Chinese government has frequently issued white papers on various topics in an attempt to communicate to the international community China's stance on various sensitive issues. The contents of these white papers range from China's domestic affairs, such as Beijing's minority policy and women's issues, to those topics of intense international concern like China's space activities and national defense. Compared to Beijing's past willingness to brush aside international concern with its domestic affairs, this is a large progression in showing its benevolent attitude.

C. Adopt a more open attitude toward sensitive domestic issues

Beijing is holding an increasingly open attitude toward its sensitive domestic issues like human rights, Tibet and Taiwan. Contrary to the past, the leaders of China are now willing to openly discuss these issues with foreign state leaders or representatives from international organizations. For example, in June 1998, U.S. President Bill Clinton and his Chinese counterpart Jiang Zemin even held an open debate over human rights issues, the 1989 Tiananmen Square crackdown, and Tibet, on Chinese TV that was broadcast live in China. Never before had China's 1.3 billion people seen a public debate between their state leader and his foreign counterpart.

D. Push for opportunity to exhibit China's achievements

The Chinese government has also made concerted efforts at publicizing China by vying to host international events. Beijing's successful bid to host the 2008 Olympic Games is an example. China tried again to bid to host another international event, Expo 2010, that will be held in Shanghai. The country also tries to expand the influences of its own culture by sponsoring or organizing cultural events in other countries, such as China-France Culture Year, China in London and Year of China in Russia. Beijing also supports performances of China's artistic troupes, participating in various exhibitions or expositions abroad. These activities are expected to showcase China's achievements since its reforms, as well as its rich culture.

E. Promote the influence of the Chinese language and culture abroad

Since 2004, the Chinese government has started sponsoring the establishment of "Confucian Institute" abroad to support the instruction of the Chinese language and culture. It is expected that 100 institutes will be created by 2010. China's Ministry of Education started a program in 2002 to donate newly published books and picture albums to foreign libraries annually. China's universities have also enlarged the pool of scholarships to attract foreign students to study in China. These arrangements are expected to help more foreigners to know the history, culture and progress of the country.

F. Use foreign public relations firms and media to publicize China

Beijing also hired foreign public relations companies to lobby for policies concerning China. The cases include hiring Hill and Knowlton to lobby U.S. Congress for the unconditional renewal of China's MFN status, Weber Shanwick Worldwide for Beijing's bid for the 2008 Olympic Games. In 2001, Beijing also cooperated with AOL Time Warner to broadcast China's English language program in the U.S.[39]

Joseph Nye attributes culture, political values and diplomacy as the sources of soft power, all being expressed in China's soft power tapping endeavors. By establishing the "Confucius Institute" abroad, Beijing aspires to extend its cultural influence; by building a "harmonious society," it aims to raise its political attractiveness; whereas by promoting cooperation with other countries, it hopes to improve its diplomacy.

Tapping Soft Power: Resources and Obstacles

Beijing's initiatives have achieved certain successes. As a result, in Southeast Asia, the China threat theory is losing credibility. More and more countries in the region are regarding China's growth as an opportunity rather than a threat. Surveys done by different agencies across the world are showing a growing positive attitude toward China's role and growth.[40] Like all other great countries in the world, China possesses a variety of assets, which may help with the realization of its soft power cultivating aim.

A.   Long history and tradition
As one of the oldest civilizations in the world and a country that has a traditionally dominant role in East Asia, China's rise may be regarded and accepted as a restoration of its historical place, thus less of a surprise to other countries in the region or even the world. For example, in an article about China, Nye argues that "re-emergence" is a more accurate description of the current growth of China, and he thinks the "rise of China" is a misnomer because the country was actually "a world leader (although without a global reach) from 500 to 1500" in terms of technological level and economic size.[41] Another scholar uses the deeply ingrained acceptance of hierarchy in Asian culture to explain why there is no regional balancing of China by other Asian countries confronting its rise. "A Sino-centric and hierarchical form of international relations" seems acceptable to these countries.[42] A scholar even comes to the point of indicating that a hierarchical international system in Asia led by China is likely to be a stable one as it once was in history that would benefit every party.[43]

B.   Cultural influence upon neighboring countries
Chinese culture has had a prolonged influence on most neighboring countries. Based on Nye's discussion of power resources, one of the intangible is "universalistic culture."[44] Though its impact is less felt in other regions of the world, Chinese cultural influence is deeply entrenched in countries such as Japan, Korea, Vietnam, Singapore and has significant impact on other Southeast Asian countries, such as Malaysia, Thailand and the Philippines.[45] The economic success of the four Asian tigers started since the 1960s and China's own economic boom since the end of the 1970s has led many observers to conclude that Confucian teachings of diligence, harmony, discipline and order are vital to economic success. Thus, it helps to propagate the favorable role of Chinese culture.[46]

C.   Economic success sets a new model
China's achievement in raising the standard of living of its citizens since its reform has won the admiration of many countries. Its rapid economic

liberalization and development in a relatively stable political and social milieu without losing independence and sovereignty seem to have paved a new way for those countries in transition, especially third world countries.[47] The compatibility between a rapid economic growth and political stability also sets up a new model for pre-Communist countries to reform without major domestic chaos, even national disintegration. This model of development has become so striking that some scholars began to discuss a Beijing Consensus that should take the place of the older Washington Consensus as new model of development for developing countries.[48] China's economic success has strengthened and will continue to solidify China's position as a leader of the third world countries.

D. Chinese diasporas in the region and their economic influence
In almost every major Southeast Asian country, there are large Chinese Diasporas who are quite economically successful. Because of cultural kinship and other connections, it is much easier for them to understand and accept China's behaviors in this region. Their well-known financial strengths can also help to spread Chinese culture and therefore strengthen the cultural universality of China.[49] There are also a certain number of Chinese communities, such as Chinatowns, in almost all major countries in the world. These overseas Chinese are the most ardent advocates, as well as vehicles, of Chinese culture abroad.

E. Benefits of sub-culture linkage
China's culture may be regarded as homogenous in general. However, the diversities in its sub-cultures are obvious, marked by different traditions, custom and habits of some national minority groups living on its periphery, such as the Muslim population, the Mongols and Koreans. These minority groups usually have connections with their kin living across the border. When properly guided, they may help China cultivate and stabilize its relations with those countries and help to proliferate Chinese culture and values across the border.

F. Stronger economy
The growth of China's wealth since the reforms enables the country to support those international programs that are able to raise China's image, such as Beijing's support in holding China-France Culture Year in Paris and paying for CNN's airing of programs that introduces the 2008 Olympic Games in Beijing. China can afford to build up its new image now more than ever before.

Despite these advantages, however, China also faces a number of obstacles in cultivating and managing its soft power. Some of them are controllable by Beijing; however, others are beyond its reach. The most significant barrier may come from within rather than from outside.

A.   Political system

As a communist country in transition, the old political ideology of Beijing makes it difficult to accept quick adjustments to new situations, especially in major political reforms. The authoritarian nature of the Chinese government, corruption, loose rule of law, and closed operation of the government are in deep conflict with the world's dominant trend of democratization and proliferation of liberal values. China's initial inaction and tardy response to the SARS outbreak in 2003 exposed the incompatibility between the operational method of its bureaucracy and the extent of the country's integration into the world community. Unexpected events like this easily damage the effort of the Chinese government in its soft power building and draw outside attention to the negative side of the regime.[50]

B.   Failure of the international communist movement

The failure of the communist movement reduces China's once-possessed luster as a supporter and patron of international socialist revolution and national liberation movements from colonial and imperialist rule. China's own transformation from a centrally-planned economy and its *de facto* act of relinquishing Marxist ideology further lessens the impact of a model of socialist revolution. Its domestic political and social changes also diminish its willingness and reduce its programs to subsidize other developing countries the way it did in the 1960s and 1970s. Thus, its way of behavior becomes less attractive to its original followers as it once did in the past.[51] Furthermore, its continuous adherence to a one-party rule also goes against the world trend of political multipolarization and democratization, which makes its persistence an anachronism.

C.   The Taiwan issue

This is perhaps the largest issue that will complicate and even interrupt Beijing's effort in soft power tapping and invalidate its "peaceful development" policy. Because of the unpredictability of the political situation on the island and Beijing's concerns about its *de jure* independence, China has increased its military spending significantly in recent years. Such an increase of military spending again becomes the evidence of the China threat theory and a source of suspicion to other countries. Thus, Beijing's effort in presenting the image of a benevolent rising power is discounted. It is true that "Clouding this prospect of a benign internal and external context for Chinese foreign policy is one central challenge: Taiwan. Beijing, until it is confident that the island will not seek formal and permanent independence, will remain prepared to exercise force and perhaps use it if that eventuality appears imminent."[52] If that happens, Beijing's soft power approach will be derailed conclusively.

D.   Historical burden of exporting communism

Beijing's history of supporting communist movements around the world during the Cold War is another negative factor for China's image building as a responsible power. The negative impact is especially noticeable in its efforts in Southeast Asian countries due to its support for the anti-government movements and guerrilla wars in those countries in the 1960s and 1970s.[53] Some countries are still suspicious of China's intentions today. They are also worried about the connection between the Chinese government and ethnic Chinese migrant population in their countries who are economically successful.[54] The Chinese Diaspora in these countries can be an asset and at the same time can turn into a liability.

E. Conflict of interest with neighboring countries

The other barrier China has to overcome is the conflict of interests with neighboring countries in the region, for example, over the gas and oil resources in East China Sea and Diaoyu Island with Japan, and the territorial disputes in the South China Sea with Southeast Asian countries. Due to the rich oil reserves in these regions, it is difficult for any country to back down from their claims. The overlapping claims of different countries about the South China Sea make the solution even more complicated.[55] For China, its phenomenal economic growth has exerted great pressure upon its oil demand; therefore, tapping the oil resources in these regions is vital for its sustainable development. Solving these disputes by any non-peaceful means will not just substantiate the China threat theory, but will also neutralize its efforts in building soft power.

F. Fear from western countries of a rising China

Finally China has to confront with the distrust of other major powers in the world, especially the U.S. and Japan, which worry that a powerful China will challenge the status quo, and therefore have strengthened their security relations.[56] The Bush administration's attempt to sell nuclear technology to India is widely believed to be "an important part of a White House strategy to accelerate New Delhi's rise as a global power and as a regional counterweight to China. As part of the strategy, the administration is also seeking ways to bolster Japan's posture in the region."[57]

The buildup of such negative responses is especially harmful since any routinization of behaviors, when added together, will eventually strengthen the hardliners in Beijing and weaken those who are in favor of soft power, self-restraint and self-improvement. Beijing may eventually draw the conclusion that the road of peaceful rise is only a one-sided dream and is not in reality viable. Hence, it will be a logical step for China to think about a rise by whatever means necessary in order to ensure the realization of its national goals. Under these circumstances, the tapping of soft power will fall into redundancy and resorting to the use of hard power will be a necessity, especially when the Taiwan issue is at stake.

IMPLICATIONS FOR THE WORLD

Ever since the end of the 1990s, China has increasingly shifted its domestic and foreign policies to the cultivation of soft power in an attempt to secure a stable international environment for its development. China's policy choice is governed by two important forces: international and domestic. The international force is the complex post-Cold War international setting that is concurrently hostile and friendly for China's growth. The friendly factor lies in the new security opportunity open for China and the new trend of globalization that provides ample chances for the growth of China's economy, in particular, access to foreign investment, markets and technology. The hostile factor is that a considerable number of countries are worried about the Chinese growth out of "security dilemma" and prejudice against a Communist Party-led growth, which incubated the China threat theory.

China's response since the end of the 1990s to international and domestic circumstances is clearly following a liberal, not a realist paradigm. The discussions above have presented extensive evidence demonstrating the shift of China's grand strategy and policies to that approach. As an emerging power that is devoted to tapping soft power and managing its rise, Beijing has accommodated the concerns and interests of other countries concerning the growth of its power in various ways. It has cooperated with all concerned countries in solving their disputes, using peaceful rather than coercive means. This is especially striking regarding the territorial disputes with ASEAN countries over the South China Sea. Kim is certainly acute when he comments: "What matters most is not so much the growth of Chinese power but how and for what purposes a rising China will actually wield its putative or actual power in the conduct of its international relations."[58] Consequently, China's devotion to soft power tapping has profound implications.

For China, these efforts toward that direction will help to foster a congenial international setting that it wants and facilitate the realization of its "peaceful rise." And its efforts have reaped preliminary rewards. Contrary to the prediction of realists that rising powers are usually counterweighed against, "a set of neighbors (of China) disinclined to balance against it..," so there exists "the puzzle of the apparent underperformance of the regional mechanism"[59] targeted at China. This provides an encouraging message for China that it is on the right track towards peaceful development and that its amicable initiative of soft power tapping is viable and fruitful.

Beijing's target at domestic politics is similarly striking, which shows promise of a propitious future for the nation and even for the world. In dealing with the Taiwan and Tibetan issues, the regime has been acting more cautiously and more cooperatively with other countries, especially the U.S., since acting like a rule-abiding player in the international community is vital for soft power building.

Among the above efforts, the experiment of democratic elections at the grassroots level has great importance. If we accept the democratic peace theory,[60] then Beijing's experiment of democracy, though at very low levels and small scales,[61] has even greater significance since it symbolizes the start of its changes following the world trend of democratization. This will imply that a democratic and strong China will coexist peacefully with the current superpower, the U.S. Such a peaceful existence is a fortune for not only the two countries, but also the world. Second, it can make the mainland more attractive to the people on Taiwan and make secession a less attractive choice. The détente across the Taiwan Straight will facilitate the peace and stability of the Asia-Pacific region.

Furthermore, China's endeavors in tapping soft power may offer something similar to what other great powers did in the past. For example, the transformation from a Communist-style country into a democracy while maintaining rapid economic growth without the chaos in the post-Soviet sphere may set a useful example for other countries in China's situation, especially former Communist countries and developing nations. The application of traditional Confucian values emphasizing social harmony to international society in settling disputes between big and small countries may create a good model that may help reduce international conflicts. These will benefit all parties involved.

However, the rise of China poses a great challenge not just for China itself and its own people, but also the world since the world's experiences with an emerging power in the past were not always pleasant. China should be fully aware of the concerns of other countries facing its "peaceful rise;" a rising giant naturally causes anxieties among other countries. It should continuously make effort to clarify its intention and keep communication channels with other countries open, especially those countries with which it is closely involved, like the U.S. and Japan. It should also follow international regimes closely and actively participate in international affairs and make its due contributions. With mutual understanding and cooperation, China's ascent will become an asset rather than a burden for the world.

For other countries, they should also realize that Beijing's stress on managing soft power is a good omen for the world because effective soft power may make the projection of its increasingly strong hard power, especially military, unnecessary. Its foreign policies will also become more cautious and predictable. Soft power building will not just act as a boost for its ascent, but also can act as a guide that leads it into the community of nations and become a "responsible stakeholder" who will share the peace dividend with everyone else. Most importantly, China's continuous interests and effort in tapping soft power is the best guarantee for its evolution toward a benign status quo power rather than an aggressive revisionist state. Thus, responding to China's drive toward that direction with approval and encouragement, rather than suspicion and rejection, might be the wisest strategy that will maximize benefits for all.

Notes

* The author would like to thank Dr. Anthony Clark, Steve Miller and Erik Wennermark for their comments and suggestions on earlier versions of this paper. He is also grateful for the invaluable support of Wang Ke while he was doing the research.

[1] See Randall L. Schweller, "Managing the Rise of Great Powers: History and Theory," in Alastair Iain Johnston and Robert S. Ross, eds., *Engaging China: the Management of Emerging Power* (New York: Routledge, 1999), pp. 1-31.

[2] In an article published in 1999 by Yong Deng who studied the possibility of change in China's conception of national interests and the impact of realist and liberal paradigms, the author had already detected such a possibility of change in China's foreign policy favoring liberal thinking. In the conclusion of the study, he pointed out that "many factors and forces are also pointing to the possibility of a conceptual shift in China's foreign policy outlook" and "...the intellectual reformulation of Chinese national interests along liberal lines can only flourish." See Yong Deng, "Conception of National Interests: Realpolitik, Liberal Dilemma, and the Possibility of Change," in Yong Deng and Fei-Ling Wang, eds., *In the Eyes of the Dragon: China Views the World* (Lamham: Rowman and Littlefield Publishers, Inc.), 1999, pp. 63-65.

[3] My discussion of China's reorientation of policy on soft power tapping since the 1990s does not refer to a formal and detailed plan or government report issued by the Communist Party of China Central Committee or the Foreign Ministry. It refers to a rough consensus on shifting emphasis in certain aspects of China's basic foreign policy which became accepted by top state leaders and other high-level policy-makers. Such consensus becomes some guide for the country's domestic and international behaviors.

[4] China's initial adjustment of foreign policy after the end of the Cold War started in 1992 after Deng Xiaoping's inspection trip to the South. The goal of the new approach is "to provide a long-term peaceful and secure environment for China's modernization and a favorable condition for its reform and opening-up policy." Current policy on the tapping of soft power still serves for this goal. For a discussion of China's foreign policy before 1993, see Chen Qimao, "New Approaches in China's Foreign Policy: The Post-Cold War Era," in *Asian Survey*, Vol. 33, No. 3. (March, 1993), pp. 237-51.

[5] This term "responsible stakeholder" was first used by former U.S. Deputy Secretary of State Robert Zoellick in a speech on U.S.-China relations in New York in September, 2005. It has since been frequently quoted and discussed as a buzzword in Sino-U.S. relations and become a description of U.S. expectation for China's future role in the world.

[6] Joseph S. Nye, Jr., *Bound to Lead: The Changing Nature of American Power* (New York: Basic Book, 1990), pp. 188-201.

[7] Joseph S. Nye, Jr., *Soft Power—the Means to Success in World Politics* (New York: Public Affairs, 2004), p. x.

[8] ibid, Nye, p. x.

[9] Joseph S. Nye, Jr., *The Paradox of American Power—Why the World's Only Superpower Can't Go It Alone* (Oxford: Oxford University Press, 2002), p. xiii.

[10] For a summary of these discussions, their authors and time, see Chen Xiangyang, "Soft Power and China's Diplomacy" [Lun ruanshili yu zhongguo waijiao], in Guo Shuyong, ed., *International Relations: A Call for China's Theories* [Guoji guanxi: huhuan zhongguo lilun], (Tianjin, China: Tianjin Renmin Chubanshe, 2005), pp. 343-55.

[11] The most striking example of the application of soft power is the seven epic sea voyages of Admiral Zheng He's fleet in the Ming dynasty (1368-1644) during the reign of Emperor Yongle (Ming Chengzu, Zhu Di, r. 1403-1424). In the twenty years between 1405-1433, with the biggest fleet built with the most advanced technology and equipped

with the cutting-edge weapons technology the world had ever seen at the time, Admiral Zheng He neither conquered other small countries nor looted treasures from other nations. His mission was peaceful and friendly, only aimed to conduct free and fair trade, and to extend and promote the nation's nobility and prestige across the world. Just as the mandate of the mission says, these sea voyages were "to proceed all the way to the end of the earth to collect tribute from the barbarians beyond the seas and unite the whole world in Confucian harmony." For detailed discussions of the mission and the voyages, see Gavin Menzies, *1421: The Year China Discovered America* (New York: William Morrow, 2003). The author of another book on China's naval history of the Ming dynasty also admits that China could have conquered the world from Taiwan to the Persian Gulf and distant Africa if it wanted. Obviously, Zheng He did not have such an agenda in his mission. See Louise Levathes, *When China Ruled the Seas* (New York: Simon and Schuster, 1994), pp. 20-21.

[12] For a comprehensive discussion of the "China threat" thesis, see Denny Roy, "The 'China Threat' Issue: Major Arguments," in *Asian Survey*, Vol. 36, No. 8. (Aug., 1996), pp. 758-771; Lin Limin, *On the Three New Features of the NewWave of 'China Threat' Theory* [Xinyibo zhongguo weixie lun de sanda tedian], http://www.china.com.cn/news/txt/2006-07/10/content_6270933.htm (accessed September 1, 2006).

[13] For example, trade volume of goods between China and the U.S. in July 2006 has surpassed those of America's traditional trading partners, including UK, France, Germany and Japan. The volume has been increasing all the time in the past two decades. For details, see U.S. Census Bureau website at: http://www.census.gov/foreign-trade/statistics/highlights/toppartners.html (accessed August 23, 2006). China has also surpassed U.K., France, Germany, and even the U.S. in 2004 as Japan's largest trading partner.

[14] For a summary and discussion of these theories, see Avery Goldstein, *Rising to the Challenge: China's Grand Strategy and International Security* (Stanford: Stanford University Press, 2005), pp. 81-101.

[15] There is a series of articles or books published by western presses that address the issue, including authors like John J. Tkacik, Jr. of the Heritage Foundation and Bill Gertz, columnist of *The Washington Times*. Both of them wrote a number of articles and books arguing for China's threat in various fields. For a discussion of Chinese interpretation of the China threat theory, see Yong Deng, "Reputation and the Security Dilemma: China Reacts to the China Threat Theory," in Alastair Iain Johnston and Robert S. Ross, eds. *New Direction in the Study of China's Foreign Policy* (Stanford: Stanford University Press, 2006), pp. 192-95.

[16] People of this group include Charles Krauthammer, "Why We Must Contain China," *Time*, July 31, 1995, p. 72, and John Mearsheimer, *The Tragedy of Great Power Politics* (New York: W. W. Norton & Company, 2001), pp. 396-402.

[17] Nye, *The Paradox*, 2002, p. 22.

[18] Yong Deng, "Reputation and the Security Dilemma," in Johnston and Ross, eds. *New Direction*, 2006, p. 187.

[19] According to the results of a recent survey released by the Pew Global Attitudes Project on September 21, 2006 that is targeted at investigating the publics' attitude toward each other in the Asian powers, a predominant percentage of people in Japan, Russia and India fear about China's growing military power. For details, see http://pewglobal.org (accessed September 30, 2006).

[20] In recent years, there are increasingly more academic works devoted to the study of relations between China's international image and its national interests. See Li Zhengguo, *The Construction of National Image* [Guojia xingxiang goujian], (Beijing, China: Zhongguo Chuanmei Daxue Chubanshe, 2006); Liu Jie, *International System and China's Soft Power* [Guoji tixi yu zhongguo de ruanliliang], (Beijing, China: Shishi Chubanshe,

2006); Chen Xiangyang, "Soft Power and China's Diplomacy" [Lun ruanshili yu zhongguo waijiao], in Guo Shuyong, ed., *International Relations: A Call for China's Theories* [Guoji guanxi: huhuan zhongguo lilun], (Tianjin, China: Tianjin Renmin Chubanshe, 2005), pp. 343-55; Liu Jinan, "National Image in International Communication" [Guoji chuanbo zhong de guojia xingxiang]," in Xiao Huanrong, ed., *International Relations in China* [Guoji guanxixue zai zhongguo], (Beijing, China: Zhongguo Chuanmei Daxue Chubanshe, 2005), pp. 345-8.

[21] C. Fred Bergsten, Bates Gill, Nicholas R. Lardy and Derek Mitchell, *China The Balance Sheet: What the World Needs to Know Now About the Emerging Superpower* (New York: Public Affairs, 2006), pp. 40-56.

[22] Other problems certainly exist, in particular, the great disparity in politics and economy between the mainland and Taiwan. Taiwan's political system has gradually evolved into a democracy and has become increasingly mature. Economically, the island's per capita GDP of about US$26,700 is significantly higher than the US$6,200 of the mainland. This great disparity between their politics and economy makes reunification of Taiwan and the mainland not just unattractive for most Taiwanese, but also a source of dissatisfaction of the people on the mainland with the government.

[23] Ever since the establishment of the PRC, overseas Chinese affairs have always been considered important to the national interest of China. For a study of the history of the PRC's overseas Chinese policy from the 1950s-80s, see C. Y. Chang, "Overseas Chinese in China's Policy," *The China Quarterly*, No. 82. (Jun., 1980), pp. 281-303.

[24] Joseph S. Nye, "The Rise of China's Soft Power," *Wall Street Journal Asia*, December 19, 2005, http://www.ksg.harvard.edu/ksgnews/Features/opeds/122905_nye.htm (accessed June 5, 2006).

[25] For a discussion of the issue, see David S. G. Goodman, "China in East Asian and World Culture," in Barry Buzan and Rosemary Foot, eds. *Does China Matter? A Reassessment: Essays in Memory of Gerald Segel* (London: Rouledge, 2004), pp. 71-86.

[26] The Jiang Zemin-Zhu Rongji administration lasted from 1989 to 2002.

[27] Such policy reiteration is frequent and can be found in foreign policy speeches of China's top state leaders from Jiang Zemin to Hu Jintao. For example, Jiang Zemin said "China will never seek hegemony. This is a solemn commitment of the Chinese people to the world" in a speech when he visited London on October 23, 1999. http://english.peopledaily.com.cn/199910/23/enc_19991023001028_TopNews.html (accessed September 24, 2006). Current president Hu also remarked that "China didn't seek hegemony in the past. It is not doing so at present. Neither will it do so in the future" when he met the heads of the seven Japan-China friendship organizations at the Great Hall of the People in Beijing on March 31, 2006. http://english.gov.cn/2006-03/31/content_242002.htm (accessed September 22, 2006).

[28] "Peaceful Rise" (*heping jueqi)* was first introduced by the former Central Party School Vice-President Zheng Bijian in November 2003 at the Bo'ao Forum for Asia. Later other state leaders of China also talked about this policy on different occasions, for example, Chinese Premier Wen used this phrase in a speech he made when he visited Washington on December 10, 2003. http://www.china-embassy.org/eng/zt/first 20beginning/t55995.htm (accessed on June 10, 2006).

[29] For a discussion of the shift of this renunciation, see Robert G. Sutter, *China's Rise in Asia: Promises and Perils* (Lanham: Rowman and Littlefield Publishers, Inc., 2005), pp. 265-66; Bergsten, et al, *China The Balance Sheet*, 2006, pp. 133-34.

[30] Bergsten, et al., *China: The Balance Sheet*, 2006, p. 133.

[31] In the tsunami relief, Beijing made a huge donation of 62 million U.S. dollars, ranking only the 8th among the donors around the world. And in the Indonesian earthquake assistance, China's donation ranked the 4th. Compared with other major donors that had a per capita GDP of between $10,000 and $40,000, such as Australia and Japan, China's

per capita GDP of $6,200 was rather low. Beijing's generosity showed from another angle its policy goals.

[32] Such policy statements can be found in almost all speeches by China's top leaders on relations with ASEAN countries. For example, President Jiang Zemin's speech "Towards a Good-Neighbourly Partnership of Mutual Trust Oriented to the 21st Century" delivered at the Informal China-ASEAN Summit held in Kuala Lumpur, Malaysia on December 16, 1997, http://wcm.fmprc.gov.cn/zdjn/eng/zywj/t270546.htm (assessed October 10, 2006) and Premier Wen Jiabao's speech "Promoting Peace and Prosperity by Deepening Cooperation in All-round Way" at the Seventh China-ASEAN Summit held in Bali, Indonesia on October 8, 2003. http://wcm.fmprc.gov.cn/zdjn/eng/zywj/t270552.htm (assessed October 11, 2006).

[33] For a discussion of the success of China's policies in Southeast Asia, see Sutter, *China's Rise in Asia*, 2005, p. 272. For a summary of its success in other countries, see Yong Deng, "Reputation and the Security Dilemma," in Johnston and Ross, eds., *New Direction*, 2006, p. 205.

[34] Cheng Li, "New Provincial Chiefs: Hu's Groundwork for the 17th Party Congress," in *China Leadership Monitor*, Winter 2005, No. 13, p. 11.

[35] For an in-depth discussion and assessment of the Hu and Wen administration in political, economic and social policies, see H. Lyman Miller, "How's Hu Doing? President Hu Jintao Continues China's Long March toward Political Reform," *Hoover Digest*, 2004, No. 1.

[36] Bergsten, et al., *China: The Balance Sheet*, 2006, pp. 57-66.

[37] Most Western observers of China hold a view that the CPC has done too little in its political reforms, but Miller believes the CPC is actually making steady, but slow progress in this aspect. Miller also thinks the Hu-Wen leadership has been taking measures in enforcing civil rights, including the incorporation of "freedom of movement" into the country's constitution.

[38] The concept of "harmonious socialist society" was first launched at the Fourth Plenary Session of the 16th Central Committee of the CPC in 2004. It was further interpreted by Chinese President Hu Jintao on several other occasions. In 2005, Premier Wen Jiabao emphasized again the goal of the government to build a harmonious socialist society in his government work report delivered at the opening meeting of the Third Session of the Tenth National People's Congress (NPC). "Building the socialist new countryside" that aims to raise the income level and standard of living of farmers was later incorporated into the scheme. A harmonious society features "democracy, the rule of law, equity, justice, sincerity, amity and vitality."

[39] For a systematic study of China's image building since the 1950s and its feedback, see Hongying Wang, "National Image Building and Chinese Foreign Policy," in Yong Deng and Fei-ling Wang, eds., *China Rising: Power and Motivation in Chinese Foreign Policy* (Lamham: Rowman and Littlefield Publishers, INC., 2005), pp. 73-102.

[40] Pew Global Attitudes Project, a project of the PewResearchCenter, "U.S. Image Up Slightly, But Still Negative-American Character Gets Mixed Reviews." http://pewglobal.org/reports/display.php?PageID=800 (accessed September 5, 2006).

[41] Nye, "China's Re-emergence and the Future of the Asia-Pacific," in Guoli Liu ed., *Chinese Foreign Policy in Transition* (New York: Aldine De Gruyter, 2004), p. 337.

[42] See Buzan, "How and to Whom does China Matter?" in Buzan and Foot, *Does China Matter?*, 2004, p. 159.

[43] See David Kang, "Hierarchy and Stability in Asian International Relations," in G. John Ikenberry and Michael Mastanduno, eds., *International Relations Theory and the Asia-Pacific* (New York: Columbia University Press, 2003), pp. 163-89.

[44] Nye, *Bound to Lead*, p. 174.

[45] For a discussion of the issue, see Goodman, "China in East Asian and world culture," in Buzan and Foot, eds., *Does China Matter?*, 2004, pp. 71-86.

[46] The father of "soft power" Nye even came to the point of saying that "China has always had an attractive traditional culture, but now it is entering the realm of global popular culture as well." See "The Rise of China's Soft Power," *Wall Street Journal Asia*, December 19, 2005. http://www.ksg.harvard.edu/ksgnews/Features/opeds/122905_nye.htm (accessed June 5, 2006).

[47] This is also recognized by Joseph S. Nye in the same article above (accessed June 5, 2006).

[48] Joshua Cooper Ramo, "The Beijing Consensus," released by the Foreign Policy Centre, UK on May 11, 2004. http://fpc.org.uk/fsblob/244.pdf#search=joshuaramobeijing (accessed September 15, 2006).

[49] For discussions of Chinese Diasporas and their political, economic and social status in a transforming Southeast Asia, see Daniel Chirot and Anthony Reid, eds. *Essential Outsiders: Chinese and Jews in the Modern Transformation of Southeast Asia and Central Europe* (Seattle and London: University of Washington Press, 1997).

[50] See Noel M. Morada, "ASEAN and the Rise of China: Engaging, While Fearing, an Emerging Regional Power," in Kokubun Ryosei and Wang Jisi, eds., *The Rise of China and a Changing East Asian Order* (Tokyo: Japan Center for International Exchange, 2004), pp. 237-8.

[51] Some authors like Segal arguably say that even China during Mao "was beacon for many in the developing world. China now is beacon to no one-and indeed, an ally to no one." See Gerald Segal, "Does China Matter?" in Buzan and Foot, eds. *Does China Matter?*, 2004, p. 18.

[52] Samuel Kim, ed. *China and the World: Chinese Foreign Policy Faces the New Millennium*, 4th edition (Boulder, Colorado: Westview Press, 1998), p. 305. Other scholars like Sutter also talks about the issue: "the PLA buildup opposite Taiwan is inconsistent with the peaceful approach..." See Sutter, *China's Rise in Asia*, 2005, p. 273.

[53] For a detailed discussion of China's relations with the revolutionary movements of Southeast Asia in the 1960s and 70s, see Jay Taylor, *China and Southeast Asia: Peking's Relations with Revolutionary Movements (Expanded and Updated Editions)* (New York: Praeger Publishers, 1976).

[54] For a more detailed discussion of the ethnic Chinese issues in the relations between China and the ASEAN States, see Leo Suryadinata, *China and the ASEAN States: The Ethnic Chinese Dimension* (Singapore: Marshall Cavendish Academic, 2005). These issues are also discussed repeatedly in other works studying China's relations with countries in this region, such as Michael Yahuda, *The International Politics of the Asia-Pacific, 1945-1995* (London and New York: Routledge, 1996), pp. 195-97.

[55] Timo Kivimaki, ed. *War or Peace in the South China Sea?* (Copenhagen: NIAS Press, 2002), provides some excellent overviews of various issues involved in the South China Sea.

[56] See Thomas J. Christensen, "China, the U.S.-Japan Alliance, and the Security Dilemma in East Asia," in Ikenberry and Mastanduno, eds., *International Relations Theory*, pp. 25-56, and Michael J. Green, "Defense or Security? The U.S.-Japan Defense Guidelines and China," in David M. Lampton, ed., *Major Power Relations in Northeast Asia: Win-Win or Zero-Sum Game* (Tokyo: Japan Center for International Exchange, 2001), pp. 73-86.

[57] Dana Milbank and Dafna Linzer, "U.S., India May Share Nuclear Technology: Bush Move to Reverse Policy on Civilian Aid Needs Hill Approval," *Washington Post*, Tuesday, July 19, 2005, page A01. http://www.washingtonpost.com/wp-dyn/content/article/2005/07/18/AR2005071801646.html (accessed on July 7, 2006). See

also Howard LaFranchi, "Why US is Shifting Nuclear Stand with India-A Bargain on Nuclear Technology may Signal View of India as Counterbalance to China," in *The Christian Science Monitor*, July 20, 2005. http://www.csmonitor.com/2005/0720/p03s01-usfp.html (accessed on July 7, 2006).

[58] Kim, *China and the World*, 1998, p. 9.

[59] Buzan, "Conclusion: How and to Whom Does China Matter?" in Buzan and Foot, eds., *Does China Matter?*, 2004, p. 158.

[60] For a detailed discussion of the democratic peace theory and empirical tests of it, see Bruce Russet and John Oneal, *Triangulating Peace: Democracy, Interdependence, and International Organizations* (New York: W.W. Norton & Company, Inc., 2001).

[61] Greg Austin, "China's Power: Searching for Stable Domestic Foundations, " in Yongjin Zhang and Greg Austin, eds., *Power and Responsibility in Chinese Foreign Policy* (Canberra: Australia National University, 2001), pp. 95-6.

Chapter 6

"Peaceful Rise:" China's Public Diplomacy and International Image Cultivation

Guoxin Xing

China has come up with the concept of "peaceful rise" to allay fears of the "China threat" which perceives a powerful China as negative influence on the world. Since it was coined in 2003 by former senior party official Zheng Bijian, "peaceful rise" has become a commonly used term. The PRC's fourth generation of the leaders, headed by President Hu Jintao and Premier Wen Jiabao, has officially adopted "peaceful development," modified from "peaceful rise" to avoid the threatening connotation, as rhetoric for explaining China's long-term foreign and security policies. The essence of "peaceful rise" is that China is rising both as a regional power and as an actor that plays an increasingly important global role without resorting to warfare or force. Even though China claims a peaceful rise, it is uncertain that this reflects China's determination to ensure its rise will be peaceful. It is certain, however, that "peaceful rise" has become the cornerstone of China's public diplomacy to gain regional, even global, acceptance for its expanding political and economic clout by allaying "China threat." It seems that most countries, including its Asian neighbors, view China positively as increasing its economic power and playing a positive role in the world. However, some other countries, particularly in the West negatively view China's economic success and its influence in the world. Perhaps the most worrisome is American public opinion towards China. According to a CNN/USA Today/Gallup poll taken in December 2005, 50 percent of Americans view China as a military threat, while 64 percent view it as an economic threat.[1] Why is China's image still perceived so negatively in the U.S.? Why has "peaceful rise" as a public diplomacy campaign failed to make a difference in the American public opinion? How is China's public diplomacy flawed?

This chapter will examine China's public diplomacy by investigating how "peaceful rise" has been represented in the U.S. news media. The findings suggest that there are discrepancies in the Chinese and U.S. accounts of "peaceful rise." The competing perspectives indicate that China has not convinced the American public that 'peaceful rise' is in reality China's long-term foreign policy goals. The failure can be linked to China's orientation toward public diplomacy which builds on a domestic tradition of political propaganda. To succeed in international public relations, it is necessary for China to realize and institute the distinction between propaganda and modern public diplomacy. Otherwise, China is trying in vain to cultivate its international image in the U.S. and the rest of the world.

INTERPRETATIONS OF "PEACEFUL RISE:" GAP BETWEEN CHINA AND U.S.

Chinese officials have made a number of remarks and scholars and media have published many studies to explain and spread the concept of peaceful rise to the outside world. They argue that the peaceful rise of China has become the country's national will. China is sincere and determined to pursue a peaceful rise. The Chinese government officials and scholars have attempted to convince the world - in particular its neighbors and the United States - of its peaceful intention as a rising power. I will summarize their points of view as follows.[2]

First, they have argued that China's increasing economic power has benefited from regional and international cooperation and globalization, and in turn, will benefit the region and the world. China's rapid economic development poses no challenge or threat to any nation; it conversely creates opportunities for expanded global cooperation. China is not the sole beneficiary of its growth. Its economic success can promote the prosperity and stability of the global economy as a whole.

Second, China is still a developing country with a population of 1.3 billion. Its economic growth is accompanied by a series of new problems and challenges in energy, ecological environment, and economic and social coordination. It will take decades, perhaps a century, for China to accomplish its long-term strategic goals of prosperity and sustainable development. As such, China needs a peaceful international environment to achieve its domestic goals. It has to live in harmony with its neighbors and other countries in our interdependent world. China has no resources and national will to wage wars against foreign countries. World peace is a prerequisite for China's endeavor to become prosperous. In other words, China's development is predicated on domestic harmony and external peace; therefore, its foreign policy goals have to be oriented toward the pursuit of peace, maintenance of stability and promotion of cooperation.

Third, China will not attempt to alter the existing international configuration by taking advantage of its rising power. In other words, China will help maintain the status quo in the world and has no intentions of challenging the U.S.– dominated existing world order. China is determined to avoid the mistake other rising powers have made in the past.

Fourth, China's foreign policy and global strategy can be traced to its traditional culture and philosophy. Culturally, China values the idea of "harmony while tolerating diversity." China will not export its ideology to the rest of the world. The ideological differences between China and the U.S. should not become barriers to the development of bilateral relations. China has no intention to export its development model into the developing world and thus expand its influence. Even though China has achieved economic success and increased its economic power, China will not compete with the U.S. for hegemony in the world, like the former Soviet Union did. Instead, China and the U.S. have primarily common interests in the short and long run, which will help forge a mutually beneficial partnership, rather than engender an unhealthy rivals, between the two countries. As the largest developing country and the largest developed country respectively, China and the U.S. have a special responsibility for peace, security and prosperity in the world, especially in the Asia and Pacific region.

Finally, the fact that China is far from having comparable military power is a clear indication that China is not able to pose any threat to the United States. China follows a defensive national defense strategy in both a strategic and policy-oriented sense. The country never has any intention of threatening any other nation with force. In terms of the total amount of dollars, money directed toward serviceman, and the ratio to the GDP, China's defense budget is smaller than any one of the major powers in the world. On the other hand, China recognizes that military modernization is necessary for the army to perform its historical missions and safeguard its sovereign and interests. Peace can be obtained through impressive military strength. One could argue that China has such a legitimate right to build its military power to protect its national interests. For example, Taiwan is a domestic issue and should be viewed as an exception for Beijing's strategy of peaceful rise, in case forces are used to seek reunification.

These five points, elaborated by Chinese leaders and scholars as official Chinese position, can be viewed as five analytical criteria in measuring representations of China's "peaceful rise" in the American media. The five points can be simplified as follows: China's rise will be a win-win game, rather than a zero-sum one; China will concentrate on domestic problems for a long time and thus need a peaceful international environment; China will be cooperative with the U.S. in the world affairs and not disrupt the current world order; China and the U.S. should co-exist peacefully, despite their ideological differences and China has no intentions to compete for influence spheres across the world with the United States; China is justified in its endeavor on military modernization for the purpose of self-defense.

How have these five vantage points been framed in the U.S. news media? According to T. Gitlin, news coverage was informed and organized by largely implicit (unspoken and unacknowledged) "frames" – "persistent patterns of cognition, interpretation, and presentation, of selection, emphasis, and exclusion, by which symbol-handlers routinely organize discourse."[3] Such frames are necessarily related to the selectivity inherent in the production of news:

Media are mobile spotlights, not passive mirrors of the society; selectivity is the instrument of their action. A news story adopts a certain frame and rejects or downplays material that is discrepant. A story is a choice, a way of seeing an event that also amounts to a way of screening from sight.[4]

It is certain that the American media would not fully spread China's conceptions of peaceful rise as their Chinese counterparts do. Instead, the American media formulate their own criteria, based on American foreign policy and national interests, to conduct a litmus test of China's strategy of peaceful rise. This study surveys 107 articles on China's peaceful rise/development listed in the U.S. newspapers section of the Lexis-Nexis professional search tool. The following newspapers are used: *International Herald Tribune* (IHT), *The New York Times* (NYT), *The Washington Post* (WP), *The Washington Times* (WT), *Newsweek* (NW), *Christian Science Monitor* (CSM) and *Los Angeles Times* (LAT). These seven news media cover significant sections of the American print media in international and China reportage. The study begins with articles since China proclaimed the concept of peaceful rise in 2003 and ends on June 30, 2006. In my sample of the articles, most of them contained opinion and editorial pieces either debating or posting warnings about China's "peaceful" rise. Based on discourse analysis, the U.S. media have constructed three interpretative frames to cast China's peaceful rise: China's deeds do not match its words; China's self-styled "peaceful rise" is a propaganda campaign; the U.S. public should not trust the liability of that slogan.

(1) China's words and deeds are at odds. In the op/ed pages, columnists and letter-writers measure what China proclaims in the concept of peaceful rise with what China actually is doing in the world. They argue that China's rise is not a win-win game as the country claims. China is expanding its influence at the expense of the U.S. interests, instead of cooperating with the U.S. in the world affairs. In an article "A rise that's not so 'win-win',"[5] Elizabeth Economy wrote:

> All the while, Hu (Chinese President Hu Jintao) and his team will advance their "win-win" diplomacy and earn praise for being the good superpower. But if you look more carefully, here is what you see: a rising power exploiting other countries' natural resources, spoiling the global environment, making economic deals but looking away from serious government mistreatment of its citizens and not delivering on promises. (16 Nov. 2005, *The International Herald Tribune*)

Economy holds a classical realist perspective of China's proclamation of peaceful rise, arguing that China is cultivating an image of a "kinder, softer, gentler" rising power and a trustworthy partner. By projecting such an image, China tends to disguise or justify its foreign policies chosen on other grounds. China denies that it is exploiting others' resources in pursuit of economic gain, while asserting that it deserves cooperation from others as it does not mix business with politics. Ms. Economy argues that there is a gap between China's word and deed. For example, China's financial and military aids contribute to conflicts in Sudan and Zimbabwe, while supporting the corrupt Dos Santos regime in Angola. China is lack of transparency in business dealings with African governments. Obviously, China's foreign polices on the ground are at odds with its promise to separate business with politics.

Others think that China proclaims "peaceful rise" to assure its neighbors while reducing U.S. influence in Asia. In its editorial "Locking Uncle Sam out of Asia,"[6] *Christian Science Monitor* commented that the U.S. absence in the first cross-Pacific summit in 2005 signaled China's political goal to marginalize the U.S. influence. Right after China proposed the concept of peaceful rise, Robert W. Radtke argued that the new initiative in Chinese foreign policy would overshadow U.S. influence in Asia, which has had a relative decline.[7] He argued that while the U.S. single-mindedly focuses on Iraq and the anti-terror war, China has laid claim to the role the U.S. played since the end of World War II in assuring the development, prosperity and stability of Asia. China sent an appealing message to Asia as it presents its rise as part of its role in promoting development and stability of Asia as a whole. Radtke argued,

> China's message was, "We're here to help," while the U.S. message was "You're either with us or against us" in the war on terror. It's not hard to imagine which was the more effective diplomatic strategy. (8 Dec. 2003, Christian Science Monitor)

This contrast between China and the U.S. couldn't have been more striking. As a result, he concluded, "Relative U.S. influence is diminished – just as China's is growing."

Many others argue that China is accumulating influence and diminishing U.S. power piecemeal. Although China has sought to portray its growing power as a "peaceful rise," the country is rapidly building up its military power.[8] China's efforts to secure supplies of oil, natural gas and other commodities in Sudan, Iran and Venezuela have undermined U.S. foreign policy goals. It seems that China is using its buying power to set up a circle of friends hostile to the U.S. interests. It raises suspicion that China is just biding its time until it possesses economic, military and strategic strength to challenge the U.S. dominance in the Pacific and beyond.

Some U.S. scholars also suspect that China is expanding its soft power to counter the U.S. influence in the world. While many developing countries become increasingly disenchanted with the so-called Washington Consensus, which asks for lowered trade barriers, privatization, democracy and free markets, China's development model, touted as the Beijing Consensus, provides an alternative. The Beijing Consensus prioritizes innovation and growth through a social-market economy, over free markets and democracy. It champions non-interference and opposes foreign meddling. Therefore, Africa and much of the third world will be drawn to "an emerging superpower that does not lecture them about democracy and human rights or interfere in what Beijing considers 'internal affairs'."[9] Although China officially denied that it is trying to pose as a rival model for other countries, it is making efforts to win friends in Africa through providing aid and training programs. For example, the Foreign Affairs University provides a three-month training program for African diplomats. Several Chinese ministries, including Science and Technology, Agriculture, Commerce and Education, provide programs to train officials and develop human resources for some African governments. China has sent medical teams to train professionals in many African countries and provide free equipment and drugs to help fight AIDs and other diseases. China's efforts to cultivate ties with Africa have political and economic purposes. Howard W. French argues,

> The classes (training African officials) are one element in a campaign by Beijing to win friends around the world and pry developing nations out of the United States' sphere of influence. Africa, with its immense oil and mineral wealth and numerous United Nations votes, lies at the heart of that effort. (20 Nov. 2005, *New York Times*)

He pointed out that China provides aid to win African hearts, while attempting to sway African minds and impart China's view of the world on development, history and democracy by providing training classes for African officials.

(2) Peaceful rise is China's propaganda to gain popularity in the world amidst the decline of America's global appeal. Being very much wedded to its own doctrine of peaceful rise, China has spared no efforts in official rhetoric and diplomacy to project an image of a new kind of superpower which has no aggressive intent. This method of propaganda is twofold: on the one hand, China can win more friends and thus break down potential U.S. containment; on the other hand, by not provoking the U.S. and neighboring countries China would buy time to manage its domestic challenges and continue high growth.

In an article "Debating China's 'peaceful rise'," Michael Vatikiotis argued that the rhetoric is carefully woven for propaganda purpose of projecting China as a "force for peace."[10] He commented in the op/ed pages:

> Although it is often dismissed as shallow propaganda, silver-tongued diplomats in Beijing have skillfully used this diplomatic lexicon to create the illusion that China is the polar opposite of a superpower that acts unilaterally and uses military power to achieve its goals. (8 Sept, 2005, *International Herald Tribune*)

Vatikiotis dismisses peaceful rise as China's propaganda to woo more countries and make them keep the U.S. at a distance. Although "peaceful rise" and "win-win" have become the most common terms to show its diplomatic amity, Vatikiotis argued, China has actually drawn away investment and capital from the rest of Asia in its growing economy and still deploys ballistic missiles off the coast of Fujian and directed toward Taiwan. China often uses symbolic gesture for making concession to Asian neighbors in solving trade disputes. For example, when Thailand complained that free trade in agricultural products harms its farmers, China expressed its willingness to concede to the farmer's demand. This loss cost China little. For Vatikiotis, China uses soft words to disguise the wielding of hard power. However, they sound insincere as China prepares to defend lines of its strategic energy supply and modernize its military power.

Even though "peaceful rise" has become a mantra among Chinese leaders, other experts argue, "China's approach is as much dictated by realism as any idealistic notions of a new-style superpower."[11] China is using soft power to set up strategic and diplomatic relationships with neighboring countries. As Bates Gill observes, China reached out and settled old scores all over its periphery, thus trying to build a benign kind of hegemony. This has become a model for China.[12]

China promises to engage South America for natural resources without causing harm to U.S. policy. But in its editorial, *the Washington Time* commented that despite China's rhetoric, the country's involvement in the Western Hemisphere is not neutral to U.S. objectives in the region. China's foreign policy has not reflected what Robert B. Zoellick calls the ideal of a "responsible stakeholder."[13] China's self-claimed state goal of peaceful rise is discordant with its military development and foreign policy. The U.S. should pay attention to China's ambitions and tactics.

(3) "Peaceful rise" is a deceptive concept and should not be believed. In this interpretation, Chinese leaders cited their pre-occupation and domestic problems to assure that China has no intention to threaten and challenge America's preeminence in the world. Through slogans like "peaceful rise," China hopes to convey this message to the United States. However, the media report that China's words could not hide the evidence that China is becoming more powerful and assertive. Therefore, the U.S. should not buy what China is selling.

In an article "Is it a 'Peaceful Rise'? U.S. Shouldn't Bet on it," Howard W. French acknowledged that China is and will consume most of its energy to address domestic problems for the foreseeable future. However, "no amount of China's stealthy diplomatic posturing can obscure the fact that the country is growing more powerful and more assertive by the day, and in the process, a new world order is being shaped."[14] Regarding China's self-claimed "peaceful rise," therefore, he advised "a word to the wise: don't believe it."

French argued that Chinese leaders have not expressed enough candors toward both the outside world and their own people. "They are still spoon-fed a saccharine-laced and ultimately dangerous form of history that paints their China as the eternal innocent: happily self-contained and fair and courtly toward others."[15] Though China's denials, he argued that China has made its way towards challenging the United States. He wrote, "The outlines of China's challenge to the United States are already beginning to take shape, and they are nothing less than sweeping."[16] He considered the concept of peaceful rise as China's stealthy approach, in which China would not stand up to the U.S. while the superpower undermines its own position in the world. As the U.S. emphasizes military forces and unilateralism, China is embracing economic multi-lateralism which the U.S. once excelled at. As a result, China, as an emerging power, has earned a positive reputation. Hence, China can counterbalance the U.S. with even calming rhetoric and pro-American policies.

For other experts, peaceful rise is China's option through doing a cost-benefit analysis. Under Pax Americana, Chinese leaders believe that China can devote itself to economic development and spend more resources on domestic problems. Being antagonistic to the United States would be too costly. Hence China has no immediate ambitions to shake the world order or challenge the United States. However, it is uncertain that China will remain moderate when it becomes a middle-class society. For some analysts, the Taiwan issue has brought out China's aggressive instincts, with unpredictable results. China's passage of the Anti-Secession Bill exposed two faces of rising China to the world. Joseph Kahn commented, "one has 19th-century notions of sovereignty and historical destiny. The other embraces 21st-century notions of global integration. The anti-secession bill looks like a victory for the former."[17]

In sum, there are discrepancies between China and the U.S. media in framing "peaceful rise." In the Chinese media coverage, "peaceful rise" aims to address the key foreign policy question – how to make Asian neighbors and then the whole world accept China as a rising power. For China, "rising" is the goal but its condition is peace and being on friendly terms with the world. China's determination to peaceful rise will rebut the China-threat theory, which seeks to vilify China's image and prevent its rise. In the American mainstream media, however, the concept of "peaceful rising" serves as a veneer to hide a more subtle and sophisticated strategy to expand China's influence in Central Asia, South Asia, Southeast Asia, Africa and South America. They argue that would be done by engaging in flurry of diplomatic and economic initiatives. China is advocating its rise as a "win-win" game, which has brought about development opportunities and tangible benefits to the rest of world. China is positioning itself as a model for developing countries, a new kind of power emphasizing economic growth and insisting non-interference in others' domestic affairs. By projecting such an image, China has actually contrasted its own policies and intentions with those of the United States. As a result, China is attempting to undermine the U.S. primacy in the world and expand its own influence. Therefore, the American media have basically framed China's peaceful rise as a self-claimed propaganda slogan, which is for the purpose of image building for China, instead of idealistic principles of its foreign policy.

INTERNATIONAL IMAGE CULTIVATION: PROPAGANDA VERSUS PUBLIC DIPLOMACY

It is evident that the American public opinion towards the strategy of China's peaceful rise is primarily suspicious. Mostly, the concept of peaceful rise is viewed as a new vocabulary, which shifts China's propaganda into global direction. In cultivating its international image, China has disadvantages inherent in its domestic propaganda system and the leaders' equation of public diplomacy and international public relations with "overseas propaganda work."

Since the 1990s, China has been concerned with its negative image in the U.S. media and the implications for Sino-U.S. relations. However, China's efforts to improve its image in the U.S. are often considered as China's propaganda associated with diplomacy. As Zhang and Cameron argue, the government's international image managing is a new dimension and an important component of China's total propaganda.[18] To manage its image in the American public, China has taken several approaches, which range from international conferences, and leaders' appearances in the U.S. major media and public relations campaigns to military visits and culture tours. From a U.S perspective, however, such activities are still conceived for propaganda purposes.

To examine how China's public relations campaigns often fall into the trap of propaganda accusations, it is necessary to separate public diplomacy from propaganda. It is hard to distinguish the two because they have common historical origins and roughly similar dimensions. Even in the Western literature, public diplomacy is sometimes seen as an outgrowth of propaganda. However, the two are fundamentally different in modern diplomatic practice. As Jan Melissen argues, the public in a liberal democracy often negatively connotes propaganda as manipulation and deceit of foreign publics. This negative understanding is reinforced by histories of Nazi and Communist propaganda and Cold War tactics. Melissen asserts that the pattern of communication can make a distinction between propaganda and public diplomacy.[19] According to M. Leonard and V. Alakeson, propaganda is a one-way messaging, because it is described as "a process that deliberately attempts through persuasion techniques to secure from the propagandee, before he can deliberate freely, the responses desired by the propagandist."[20] By contrast, Melissen describes modern public diplomacy as a "two-way street," in which foreign publics are persuaded to recognize one country's interests and foreign policy goals by means of dialogue. Both propaganda and public diplomacy attempt to persuade people what to think, but Melissen sees the difference in the latter's willing to listen to what people have to say. In Jay Black's argument, public relations and persuasion campaigns are meaningful communication between official agents and foreign publics, in which pluralism is accepted and receivers are expected to conduct further investigations.[21] For example, when Western Europe launches public campaign aimed at civil society building, rule of law and improving democracy, few would view their activities as propaganda.

Non-state actors play an increasingly important role in conducting public diplomacy. Hans Tuch defines public diplomacy as "a government's process of communicating with foreign publics in an attempt to bring about understanding for its nation's ideas and ideals, its institutions and culture, as well as its national goals and policies."[22] However, public diplomacy is not the practice uniquely done by the state representatives. In Melissen's opinion, civil society, ordinary individuals and loosely organized groups are more capable and agile in mobilizing support among foreign publics than official players. As Paul Sharp argues, public diplomacy can be described as "the process by which direct relations with people in a county are pursued to advance the interests and extend the values of those being represented."[23] Thus, public diplomacy targets general public in foreign societies, more specific non-official groups, organizations and individuals. Accordingly, it is important to enhance communication between non-official players. As public diplomacy targets foreign publics, Melissen argues, persuasion techniques used for dealing with them should be different from that used for dealing with domestic socialization.

Conceiving of public diplomacy as lip service may damage one country's trust and credibility in its communications with foreign publics. As a result, Melissen argues that public diplomacy and foreign policy should be closely tied to each other. In other words, public diplomacy should take a country's foreign policy into considerations. It should tune to medium-term and long-term foreign policy objectives. Otherwise, public diplomacy is reduced to propaganda for foreign publics.

Bearing in mind the above theoretical framework of public diplomacy, we can examine the strengths and weaknesses of China's public diplomacy practice with the concept of peaceful rise as the cornerstone. China has advantages in central coordination of its public diplomacy activities. Ingrid d'Hooghe argues that as a one-party state, China has a centralist authoritarian regime which can control public diplomacy instruments and build on a tradition of political propaganda.[24] Because of these characteristics, China concentrates on formal intergovernmental contacts. When promoting the concept of peaceful rise overseas, obviously, Chinese leaders, senior officials, diplomats and scholars of the government-run think tanks are primary actors in the international arena and conferences. China is typical of what B. Hocking calls "the state-centered, hierarchical model of diplomacy" and Jarol B. Manheim terms "strategic public diplomacy" – the government of one country uses strategic political communication to influence opinion in another country.[25] As China discourages the development of civil society and allows no role for private actors in diplomacy, it faces a structural deficiency in conducting public diplomacy activities, in which public and private actors usually play an active role. Although the Chinese people's Association for Friendship with Foreign Countries (CPAFFC) and the Institute of Foreign Affairs (IFA) claim them to commit to "people-to-people diplomacy" and non-governmental exchanges, they are still semi-official, rather than independent, institutions. They mainly invited retired senior leaders of foreign countries to visit China.

China seems to equate public diplomacy and national image building with "external propaganda." Chinese leaders re-apply domestic mechanism of propaganda to their goals of creating a positive image abroad. China applies the mindset and ideas of communist propaganda to set up its institutions responsible for improving its overseas images. The most powerful is the Central Committee Foreign Propaganda Office, in charge of the overall oversees publicity work. In the central government, the State Council Information Office plays a major role in orchestrating China's public diplomacy activities. It aims to improve and shape a favorable image of China in world opinion through publicizing China's economic and social achievements and interpreting China's policies to foreign audiences. Even Zheng Bijian, who coined the concept of peaceful rise, is a former Communist Party propaganda chief. In China, propaganda chiefs who know little about diplomacy and international relations have the task of explaining China to the outside world and improving the image of China through public diplomacy. As a result, the messages relayed from such institutions to the outside world are full of propagandistic tone. The English-language media in China which convey the messages to the outside world include Beijing Review, China Daily, China International Radio Broadcasting, CCTV-4, Overseas News Editorial Department of Xinhua News Agency, and English Edition of People's Daily Online. These media organizations are primary mouthpieces of the party. As propaganda tools of the party, their news coverage and texts are often staid and not appealing even to domestic audiences and readers, let alone foreigners. As a result, first-hand messages about China are accessible to foreign publics mainly through coverage and reportages by foreign media organizations which have journalists stationed in China. As these media organizations target their domestic audiences and readers, they frame and represent China through their own perspectives, thus distorting China's existential reality and truth. The messages which the Chinese government hopes to convey cannot be accurately received by foreign publics. When Chinese leaders and scholars have the chance to conduct face-to-face communication with foreign publics, their remarks and speeches are elusive to foreign audiences. The problem lies in inter-cultural communication, as well as ideological differences. The two sides do not have the opportunity to dialogue on substantive issues. Successful public diplomacy requires consonance between the actual message and what the audience comprehends. Chinese officials and scholars still have a long way to go to learn to use rhetoric and expressions which foreign publics are accustomed to. They also should respond to foreign publics and conduct dialogue with them on their concerns about China.

Although China has initiated commercialization of its media system, it still follows a propaganda model to distribute messages about China to the outside world. Thus in the international flow of news, China is at a disadvantage in influencing the standard processes of gathering and selecting information. Given this structural condition, China often has a negative image in the global information network dominated by the major Western media. According to Michael Kunczik, structural communication deficits can be offset through public relations (PR) for states. Kunczik argued, "this form of PR for states, meant primarily to compensate for structural communication deficits, aims mainly at adapting the image to news values by trying to influence mass media reporting."[26] What Kunczik calls "structural international PR" could correct the "false" images previously created by the mass media. Obviously, China has realized the importance of international public relations campaigns in improving China's image abroad. During Jiang Zemin's leadership, for example, the Chinese government launched a $7 million public relations campaign, called "2000, Experience China in the United States" to introduce Americans to China. The New York Times commented that the touring cultural extravaganza "is the first large-scale attempt by the Chinese government at public relations and marketing in the United States, skills that were largely irrelevant and ignored there when it was an isolated Communist state."[27] Certainly, as d'Hooghe argues, China's culture has enormous potential from a public diplomacy perspective. However, the Chinese government under Hu's leadership does not continue to take advantage of culture as a good theme to push forward China's public diplomacy and international public relations campaigns in the United States. Instead, the current leadership has adopted the concept of peaceful rise as the cornerstone of China's public diplomacy. As this theme overlaps foreign policy issues, it would damage China's credibility when its assertions are contradictory with the country's foreign policy goals in reality.

While China's public diplomacy aims to project an image of China as a trustworthy, cooperative, responsible and peace-loving power through promoting the concept of peaceful rise to the outside world, the country's real foreign policy goals and means are inconsistent. The contradiction will damage China's image building endeavor. For example, China is advancing its foreign policy in the developing world to secure future energy supplies and raw materials for its economic growth. China is accused of exploiting others' resources in pursuing its own economic gain. Also, critics say that China's hunger for oil has led it to cooperate with some unsavory regimes in defiance of international pressure. China is accused of fuelling conflicts and human rights violations by selling arms to repressive regimes like Sudan and Zimbabwe in exchange for oil and minerals. For the American public, China's voracious appetite for petroleum has aligned it with what the U.S. government labels "oil-rich bad-boy" countries such as Venezuela, Sudan and Iran. To seek energy supply for its economy, China is indifferent to these countries' human rights abuses or autocratic ways. These accusations against China have damaged its credibility and sincerity in the strategy of peaceful rise. China has defended its record by arguing that it is selfless in its desire to provide help and serve as a development model for poor countries. This justification looks hypocritical and will raise new suspicions of a "China threat." The Western public is not naive and does not believe that there are no self-interests involved. The discourse of selflessness used in international relations would only raise further doubts about China's orientation. If China says that it serves as a development model for African countries, it will justify the U.S. fear that Beijing would challenge the "Washington Consensus" with a "Beijing Consensus" and thus expand its influence in the world by pushing forward the soft power.

In sum, the American media framing of China's "peaceful rise" has not delivered a positive message for the American public. The concept "peaceful rise" has not convinced the American public. As Lanxin Xiang argues, "China's leaders must prove - rather than just assert - that China's restoration will not produce an inevitable conflict with the superpower of the day."[28]

CONCLUSION

The discrepancies between China and the U.S. in the presentation of "peaceful rise" expose the structural limitations of China's public diplomacy. First, it is tempting for China to see public diplomacy as just another dimension of propaganda in attaining its foreign policy goals. This temptation has led China to equate image building with the task of external propaganda. In the case of peaceful rise, China seems to overlap the boundaries between public diplomacy and foreign policy. In other words, it is difficult for the outside world to clarify whether the concept of peaceful rise is a discourse of China's public diplomacy or a principle and objective of its foreign policy. This confusion is heightened by the unexplained contradiction between China's moderate assertions and its ambitious foreign policy practices in the world. As a result, China's public diplomacy, with "peaceful rise" as the cornerstone, may fail in the U.S. because it cannot reach consonance between the actual message and what the audience comprehends.

Second, China has recognized the vital role of soft power for a country, but still has misunderstandings of public diplomacy as one of soft power's key instruments. As J. Nye argued, countries that are likely to be more attractive in post-modern international relations are those that help to frame issues, whose culture and ideas are closer to prevailing international norms, and whose credibility abroad is reinforced by their values and policies.[29] If China attempts to enhance its soft power in the world, it is important for China to strengthen the rule of law and develop democratic institutions domestically. China should launch political reform to fight corruption, solve wealth gaps, reform its judiciary, encourage the development of civil society, expand religious freedom, guarantee press freedom and hold its government accountable to the people. The political reform, which matches China's economic growth, will become part of China's soft power. It will also buttress China's promise of peaceful rise through institutional arrangements. For the outside world, China will not just pay lip service to the concept of peaceful rise. The openness of China's society will also expand the room for the growth of civil society. This will allow public and private actors to play an active role in engaging in China's public diplomacy. The participation of non-governmental actors will change China's highly centralized and state-controlled public diplomacy and water down this form of propaganda.

Third, China is still lack of mechanism in structural international PR to cultivate its international image. China has realized the increasing importance of image building in seeking acceptance in the world arena, but it should be clear-minded about theme options in structural international PR. According to d'Hooghe, China's human rights records, its minority policies and the Taiwan issue are its biggest liabilities that hamper selling the country.[30] By contrast, China's culture and economic success are powerful assets in creating a positive image abroad. However, China faces a dilemma for choosing economic success as one of public diplomacy themes. On the one hand, it is tempting to showcase the economic development that will increase the legitimacy of the Communist Party and the appeal of China's development model to the developing world; on the other hand, playing the card of economic success may heighten the "China threat." China's economic growth has whetted its appetite for oil and raw materials, caused environmental pollution, brought about a growing gap between the rich and poor. Without a doubt, therefore, culture is a good theme for China's public diplomacy. However, China's current leadership seems not to pay particular attention to this dimension and continues the platform established under Jiang's rule. Instead, the Chinese leadership under Hu Jintao resorts to the concept of peaceful rise. It is difficult to manage it as the theme of public diplomacy because this concept overlaps domestic politics, national security and foreign policy. China must match its words in public diplomacy with actions in domestic political affairs and foreign policy. Otherwise, the main objective of international public relations – projecting an image of China trustworthy to other actors in the world system – will be hampered.

Peace, harmony, reconciliation are topping China's agenda and official rhetoric. Like such slogans, the concept of peaceful rise is adopted by China to convince the world that the country has chosen an unprecedented development road different from one pursued by other countries that rose in the last few centuries. The Chinese leaders have ever been fond of slogans for propaganda and political purposes. If "peaceful rise" is China's long-term national strategy and foreign policy, it will not lose its luster like other slogans the Chinese leaders had ever trumpeted. China must let the outside world understand what progress it has made in social development and political democratization and justify its security and foreign policy goals. However, it is unfortunate that the task of explaining China to the world is still in the hands of propaganda chiefs. To cultivate a positive image in the world, China has to learn how to conduct public diplomacy and international public relations, other than perceiving them as "external propaganda work."

Notes:

[1] BBC News International at news.bbc.co.uk; CNN/USA Today/Gallup Poll at PollingReport.com.

[2] These articles on peaceful rise can be retrieved from *People's Daily* online and special edition on peaceful rise at xinhuanet.com.

[3] T. Gitlin, (1980). *The Whole World is Watching: Mass Media in the Making and Unmaking of the New Left* (Berkeley, Los Angeles and London: University of California Press, 1980), p. 7.

[4] Gitlin, *The Whole World is Watching*, 1980, pp. 49-51.

[5] Elizabeth Economy, "A Rise that's not so 'Win-Win'", *The International Herald Tribune*, Nov 16, 2005.

[6] "Locking Uncle Sam out of Asia", *Christian Science Monitor*, Sept 8, 2005.

[7] Robert W. Radtke, "China's 'Peaceful Rise' Overshadowing US Influence in Asia?" *Christian Science Monitor*, Dec 8, 2003.

[8] Joseph Kahn, "Friend or Foe? Hu Visit to Test Ties with U.S.", *New York Times*, April 17, 2006.

[9] Howard W. French, "China Wages Classroom Struggle to Win Friends in Africa", *New York Times*, November 20, 2005.

[10] Michael Vatikiotis, "Debating China's 'Peaceful Rise'", *International Herald Tribune*, Sept 8, 2005.

11 Howard W. French, "China Moves toward another West: Central Asia," *New York Times*, March 28, 2004.

12 Ibid.

13 "China in the West", *Washington Time*, May 30, 2006.

14 Howard W. French, "Is it a 'Peaceful Rise'? U.S. Shouldn't Bet on it," *International Herald Tribune*, April 20, 2006.

15 Ibid.

16 Ibid.

17 Joseph Kahn, "The Two Faces of Rising China", *New York Times*, March 14, 2005.

18 Juyan Zhang and Glen T. Cameron, "The Structural Transformation of China's Propaganda: An Ellulian Perspective," *Journal of Communication Management*, Vol. 8, No. 3, 2004.

19 Jan Melissen. "The New Public Diplomacy: Between Theory and Practice," in Jan Melissen, ed., *The New Public Diplomacy: Soft Power in International Relations* (New York: Palgrave Macmillan, 2005), pp. 17-19.

20 M. Leonard and V. Alakeson, *Going Public: Diplomacy for the Information Society* (London: Foreign Policy Center, 2000), pp. 86-98.

21 Jay Black, "Semantics and Ethics of Propaganda," *Journal of Mass Media Ethics*, vol. 16, nos.2-3, 1986, p. 133 and p. 135.

22 Hans Tuch, *Communicating with the World: US Public Diplomacy Overseas* (New York: St Martin's Press, 1990), p.3.

23 Paul Sharp, "Revolutionary States, Outlaw Regimes and the Techniques of Public Diplomacy", in Jan Melissen, ed., *The New Public Diplomacy: Soft Power in International Relations* (New York: Palgrave Macmillan, 2005), p. 106.

24 Ingrid d'Hooghe, "Public Diplomacy in the People's Republic of China", in Jan Melissen, ed., *The New Public Diplomacy: Soft Power in International Relations* (New York: Palgrave Macmillan, 2005), pp. 88-103.

25 B. Hocking and Jarol B. Manheim, *Strategic Public Diplomacy and American Foreign Policy: the Evolution of Influence* (New York: Oxford University Press, 1994).

26 Michael Kunczik, *Images of Nations and International Public Relations* (Mahwah, N.J.: Lawrence Erlbaum Associates, 1997), p.25.

27 Elisabeth Rosenthal, "China's U.S. Road Show, Aimed at Making Friends," *New York Times*, August 23, 2000.

28 Lanxin Xiang, "Why Washington Can't Speak Chinese," *The Washington Post*, April 16, 2006.

29 Joseph S. Nye, *Soft Power: The Means to Success in World Politics* (PublicAffairs, 2004), pp. 31-32.

30 Ingrid d'Hooghe, "Public Diplomacy in the People's Republic of China", in Jan Melissen, ed., *The New Public Diplomacy: Soft Power in International Relations* (New York: Palgrave Macmillan, 2005), pp. 94-95.

Chapter 7

China's New Approach to North Korean Nuclear Issue: An Economic Interdependence

Han Lheem

INTRODUCTION

This chapter attempts to analyze the nature of North Korean nuclear crisis and introduce China's new economic strategy to the North, which is looking beyond the six-sided talks and the American approach. Unlike U.S. approach that Washington tries to squeeze and force Kim Jong Il to drop his nuclear ambitions, Chinese new agenda on North Korea has different orientations of massive investment and gaining Kim's confidence. Indeed, Beijing dramatically pumped up investment to some $2 billion in 2005 from $1.3 million and $200 million in 2003 and 2004 respectively, and is helping to create factories and modernize energy sectors in what Washington diplomats call a "massive carrot-giving operation."[1] On January 18, 2006, for the first time, Korean Central News Agency (KCNA) commented positively about China's opening and reform after Kim's visit to the model reform cities of Shenzhen, Guanzhou, and Zhuhai in China's southern Pearl River Delta.[2] Five years ago, after Kim went to Shanghai in 2001, the North Korean leader called China's historic move to market reform, engineered by paramount leader Deng Xiaoping in a visit to the same cities that Kim visited, a "betrayal of socialism," and KCNA also stated that "while market reforms might be good for China, they were not correct for us [North Korea]."[3] However, the 2006 visit made Kim confess that, "our visit to the southern part of China convinced us . . . that China has a rosier future thanks to the correct line and policies advanced by the Communist Party of China."[4] Chinese President Hu Jintao's visit to Pyongyang in October 2005 and Kim Jong Il's return visit in January 2006 highlighted deepening economic relations. China is undertaking a range of infrastructure projects in and around North Korea and now accounts for 48 per cent of North Korean foreign trade. Since 2003, over 150 Chinese firms have begun operating in or trading with North Korea. As much as 80 per cent of the consumer goods found in the country's markets are made in China, which will keep trying to gradually normalize the economy, with the long-term goal of a reformed, China-friendly North Korea.[5]

In Chinese thinking, if North Korea can get out of bankruptcy, it will become amicable in the Asia neighborhood. China's new strategy is trying to do business with North Korea, while U.S. approach has been in a hurry to resolve the nuclear issue over night. A study of the Asia-Pacific Center for Security Studies in Honolulu also states, "[China] wants to go its own way, and has decided to raise up North Korea again, to rebuild and reinvent it."[6]

The remainder of this research is constructed as follows. First, this study will introduce two different explanations for the North Korean nuclear crisis, and try to identify the nature of the problem and its parameters. Second, it will analyze the arguments of two protagonists, the United States and North Korea, and the six-sided talks since 2003, along with reviewing changes in U.S. policies on the North throughout the Clinton and Bush Administrations.[7] Third, it will introduce China's new agenda of economic engagement and interdependence on the North Korean issue, which are based upon dialogue and consultation rather than pressure or sanctions.

THE NATURE OF NORTH KOREAN NUCLEAR CRISIS

There are two different approaches to view and explain the North Korean nuclear crisis. Although both approaches, the hawkish and the dovish, offer different assumptions on the North Korean regime and its foreign policy strategy, they believe that engagement represents the only rational policy for not only the United States, but for the other four participants in the six-sided talks as well.[8]

The hawkish camp, on the one hand, is suspicious of the North Korean regime's principles to the six-sided talks and the apparent desire to be friendlier to South Korea since South Korean president Kim Dae Jung's visit to Pyongyang in 2000. It believes that North Korea's stance on the talks is a tactical maneuver rather than a strategic shift, and the North will break the agreements and walk back to its nuclear programs if needed at any time, because the fundamentals of North Korean foreign policy are based upon the pure Machiavellian *realpolitik*. The hawks, therefore, argue that the United States needs to continue to apply harsh measures: containment plus isolation, coercion, and sanctions in order to attain a total surrender of the North. Ex-U.S. arms control envoy John Bolton, now the U.S. Ambassador to the United Nations, said, the central issue in the six-sided talks was "whether North Korea is prepared to make the commitment for the complete, verifiable, irreversible dismantlement of its program," and the United States wanted a complete end to the program, while a freeze of nuclear reactors was desirable.[9]

In fact, with the hawkish approach of the Bush Administration, the North began to feel it was losing everything. The completion of new power stations had been delayed and eventually expired in June 2006, and Washington was refusing to let the South sell electricity to the North, while the economic embargo continued. North Korea, consequently, has been trying to use the nuclear issue as a hard-line ploy to negotiate a non-aggression pact and improved economic aid from the United States.

The dovish camp, on the other hand, believes that the North does not wish to go nuclear; that if it had wanted to, Pyongyang would have done so long ago. But the North does have genuine security concerns, inflamed by a U.S. administration fond of hyperbolic rhetoric and a National Security Strategy praising the efficacy of preemptive strikes. Unless Washington addresses these entirely understandable fears, North Korea will quite logically conclude that it has no alternative but to develop a nuclear deterrent sufficient to convince the United States that armed action against the North would be insupportably costly. It continues that U.S. pressure will exacerbate North Korean security fears, and being ordered to disarm by the world's sole superpower will only increase the North's incentives not to disarm. This essentially defensive explanation for Pyongyang's nuclear weapons program, needless to say, will not find many adherents in the Bush Administration. The dovish engagement, however, has a number of important points in its favor: it avoids the likelihood of war because it lengthens time horizons, it reduces the threat of imminent attack, and ultimately it changes the North's terms of reference. This was what was so remarkable about the Clinton diplomacy. Built on Jimmy Carter's pact with the late Kim Il Sung it achieved breakthroughs in the North's posture on nuclear weapons.[10]

Despite their different views on North Korea, the hawkish and the dovish camps believe engagement is needed and that the military option could trigger a catastrophe. Fears about regime survival, imminent collapse, or inevitable absorption by the South could all prompt the North to lash out. A policy of engagement is the only means of avoiding a situation where Pyongyang could view armed force as a "rational" course of action, even if military victory were impossible. North Korea understands the suicidal nature of a 1950-style invasion across the DMZ (Demilitarized Zone) separating the two Koreas. If the status quo is sufficiently threatening, both camp argue, violence becomes rational as a means of inducing the United States to negotiate a new status quo more to Pyongyang's desire. The limited use of force represents a rational, even an optimal, choice. It is in the U.S. interest to give the North a stake in the status quo, if Pyongyang makes this possible. A strategy based on isolation, threats, and coercion fails this test. They project, accordingly, that if engagement were to work, it would produce regime change, in effect, if not in fact.

The North Korean nuclear crisis, actually, comes down to one essential question: Does North Korea have genuine security fears or not? If they don't, if they're making up a threat from the United States, then they are trying to blackmail Washington; they're trying to extort money by creating a threat and hoping to get something in return. However, if North Korea does have genuine security concerns, as the doves believe they do, then without resolving those security concerns we will not resolve the nuclear issue, because it's unlikely that North Korea will unilaterally disarm and trust the United States to do the right thing by them.

It is true and has been verified that the North is a reprehensible, corrupt, brutal regime. The regime *should* go away and the Korean peninsula *should* be denuclearized. However, even a corrupt and morally reprehensible regime can still have genuine security concerns. The United States had the Korean War with the North; it signed a truce in 1953, but they are still technically at war with North Korea. No peace treaty has ever been signed. The United States specifically targeted North Korea with nuclear weapons in the 2002 nuclear posture review despite having said in the 1994 Agreed Framework that the United States would provide assurances against first use. The United States also displays, still, about 36,000 troops in the South, and it is very obvious that the United States, as a hegemonic power house, has been playing a critical role in the region since the beginning of WW II. And also, since the collapse of global communism during 1990s, North Korea has lost both its allies, China and the Soviet Union, and has experienced economic disasters for the last decade. So the North justifiably has reason to have security concerns. It is not a surprise then that what they don't want to do is to give up those weapons and hope that the United States won't take advantage of that. If the United States continues to press Kim's regime, it *might* end up with precisely an outcome nobody wants, which is what North Korea says; "There is no way we can give up these nuclear weapons. This is the only thing that we can do."[11] David Kang also cautiously warns that too much pressure would provoke a counter response, rather than generating a total surrender from the North.[12]

In fact, on the other side of spectrum, there have been positive changes that are going on in North Korea, and the United States should encourage these trends and not retard them. Because the United States is not paying a lot of attention to North Korea, the world only focuses on the North when there's a military security issue, but one thing that tends to be overlooked is that North Korea has had a real and profound economic reform that has gone on in the last five or more years. The North Korea of today does not look at all like the North Korea that it used to be. Since July 2002 North Korea has tried to implement a market system, abandoning the centrally planned economy. No longer is there a ration system, supply and demand now determine prices. Since then there has been significant economic cooperation, mostly with China and South Korea. This is a dramatic paradigm shift in Kim's regime. The railroads have been reconnected through the DMZ between the North and the South, there are special economic zones, there are private markets, there are over a billion U.S. dollars in circulation in North Korea that are used in buying foreign goods. Yet, of all these changes that were completely unthinkable a decade ago, the most important change is ending Marxist economic orders. When Deng Xiaoping said in 1978, "to get rich is glorious," China did not instantly become a market economy and, in fact, it is not truly one even now. Although there are still state owned enterprises, enormous government control and a repressive regime in China, we are not nearly as worried about reforming China as we were when they were Red China. It is because today's China is a crucial member of the global community. They became capitalists, trading partners, and we have a lot of knowledge about them and there are Chinese everywhere. China is no longer separated from the world. It was Nixon who went to China, not the other way around. China did not make an instant transition to capitalism in 1978. China's opening to the world has been a decades-long process of gradual reform and opening, but it has also been successful beyond anyone's hopes. The United States engaged them first to the benefit of both the United States and China, gradually bringing Red China back into the world. China's example can be a vital lesson for the United States, and seems the safest and most humane way to relate to the North Koreans. After all, the nuclear standoff and quarrel are not with the North Korean citizens but with the regime. As O'Hanlon and Mochizuki explain, North Korea can be induced to be a member of world community, just as the leaders of China and Vietnam have embraced elements of economic reform without abandoning their communist ideology. They continue: "North Korean leaders seem to want to change, - they just cannot figure out how to do so successfully while also holding onto power."[13] Kang also agrees, North Korea is truly trying to reach a *modus vivendi* with the rest of the word. "Above all," he asserts, Pyongyang wants better ties with the United States.[14]

Indeed, North Korea has rapidly increased its relations with the South: North-South trade was $440 million in the first six months of 2006, and trucks on a road that goes through the DMZ carried some of that trade.[15] Over 150,000 South Koreans have visited North Korea in the past three years.[16] To cap all of these developments, Kim Jong Il finally admitted in September 2005 — after three decades of denials — that the North kidnapped Japanese citizens in the 1970s. The United States should encourage these trends and such candor, not retard them with a policy of pressure and isolation. Focusing on economic change is the best strategy for the United States to follow, because it is transforming, gradual and peaceful. Capitalism is a powerful force, and when it is unleashed, it is very difficult to turn back. This will also transform the mindset of all North Korean citizens, not just the leadership. Give North Koreans a taste of economic freedoms and outside ideas and the next generation will view their own leadership and the outside world in different terms. Engagement that is gradual, will allow the world to bring North Korea slowly back into the world. Economic transformation will also be peaceful.

THE U.S. – NORTH KOREA DISPUTES AND SIX-PARTY TALKS

The relations between the United States and North Korea have deteriorated since President Bush labeled North Korea part of an "axis of evil" in January 2002. Tensions really started escalating the following October, when the United States accused North Korea of developing a secret, uranium-based nuclear weapons program. Washington was not only concerned about the development of such weapons in North Korea, but also wanted to curb Pyongyang's capacity to export missile and nuclear technology to other states or organizations. Since the October 2002 confrontation, the North has restarted a mothballed nuclear power station, thrown out inspectors from the UN's International Atomic Energy

Agency (IAEA) and pulled out of the Nuclear Non-proliferation Treaty (NPT). In the middle of this confrontation, China started to host the "Six-Sided Talks" with the United States, Russia, Japan, and North and South Koreas in August 2003. The key protagonists of the talks, of course, are the United States and North Korea.[17] For the United States, elimination of any North Korean nuclear weapons and related programs is the overriding goal, but the United States also seems to want to deny North Korea any right to a civilian nuclear energy program, while dealing with its missile program and human rights record. Beyond this, there are also within the Bush Administration those who are absolutely committed to regime change in North Korea. For North Korea, the nuclear weapons issue is probably secondary. It is the means to try to achieve resolution of the problems that have plagued it for so long: isolation, intimidation and sanctions. What it wants above all is to convert the ceasefire of 1953 into a permanent peace treaty and to "normalize" relations of all kinds – security, political, diplomatic, economic - with the United States and Japan. The memory of a previous attempt at a comprehensive deal, a trade-off of nuclear programs for security, is fresh: in 1994 North Korea suspended its reactors and froze its plutonium wastes under international inspection, in return for a promise of two light-water reactors, heavy oil, and diplomatic and economic normalization. All it got in more than ten years was the supply of heavy oil, so it wants to be sure of a better outcome this time.

The United States has issued many demands, but refuses to negotiate with the North on a one-on-one basis. Former Deputy Secretary of State Richard Armitage criticized the chief U.S. representative at talks between 2002 and 2004, James Kelly, for behaving at the Beijing conferences like an envoy of the former Soviet Union, as if he were constantly under surveillance and had no leeway to say anything but what was in his brief.[18] After the August 2003 session, the Chinese Chair, Wang Yi, also expressed that the biggest obstacle in the negotiations had been "the American policy towards DPRK (Democratic People's Republic of Korea). This is the main problem we are facing."[19] The demand for "CVID" (complete, verifiable, irreversible, dismantling) was repeated like a mantra. North Korea was told that it would have to satisfy the United States on missiles, conventional force reduction, counterfeiting, drug smuggling, terrorism, human rights and abduction, while Washington believed that Pyongyang's demand for a guarantee it would not be attacked, let alone its demand for comprehensive normalization, was seen as unnecessary, irrelevant, or premature. It is no surprise that talks on such a basis were fruitless.

In the agreements of the Fourth Round six-sided talks in September 2005, which were the most successful outcome so far, the positions of the two antagonists seemed to be as follows. The United States had softened its rhetoric and ceased its abuse, showing a new readiness to actually talk with the North Koreans. North Korea, for its part, declared its readiness for "strategic decisions" to resolve the problems. However, on matters of substance the United States seems not to have softened its line.[20] The United States continued to call for complete, verifiable, irreversible dismantling (CVID) of North Korea's nuclear programs and installations as something to which North Korea would have to yield unconditionally in advance of negotiations; only then could other matters be addressed. The United States believed that North Korea would have to declare and abandon both plutonium and uranium-based weapons programs, return to the IAEA and the inspections mandated under it, abandon its program of nuclear energy generation, abandon its long-range missile program, and, although it is not at all clear precisely how this is addressed in the draft agreement, address human rights concerns.[21] North Korea, on the other hand, sought security guarantees, normalization of political and economic relations with the United States and Japan, and cooperation in its economic reconstruction programs first.

Even among the five parties to the talks with North Korea there was no substantial consensus. Early in August 2005, reports from Beijing referred to the five parties all signing off on a draft agreement, which was surprising. Despite regular statements from Washington about the unity of the five countries that sit with North Korea around the table, and the insistence that responsibility for the crisis rests exclusively with North Korea, disunity has in fact been characteristic and blame is shared. All parties undoubtedly agree on the desirability of a nuclear weapon-free peninsula, but unity stops there. There was no other step forward to easing the crisis. Accordingly, although the 2005 preliminary agreement was announced, the provisional conclusion was designed to be ambiguous, allowing each to interpret it to suit their own position. Not only did serious differences remain on the part of the "Five," but the matters most urgent for North Korea – security, especially from nuclear threats, and steps towards diplomatic and economic normalization – remained, so far as is known, unresolved.

TWO REALITIES FROM TWO ADMINISTRATIONS

In 1994, the first nuclear confrontation between the United States and North Korea degenerated to the brink of war, staved off only at the last minute by an accommodation known as the Geneva "Agreed Framework." Under the framework, North Korea froze its graphite reactors and accepted international inspection of its plutonium wastes, while the United States promised to construct two alternative, light water reactors, supply heavy oil for energy generation till the reactors came on stream, and to move towards political and economic normalization. Since the "1994 Agreed Framework," the relations between the United States and North Korea had been improved during the Clinton Administration. In fact, President Clinton welcomed the North's second-ranking leader, Marshal Jo Myong Rok, to the White House in October, 2000, and a month later, Kim Jong Il gave a warm hearted welcome to visiting then-Secretary of State Madeleine Albright. The U.S. commitment to normalized relations with Pyongyang at that time was symbolized by the fact that Secretary Albright paid her respects at the late Kim Il Sung's mausoleum, which former South Korean President Kim Dae Jung had not done in June 2000.[22]

However, from the start, the Bush Administration has been divided over whether to continue the Clinton policy. Former Secretary of State Colin Powell declared on March 6, 2001, that "we do plan to engage with North Korea and to pick up where President Clinton and his Administration left off," only to be promptly countermanded by the White House. Two days later, in the presence of Kim Dae Jung, Bush pointedly questioned whether North Korea was honoring its existing agreements and, specifically, whether its "secretive" leader, Kim Jong Il, could be trusted to honor any new agreements. In reality, North Korea had scrupulously observed the inspection provisions of the Agreed Framework, as the IAEA and U.S. ACDA (Arms Control and Disarmament Agency) inspectors had frequently declared. Bush's attack on North Korea, Iraq and Iran as an "Axis of Evil" in his 2002 State of the Union address was followed by increasingly explicit indications during 2002 that the White House goal was not to continue the pursuit of normalized relations with North Korea but, on the contrary, to promote its collapse.

The Framework broke down over the United States persistence that Pyongyang had been pursuing a two-track nuclear weapons program and exporting nuclear technology. One track was a program that was subject of the 1994 Agreement, using the wastes from the Yongbyon reactors to process plutonium for "Nagasaki-type" nuclear devices, and the other was a covert program using uranium enrichment to produce "Hiroshima-type" devices. Assistant Secretary of State James Kelly in October 2002 insisted that officials in Pyongyang had confessed such a program to him. It eventually led the United States in November 2002 to suspend its commitments under the Framework, which in turn prompted North Korea in the following January to withdraw from the NPT and resume its weapons program, while expressing willingness to abandon that program only if the United States and other parties are prepared to return to something like the 1994 Agreement. Pyongyang has also consistently denied the covert uranium enrichment program, saying instead that Kelly misunderstood its statement of the right to such a program as a statement of its possession.

In the next two years to late 2004, Washington signally failed to convince its other partners of this crucial claim of Pyongyang's development of the two-tract nuclear weapons program. Late in 2004, the Second Bush administration launched a renewed diplomatic effort. By this time, the United States manipulation of intelligence on Iraq to justify the war was well known, and suspicion naturally attached to the intelligence on North Korea too. After Michael Green, the senior director for Asia policy at the White House had been dispatched around Asian capitals with "conclusive" evidence in February 2005, the Asahi Shimbun reported that China had at last been persuaded. However, the Chinese Foreign Minister Li Zhaoxing himself intervened to deny it.[23] The Director of South Korea's National Intelligence Service likewise intervened to refute the United States claim.[24] The Washington Post wrote: "U.S. misled allies about nuclear export."[25] Selig Harrison also pronounced the evidence still inconclusive, based on a deliberate favoring of "worst case scenarios."[26]

In addition, the head of the U.S. delegation, Christopher Hill, insisted that North Korea had to abandon not only its weapons programs but also all its civilian, energy-related nuclear programs.[27] However, South Korea, Russia and China were all reported to take the view that North Korea should enjoy its right to a civil, energy program once it returned to the Treaty.[28] As Russia's deputy head of delegation, Valery Yermolov, put it, "Denuclearization does not imply the renunciation of peaceful nuclear programs. We would want this basic notion to be included in the final document."[29] North Korea's claim to the right to develop peaceful nuclear energy is not only one found in the explicit terms of the NPT but is in line with a growing regional commitment to nuclear power generation. Both Japan and South Korea currently produce around 40 per cent of their electricity from nuclear power stations. In China the current proportion is still low, around 2.3 per cent, but massive expansion is planned.[30] The wisdom, economics, and safety of nuclear power generation may be open to serious question, and the provisions of Article 4 of the NPT may deserve revision, but it is scarcely credible for the United States (and Japan) to demand that North Korea alone should be deprived of a right that is generally recognized and is even entrenched in the very treaty that it is being told it must return to.[31]

Furthermore, there were other issues that should be reexamined. Although the Koizumi Government and the Bush Administration were reported to have urged the other participants to include human rights and missile development issues in the 2005 agreements, the reluctance to include any reference to "human rights" on the part of those countries is well known. China in particular views American "human rights" campaigns as a cloak for attempts to achieve regime change and extend U.S. influence, and South Korea has long insisted that the "Sunshine" policy and non-interference is the best way to achieve improvement in human rights matters in North Korea. The interpretation of North Korean missile development may be the more complicated issue. However, the fact is that missile programs are one of the North Korea's few, profitable industrial export items, and Kim Jong Il specifically declared a readiness to scrap his long-range missile programs when meeting with South Korea's Unification Minister in mid-June 2005.[32]

THE DIVERGENCE OF PERSPECTIVES FROM THE U.S. AND CHINA

The divergence between Chinese policy toward the North Korean nuclear issue and the Bush approach has increased steadily since the late 2002, when the United States took a series of steps that culminated in the abrogation of the Agreed Framework. The accusation that North Korea had cheated on the Agreed Framework was used to justify a termination of the oil shipments to the North required under the 1994 agreement.[33] The so-called "second nuclear crisis" with North Korea that has subsequently intensified was welcome to Washington hard-liners, who wanted to shift to a confrontational posture toward Pyongyang that would set the stage for overt efforts to bring about "regime change," or at a minimum, to forestall economic help for North Korea as part of a denuclearization agreement.[34] However, the Washington hard-liners' assumptions were far beyond what the North was capable of. In fact, Pakistan made clear on September 15, 2005, that it provided only 12 prototype centrifuges to Pyongyang, not the thousands of already-manufactured, ready-to-use centrifuges that would be necessary to make weapons-grade uranium. Even before this, in February, 2005, the South Korean National Intelligence Service announced its conclusion that North Korea did not have a weapons-grade uranium capability. China had been more circumspect, but had increasingly signaled that it shares the South Korean assessment. Beijing also questioned whether Pyongyang had so far developed a militarily operational, plutonium-based nuclear weapons capability.

The underlying assumption of the hard-liners approach in the Bush Administration was originally that China would cooperate in bringing about a collapse of the Kim Jong Il regime by putting economic pressure on Pyongyang. China instead began stepping up its economic help to Pyongyang, made clear that it did not want North Korea to collapse, and criticized the United States for hamstringing the six-party nuclear negotiations. In 2003, Chinese Foreign Ministry urged Pyongyang and Washington to revert to the 1994 Agreed Framework as a way out of the festering crisis. Its spokesman Kong Quan stateed, "China believes the situation on the Korean peninsula is at a critical moment, we hope the international community and parties concerned can exercise restraint and calm and stick to the peaceful direction of seeking settlement through dialogue.[35]

The hard-liners then staged a temporary tactical retreat. They permitted Assistant Secretary of State Christopher Hill to launch a serious negotiating initiative with Pyongyang in mid-2005. The result was the Beijing Declaration on September 19, which envisaged the eventual normalization of U.S.-North Korean relations. Immediately thereafter, however, the hard-liners deliberately set out to undermine Hill's effort. The hard-liners have orchestrated a campaign to depict North Korea as a "criminal regime" with which normalized relations are not possible.[36] The base goal of hard-liners is to implement a "regime change" policy. The Bush administration doesn't want a deal that could prolong North Korea's dictatorial regime. "The United States does not want a solution. It wants a North Korean surrender."[37]

This is clearly different from the Chinese priority. The Chinese priority objective, along with Sun Shine and Engagement policies of Kim and Roh Administrations in South Korea respectively, is to stabilize and to some extent to liberalize the existing regime in Pyongyang, a "changing regime" policy, leading to a confederation and eventual reunification of two Koreas. By contrast, the U.S. policy is "regime change." China also welcomed President Roh's expression of explicit disagreement with the United States, declaring that it was "understandable" for Pyongyang to pursue the development of nuclear weapons, "considering the security environment they live in," a reference, in part, to the Bush National Security Doctrine with its explicit threat of preemptive military action against potential U.S. adversaries.[38]

The bottom line of the China's agenda to the North is that the U.S. approach would lead to instability, would not dislodge the regime but would damage the nascent process of market reforms not only in the North but in China and harm Kim's confidence in China.[39] One factor shaping China's preference for the status quo in North Korea through dialogues and economic engagement is the presence of more than `two million ethnic Koreans in the country including an estimated 50,000 refugees and migrants at any one time. Although refugee flows are perceived to present one of the greatest threats to China in case of political or economic collapse in the North, most Chinese analysts and officials are unconcerned about the short-term threat posed by border crossers. Meanwhile, genuine political refugees are now quietly leaving China and being resettled in South Korea without Chinese opposition – sometimes even with its assistance -- so long as they depart without causing embarrassment.

Although China's approach cannot deliver a rapid end to Pyongyang's weapons program, it still tries to be an integral component of any strategy with a chance of reducing the threat of a nuclear North Korea. No other country has the interest and political position in North Korea to facilitate and mediate negotiations. It is also the key to preventing transfers of the North's nuclear materials and other illicit goods, although its ability to do this is limited by logistical and intelligence weaknesses and unwillingness to curb border trade. Over the long-term, Chinese economic interaction with the North may be the best hope for sparking deeper systemic reform and liberalization there.

CHINA'S ECONOMIC ENGAGEMENTS AND INITIATIVES IN NORTH KOREA

While Washington has kept its harsh measures to the North, Chinese engagement and policy towards the North has been dramatically changing since 2003. Chinese investment in North Korea has jumped from $1.3 million in 2003 to $200 million, 2004 and to some $2 billion, 2005.[40] In fact, China is investing in entertainment projects, hotels, restaurants and light industry, and is taking advantage of lower North Korean labor costs and recent changes that have opened the economy to private enterprise. China is also North Korea's biggest trading partner and provides its fuel and much of its food.[41] The North Korean share of trade with China is likely to reach 48 per cent of all North Korean foreign trade. With the investment, China's share is even higher, some 85 per cent.[42] China and North Korea have also signed a 50-year agreement that will give the Chinese border city of Hunchun exclusive rights over the North Korean port of Rajin, according to Chinese and South Korean reports.[43] The deal is seen as a boost to this underdeveloped region of China and to Hunchun in particular which is about 80 km inland on the Tumen River. It also envisages that Hunchun will establish a 5-10 sq km industrial zone in Rajin and for a highway to be built between the two cities.

With floods of cash and a new policy of patience and friendly support, China has quietly penetrated the thick wall surrounding North Korean leader

Kim Jong Il's regime, gaining significant leverage for the first time in one of the world's most closed societies. Beijing believes that such economic engagements and interdependence will bring North Korea back to the table and eventually denuclearize the Korean peninsular. Those growing economic initiatives are frustrating U.S. efforts to impose measures in the context of nuclear disputes. China wants to deal with North Korea's nuclear program "through dialogue and consultation rather than through pressure or sanctions," says Chu Mao Ming, a Chinese spokesman in Washington. Alexandre Mansourov of the Asia-Pacific Center for Security Studies in Honolulu also points out that China has decided to change its strategy on North Korea and implemented their own way to rebuild and reinvent North Korea again.[44] He adds, this strategy has accelerated Kim's attention to the possibility of economic reforms in North Korea, and for the first time, Kim fully embraced Chinese way of economic reforms, as well as KCNA's positive comments about China's opening and reform.[45] Indeed, following Kim's 2006 visit to China, North Korea seems to be behaving nearly like a Chinese "client state," indicating the close nature of the relationship.[46] South Korean media also reported that the impoverished North, whose economy is in shambles, was gearing up to make its border region of Sinuiju a "special economic zone."[47]

"Chinese leaders repeatedly state they want a free and more open North Korea," says Jin Linbo, director of Asia policy at the China Institute of International Studies in Beijing. China is trying to help the North out of a desperate situation. The Chinese think that if North Korea can overcome the hard economic conditions and security matters, it will be harmonious not only with the Asia neighborhood but with the global community. China is trying to open the closed door of the North, while not being in a hurry to resolve the nuclear issue. China believes that dialogues and consultation rather than harsh measures of pressure and sanctions are the only option for everybody, and generate the best interest for China.[48] Unlike the Bush approach that might, China's leaders believe, bring in a worst scenario of nuclear North Korea, China's approach of economic interdependence marks several incentives not only for the strategic stability in the region but for Chinese direct interests. In terms of economic calculation, the approach of economic interdependence can secure the stability of its three economically weak northeastern provinces by incorporating North Korea into their development plans and avoid the economic costs of an explosion on the Korean Peninsula. It can also reduce the financial burden of the bilateral relationship by replacing aid with trade and investment. In terms of strategic concerns, it hopes to sustain the two-Korea status quo so long as it can maintain influence in both and use the North to avoid a situation where a nuclear North Korea leads Japan and/or Taiwan to become nuclear powers.

Indeed, North Korea said on October 8, 2006, it had performed its first nuclear weapons test. Now is the most critical time for policy makers to reexamine the potential consequences of nuclear North Korea, while rescrutinizing two different approaches, the hawkish U.S. approach or the dovish Chinese approach.

Notes

[1] Barbara Slavin, "China, U.S. come at N. Korea from different angles," USA Today, June 2, 2005, p. A 3; Robert Marquand, "China's New North Korea Agenda: Economic reform trumps anti-nuclear message," The Christian Science Monitor, March 1, 2006, p. A 3, and Japan Focus, March 19, 2005; Andrei Lankov, "China raises its stake in North Korea," ChoSun Ilbo, December 17, 2005, p. A 1.

[2] Kim Jong Il's entourage to China to discuss the crisis over Pyongyang's nuclear-weapons programs and economic cooperation with China included senior regime figures such as Vice Marshal Kim Yong-chun, the chief of the general staff of the Korean People's Army (KPA) and a member of the powerful National Defense Commission (NDC); Yon Hyong-muk, vice chairman of the NDC; Prime Minister Pak Pong-ju; and First Vice Foreign Minister Kang Sok-ju. About 40 other economic, diplomatic, and security officials were part of the North Korean delegation.

[3] "China and Socialism," Korean Central News Agency (KCNA), January 22, 2001, p. A 1.

[4] "Our Leader's Visit to China," KCNA, January 18, 2006, p. A 1.

[5] "China and North Korea: Comrades forever?" Asia Report N-112, International Crisis Group, February 1, 2006. http://www.reliefweb.int/rw/RWB.NSF/db900SID/KHII-6LM53K?OpenDocument

[6] Denny Roy, "China and Nuclear Nonproliferation," Asia-Pacific Center for Security Studies, Honolulu, HI, February, 2006
http://www.apcss.org/graphics/graphics_research.htm

[7] Since August 2003, China has hosted the "Six-Sided Talks" with the United States, Russia, Japan, and North and South Koreas. The first round was held in August 2003, the second round in February 2004, the third round in June 2004, the fourth round in July, August and September 2005, and the fifth round in November 2005.

[8] For more details of the debates between the hawkish and the dovish arguments, see Victor D. Cha, "Korea's Place in the Axis," Foreign Affairs, vol. 81 n. 3 (May/June 2002), pp. 79–92; V. Cha and D. Kang, Nuclear North Korea: A Debate on Engagement Strategies (New York: Columbia University Press, 2003); Gavan McCormack, Target North Korea (New York: Nation Books, 2004); Michael O'Hanlon and Mike Mochizuki, Crisis on the Korean Peninsula (New York: McGraw-Hill, 2003).

[9] Op-ed page, "The Present and Future of the Six-Sided Talks," Hangeoyrei Shinmun, February 18, 2004, p. 12.

[10] After Carter's meeting with Kim Il Sung, the United States and North Korea signed the Agreed Framework in Geneva, 2004. More details on this issue will be presented later in this chapter.

[11] Op-ed page, "Our Rights," KCNA, September 20, 2005, p. 12

[12] David Kang, "North Korea's Nuclear Program," Washing Post, May 4, 2005, p. A. 3.

[13] O'Hanlon and Mochizuki, Crisis on the Korean Peninsula, 2003.

[14] David Kang, "North Korea's quest for economic and military security," in B.C. Koh, ed., North Korea and the World: Explaining Pyongyang's Foreign Policy (Seoul: Kyungnam University Press, 2005).

[15] Although South Korea is increasing investment in North Korea, setting up factories in a special industrial zone near the border between the two countries, it is inhibited by restrictions on the export of machinery without U.S. content.

[16] Op-ed page, "The Exchange of the North and the South," Hangeoyrei Shinmun, August 20, 2006, p. 12.

[17] The nature of two protagonists is as asymmetrical as any two countries could be, on one side the greatest military and industrial power in history and on the other one of the world's poorest and most isolated small states.

[18] Hamish McDonald, "US backs away from another regime change," Sydney Morning Herald, July 27, 2005, p. A 5.

[19] "South Korea, Russia wants diplomatic push, China blames US Policy," Agence France-Presse, September 1, 2003.

[20] On September 19, 2005, as the conclusion of the fourth round, negotiators from all six sides announced that they had finally reached a preliminary agreement. Highlights of the agreement include: 1) North Korea agreeing to abandon all nuclear weapons and nuclear programs; 2) the United States and South Korea declaring they have no nuclear weapons on the Korean Peninsula; 3) the United States has no intention of attacking and/or invading North Korea; 4) Japan and the United States will work to normalize ties with North Korea.

[21] Thus forfeiting a right described in Article 4 of the NPT as "inalienable," one that the United States was not disputing on the part of Iran

[22] The policy of engagement with North Korea during Kim Dae Jung Administration was called the Sunshine Policy. In June 2000, he participated in the first North-South presidential summit with North Korea's leader Kim Jong Il, talks for which he won the Nobel Peace Prize.

[23] Selig Harrison, "Crafting Intelligence: Iraq, North Korea, and the Road to War," Japan Focus, March 15, 2005, http://www.japanfocus.org/products/details/1915; S. Harrison, "Crafting Intelligence,"The Asahi Shimbun, February 28, 2005, p. A 7.

[24] Harrison, "Crafting Intelligence: Iraq, North Korea, and the Road to War," 2005.

[25] "The U.S. and North Korean Crisis," The Washington Post, March 20, 2005, p. A 5.

[26] Selig Harrison, "Did North Korea cheat?" Foreign Affairs, January-February 2005, pp. 87-93.

[27] "N.K has right to peaceful nuclear use," The Korea Herald, August 12, 2005, p. A 1.

[28] Yu Yoshitake, "North Korea and Nuclear Crisis," Asahi shimbun, July 26, 2005, p. A 3.

[29] Yu Yoshitake, "6-way talks split on final wording," Asahi shimbun. August 1, 2005, p. A 5. South Korea's Unification Minister and head of its National Security Council, Chung Dong-young, also made clear Seoul's position that North Korea was entitled to use nuclear energy for peaceful purposes. "N.K has right to peaceful nuclear use: Chung," Korea Herald, August 12, 2005, p. A 1.

[30] China currently has six nuclear power plants, with nine operating sets in operation and two under construction. Its plans to construct 30 new reactors between 2005 and 2020, and to raise the nuclear component of the national grid from its current 2.3 per cent to 4 per cent (from 8,700 MW to 36,000 MW). "China accelerates nuclear energy development," *People's Daily* Online, 27 September 2004, http://www.people.com.cn/english, and "Nuclear power industry faces development opportunity," China Economic News, 11 May 2005, p. B 1.

[31] Article IV of the treaty says: 1). Nothing in this Treaty shall be interpreted as affecting the inalienable right of all the Parties to the Treaty to develop research, production and use of nuclear energy for peaceful purposes without discrimination and in conformity with Articles I and II of this Treaty; 2). All the Parties to the Treaty undertake to facilitate, and have the right to participate in, the fullest possible exchange of equipment, materials and scientific and technological information for the peaceful uses of nuclear energy. Parties to the Treaty in a position to do so shall also co-operate in contributing alone or together with other States or international organizations to the further development of the applications of nuclear energy for peaceful purposes, especially in the territories of non-nuclear-weapon States Party to the Treaty, with due consideration for

the   needs   of   the   developing   areas   of   the   world.   See,
http://www.un.org/events/npt2005/npttreaty.html.

[32] J. Glansbeek, "In the Conflict with North Korea," *Freedom Socialist*, vol. 24, n. 1, pp
21-29, http://www.socialism.com/fsarticles/vol24no1/korea.html.

[33] Only sketchy, inconclusive evidence in support of this assessment was presented to
South Korean intelligence officials during intelligence exchanges with the CIA both
before and after the publication of this assessment. However, the Bush Administration
has yet to present evidence sufficient to establish that a weapons-grade uranium
enrichment program exists. See for more details, .Selig Harrison, "The New Face of the
South Korea-U.S. alliance and the North Korea Question," *The Korea Policy Review*,
February 2006, http://www.korea-is-one.org/article.php3?id_article=2459.

[34] Among them within the administration include David Addington, Vice-President
Cheney's Chief of Staff; J.W. Crouch, Deputy National Security Adviser, and Robert
Joseph, John Bolton's successor as Undersecretary of State for Arms Control and
National Security.

[35] King Quan, "China urges N. Korea, US to revert to the 1994 accord"
http://www.dawn.com/2003/07/18/top17.htm

[36] The cutting edge of this campaign has been the crackdown on a Macau bank linked to
alleged North Korean counterfeiting and drug trafficking. The hard-liners in Washington
accused North Korea as the only government in the world today that can be identified as
being actively involved in directing crime as a central part of its national economic
strategy and foreign policy.

[37] Hamm Taik-young, "A way of reaching agreement: The United States and North
Korea," ChoSun Ilbo, June 18, 2005, p. A 5.

[38] President Roh's speech during the Asia-Pacific Economic Cooperative (APEC)
meeting, November 2004, Los Angeles.

[39] David Shambaugh, "China and the Korean Peninsula: Playing for the Long Term,"
Washington Quarterly, vol. 26 (spring 2003), pp. 43–56.

[40] Slavin, "China, U.S. come at N. Korea from different angles," 2005; Marquand,
"China's New North Korea Agenda: Economic reform trumps anti-nuclear message,"
2006.

[41] Slavin, "China, U.S. come at N. Korea from different angles," 2005, p. A 3.

[42] Lankov, "China raises its stake in North Korea," 2005, p. A 1; Annual Report "North
Korean Economy," Korea Trade-Investment Promotion Agency (KOTRA), March, 2006.

[43] Michael Rank, "China-NK relations, Economic policy", Jung Ahng Daily, September
23, 2005, p. A 4.

[44] Alexandre Mansourov, "Bytes and Bullets: Information Technology and Revolution
and National Security on the Korean Peninsular," The Asia-Pacific Center for Security
Studies, 2005, http://www.apcss.org/graphics/graphics_research.htm.

[45] "Our Leader's Visit to China," Korean Central News Agency (KCNA), January 18,
2006, p. A 1.; Mansourov, "Bytes and Bullets: Information Technology and Revolution
and National Security on the Korean Peninsular," 2005.

[46] Marquand, "China's New North Korea Agenda: Economic reform trumps anti-nuclear
message," 2006, p. A 3.

[47] Op-ed page, "New Road for North Korea," Hangeoyrei Shinmun, January 20, 2006, p.
12.

[48] There is another reason that China rejects economic sanctions on North Korea. It fears
that sanctions would provoke an economic collapse in North Korea that would send an
exodus of refugees into China. On this issue, see "The Invisible Exodus: North Koreans
in the People's Republic of China," Human Rights Watch, vol. 14, n. 8 (c), 2002.
http://www.hrw.org/reports/2002/northkorea/

Chapter 8

China's Middle East Policy and Its Implications for US-China Relations

Zhiqun Zhu

INTRODUCION

In a talk given at Yale University, *The New York Times* columnist Thomas L. Friedman succinctly captured two major objectives of Chinese foreign policy in the 21st century: unifying with Taiwan and looking for oil.[1] Both issues are of great concern to the United States. In recent years, China and the United States have found more common ground on the question of Taiwan, traditionally the most difficult and explosive issue between the two powers. With both China and the United States opposing *de jure* Taiwanese independence, the independence movement is unlikely to go very far in Taiwan, thus greatly easing tension between the United States and China.[2] But China's hunger for energy and its active hunt for oil are already creating a new and perhaps a more intractable problem between the two great powers.

Though China's current consumption of about 6 million barrels of oil per day is less than one-third of America's usage of about 20 million barrels per day, as its economy continues to grow at a high rate, China is becoming increasingly thirsty for energy from abroad. In 2003 China supplanted Japan to become the second largest oil consumer in the world after the United States. The Daqing oilfield in Northeast China, which had produced enough oil to keep China self-sufficient after it was discovered in 1959, had become mature and unable to satisfy domestic needs. Since China became an oil importer in 1993, Chinese leaders have considered developing relations with oil rich countries, including the Middle East oil producers, to be a diplomatic priority.

China's foreign policy has become multidimensional since the end of the 1990s.[3] In addition to its strategic focus on great power relations and its traditional emphasis on relations with Asian neighbors, Chinese diplomatic activities have been expanded to Latin America, Africa and the Middle East. Aware of its vulnerability on the energy front, China has attempted to diversify sources of energy supply as much as possible. China has oil and other energy deals with many energy rich countries around the world such as Canada, Mexico, Russia, Indonesia, Angola, Nigeria, Saudi Arabia, Sudan, Iran, Kazakhstan, Turkmenistan, Libya, Myanmar, and Venezuela. What concerns the United States most is that China not only seems to be competing with the United States for energy around the world, but is cozying up to some of the "problem states" such as Sudan and Venezuela, which may undermine America's global interests.

This chapter focuses on China's foreign policy towards the Middle East and explores its impact on US-China relations. The study contends that China's policy has largely been driven by economic interests so far. But with its growing power, China will expand its political, diplomatic and cultural influence in the region. Though China and the United States have their own interests in the Middle East, the two countries also share much common ground in the region such as fighting against terror, maintaining oil security, and promoting peaceful resolution of the Arab-Israel conflict. The challenge for China and the United States is how to turn the Middle East into another venue for cooperation in their joint efforts to advance international peace and prosperity as well as their own political and economic interests.

CHINA'S FOREIGN POLICY TOWARD THE MIDDLE EAST

With growing political and economic power, Chinese foreign policy is undergoing some significant transformation. As Wu Jianmin, a senior diplomat and president of the China Foreign Affairs University has observed, China is moving from "responsive diplomacy" (*fanying shi waijiao*) to "proactive diplomacy" (*zhudong shi waijiao*).[4] The Middle East, once considered too distant for any significant economic and political investments, has become a newfound location to implement key objectives of China's new multidimensional foreign policy.

Chinese-Middle Eastern relationship has experienced many changes since 1949. By the late 1990s, it had reached the point that not knowing China's Middle East policies means not understanding Chinese diplomacy as a whole. Nor can one understand the Middle East without knowledge of that region's relations with China.[5] China's economic and political activities in the Middle East are part of its new global diplomacy. China's current policy towards the Middle East is largely driven by its need for economic and military modernizations. Its overriding foreign policy objective in the region is to secure energy to fuel domestic growth.

Indeed, a major pillar of China's Middle East policy is seeking oil. Thirst for oil has made China an active player in oil-rich regions. More than 45% of China's oil imports were estimated to come from the Middle East in 2004.[6] Top three suppliers of crude oil to China are Saudi Arabia, Oman, and Iran. Iran alone already accounts for about 11% of China's oil imports, and in October 2004, Sinopec, China's state-controlled petroleum and chemical corporation, signed an agreement with Iran that could be worth as much as $70 billion—

China's biggest energy deal yet with any major OPEC producer. China also committed to develop the giant Yadavaran oil field in Iran and buy 250 million tons of liquefied natural gas over the next 30 years; in return, Iran agreed to export to China 150,000 barrels of oil per day, at market prices, for 25 years.[7]

China's relations with Saudi Arabia, the largest oil producer, are strong. Sino-Saudi oil cooperation has been expanding in recent years, and Saudi Oil Minister Ali al-Naimi has made at least six trips to China in 2004 and 2005.[8] King Abdullah bin abdul-Aziz's first official visit abroad was to Asia in January 2006 since he succeeded to the throne following the death of his half-brother, King Fahd, in August 2005, and his first stop was China. It was also the first visit to China by a Saudi head of state since the two countries established diplomatic links in 1990.

An oil refining project jointly invested by Saudi Arabian and Chinese companies has been put into production in Saudi Arabia as of the beginning of 2006. State oil firm Saudi Aramco is already in talks over joint refinery projects in China to deal with heavier oil that is more difficult to refine.[9] China imports about 450,000 barrels of oil from Saudi Arabia daily, accounting for 14 percent of its overall oil import. Saudi-Chinese trade exchange reached $14.5 billion in the first 11 months of 2005.[10] During the Saudi King's Beijing visit in January 2006, the two countries signed an agreement on oil, natural gas and mineral cooperation, in which Saudi Arabia promised to increase the annual oil and gas exports to China by 39%. As part of the agreement, a 100-million-ton crude oil storage facility is planned for construction in China's Hainan province.[11]

From Saudi Arabia's perspective, China could be used as a valuable source of support as Riyadh continues on a path of cautious and selective economic liberalization while seeking to deflect US pressure in the area of political reform. The sometimes strained Saudi-US relations provide the opportunity for China to consolidate its relations with the Saudi leadership. Though China and Saudi Arabia are likely to expand their ties to other areas such as education, investment, anti-terrorism, and military cooperation, Saudi Arabia will probably attempt to strike a balance between the United States and China and avoid compromising US interests to please China in the near future.

China has also invested heavily in Sudan's oil industry. Since 2000, China has developed several oil fields, built a 930-mile (1,512 kilometer) pipeline, a refinery and a port. By far, Sudan represents one of China's largest overseas investments.[12] Chinese companies have been pumping crude oil from oilfields in Sudan, sending it through the Chinese-made pipeline to the Red Sea, where tankers wait to ferry it to China's industrial centers. Oil from Sudan makes up one-tenth of all of China's imported oil.[13]

China views the Middle East not only in terms of its value as a source of oil but also in the context of its huge potential as an oil services market and trade partner. By 2001, China had signed almost 3,000 contracts with all six Gulf Cooperation Council states for labor services worth $2.7 billion. And in July 2004, the six Gulf Cooperation Council finance ministers visited China where they signed a "Framework Agreement on Economic, Trade, Investment, and

Technological Cooperation" with China and agreed to negotiate a China-Gulf Cooperation Council free trade zone.[14]

Comparatively speaking, the Middle East is more important to China than to the United States as a source of oil supply. Three of the top four suppliers of oil to the United States are in the Western Hemisphere (Canada, Mexico, and Venezuela), which currently comprise over 48% of total US petroleum imports, and Saudi Arabia only supplies about 8% of total US demand.[15] The Middle East as a region has been China's largest supplier of oil. In 1998 and 1999, for example, the import from there accounted for about 60% of the total Chinese imports,[16] though since 2000 China has attempted to diversify sources of energy and has increased imports from other regions.

A second pillar of China's Middle East policy is its arms trade with countries in the region. Chinese weapons started to enter the Middle Eastern market as early as the 1970s with major buyers in Egypt, Iraq, Iran, Saudi Arabia, and Sudan. That China is both the recipient of advanced weapons from Israel and an alleged proliferator of weapons to the Middle East creates serious security challenges to the United States and frustrates global nonproliferation efforts.

Israel has been China's second largest weapons supplier next only to Russia. China's interest in Israel's, and through it, America's weapons is always high. Despite its small size, Israel is an important investor in Chinese development projects and supplier of high-technology weapons. Former Prime Minister Benjamin Netanyahu once told Chinese visitors that "Israeli know-how is more valuable than Arab oil."[17]

In the Israeli-Palestinian conflict, China has taken a more balanced position now than its pro-Palestine stand in the past. Israeli-Chinese relations started relatively well at the very beginning. The Chinese press welcomed the establishment of the state of Israel in 1948, and Israel was one of the very first countries to recognize the PRC after the latter's founding in 1949. The two countries would have established diplomatic relations in the early 1950s if Israel had not been pressured by the United States and China had not readjusted its foreign policy following the Bandung Conference of Asian and African states.[18] Since the mid-1950s, the PRC had taken a strongly anti-Israel stance. It eschewed bilateral contacts with "the Zionist entity". Even trade with Israel was banned. After the Suez Canal crisis, Beijing denounced Israel as "the tool of imperialist policies," and all contacts between the two countries came to an end.[19]

China's policy re-orientation towards Israel since the mid-1980s has clearly been driven by realism and pragmatism associated with its opening door policy. An emerging superpower and an increasingly important player in the region, China's attitude toward the Israeli-Palestinian issue may influence or complicate the final resolution of the issue. China both supports the concept of "land for peace" and recognizes the need for an independent Palestinian state. It also emphasizes the importance of guaranteeing Israel's security, a position the Chinese government has enunciated since the early 1990s.[20]

After Hamas, a militant Islamic group, swept to victory over the long-dominant Fatah party in the January 2006 parliamentary elections in Palestine, Chinese official response was mild compared to strong statements from the United States and EU countries that condemned Hamas' anti-Israel stance and demanded it to disarm. Consistent with its balanced approach, Chinese Foreign Ministry issued a statement that "welcomes the smooth completion of the election of the Palestinian Legislative Council"; meanwhile, China hopes "all Palestinian factions will maintain unity and solve the dispute with Israel through peaceful negotiations and political means."[21]

China-Israel relations have been warming up since the two countries established diplomatic relations in 1992.[22] Trade volume kept two-digit growth since 2000. By 2004, Israel's trade with China totaled $2.63 billion.[23] China plays a significant role in the contracted engineering market in the Middle East, with constructed projects valued at more than $1 billion, and more than 10,000 Chinese holding work permits in Israel's construction and agricultural sectors.[24]

High-level visits are often exchanged. Every Israeli president since Chaim Herzog, as well as prime ministers Yitzhak Rabin and Benjamin Netanyahu, has visited China. In June 2004, Israel's then deputy prime minister Ehud Olmert visited Beijing. Chinese President Jiang Zemin and Vice Premier Qian Qichen visited Israel in 2000. In December 2004, Chinese state councilor and former foreign minister Tang Jiaxuan visited Israel.

To obtain hi-technology weapons from Israel is not the only incentive for China to develop its relations with the Jewish state. Like many other countries, China may figure that good relations with Israel would help its relations with the United States, given the special and close ties between Israel and the United States.

China's record in weapons proliferation in the Middle East is mixed. Since China was found to have delivered 36 CSS-2 missiles and nine launchers to Saudi Arabia in 1988, there has been no documented evidence of transactions of a similar nature. Nor have there been credible reports of sales by China of significant quantities of conventional arms to Saudi Arabia, Iraq, Iran or other countries since then. But there are still occasional reports in Western media of weapons or technology sales and transfers to the region by Chinese companies, though these activities may have not been authorized by the Chinese government.[25]

It is believed that China remains Sudan's largest supplier of arms, according to a former Sudan government minister. Chinese-made tanks, fighter planes, bombers, helicopters, machine guns and rocket-propelled grenades have intensified Sudan's two-decade-old North-South civil war.[26]

China's political and military ties with Egypt are also solid. Sino-Egyptian cooperation extends to military affairs in the form of regular high-level contacts between Beijing and Cairo. In response to Israel's powerful nuclear arsenal and Iran's weapons program, Egypt is often cited as a likely candidate to pursue its own nuclear option down the road. Egypt reportedly approached China and Russia in 2002 for assistance in the development of a nuclear reactor in Alexandria. China's history of weapons proliferation and nuclear cooperation in the region may portend closer ties with Egypt in this area, should Egypt decides on a course of action.[27]

As a footnote, Taiwan is reportedly considering selling weapons to the United Arab Emirates (UAE). The UAE has official relations with the PRC. Its diplomatic flirtation with Taiwan is not only irritating to Beijing but will also complicate the non-proliferation efforts in the region.[28]

A third pillar of China's Middle East policy is fighting against separatism linked to the Middle East. While the United States has focused on weeding out global terrorist networks such as Al Qaeda in the Middle East, China is more interested in maintaining security by defeating radical separatists within its borders.

China has serious security concerns along its northwestern border. China's political and intelligence support for US-led war against the Taliban after the 9/11 terrorist attacks is part of its own efforts to seek international and regional cooperation to crush the separatist movement in the western Xinjiang autonomous region. China shares a 20-mile long border with Afghanistan. The 7 to 10 million Uighurs in Xinjiang are Muslims and have preserved a distinct, non-Chinese ethnic identity. Radical separatists in Xinjiang have sparked riots, assassinations, and bombings since 1990. The East Turkestan Islamic Movement has sought to establish an Islamic Republic of East Turkestan in Xinjiang. According to Chinese official sources, between 1990 and 2001, East Turkestan terrorist groups staged more than 200 attacks in Xinjiang, killing 162 people, including local community leaders and religious personnel.[29] The Chinese government seeks diplomatic support from Muslim countries in the Middle East to cut off any financial, political, or other support for these extremist groups. One major aim of the Shanghai Cooperation Organization is also to stop terrorism from infiltrating into China from Central Asia and the Middle East.[30] The US Department of State eventually labeled the East Turkestan Movement a terrorist group in 2002, but many in and outside the Bush administration are concerned that China may tighten its ethnic policies in Xinjiang and other restive regions in the name of fighting against terrorism and separatism.

China has also been involved in the Middle East in other aspects. Beijing has become politically and diplomatically more active and assertive in the 21st century. In September 2002, Chinese Foreign Ministry declared to appoint a special envoy to the Middle East "at the request of several Arab states."[31] In May 2004, China's UN mission raised a proposal to enhance the Iraqi government's real power by setting a date for a US military withdrawal. Russia, France, and Germany supported China's proposal, which was reflected in the final text of UN Security Council Resolution 1546. For China watchers, Beijing's actions are highly significant because China's Middle East policy had been passive in the past and China seldom raises its own proposals on issues relating to the Middle East.[32]

There is a clear trend of cultural, religious, educational, and other forms of exchanges between China and the Middle East. Chinese *hajj* pilgrims have traveled to Saudi Arabia every year since 1955; their number regularly exceeded 6,000 in the 1990s, and by 2003 had ballooned to over 10,000.[33]

China's growing influence in the Middle East is unmistakably evident. In Egypt, the most populous Arab country and a political and cultural hub of the Arab world, China is considered a trusted friend and has been invited to participate in the joint development of the Suez Special Economic Zone.[34]

Modern Sino-Egyptian relations were initiated by President Gamal Abdel Nasser and Premier Zhou Enlai during the historic 1955 Afro-Asian Conference in Bandung, Indonesia. To a large extent, Egypt and China have become political and economic allies today. Sino-Egyptian trade was expected to reach $2billion by the end of 2005.[35] China supports Egypt's strong interest in assuming the role of representing Africa and the Middle East alongside the five permanent members of the UN Security Council. Cultural and educational exchanges are robust. China and Egypt have agreed to establish the Egyptian Chinese University in Cairo, the first Chinese university in the Middle East.[36] Like Saudi Arabia, Egypt resents growing American pressure to implement democratic reforms and criticism of its human rights record. And like Saudi Arabia, Egypt finds moral and political support from China on these issues.

China has also entered the Middle Eastern financial market. The Bank of China (BOC), China's central bank, was approved by the Bahrain authority to set up a branch in Bahrain in 2004, the BOC's first overseas branch in the Middle East region.[37]

APPRAISAL

According to China's own calculation, 94% of its energy need is still met by domestic supply as of 2005. Only 6% of its energy need is imported, and 67% of China's energy supply is still from coal burning.[38] Currently China is estimated to import close to 3 million barrels of oil a day.[39]

However, with the continued modernization of Chinese economy and its energy sector and rising standards of living of ordinary Chinese, the demand for oil, gas and other types of energy is expected to increase tremendously. In 2004 and 2005, 35% of the increment in the world's consumption of petroleum had been China's, and China's automobile population is expected to be the world's second largest market within a decade.[40] According to Andy Xie, chief economist at Morgan Stanley Asia, China's daily consumption of oil was expected to reach 7 million barrels by the end of 2005, and 14 million barrels over the next decade, bringing Chinese oil consumption to US and European levels.[41] China may decide to produce more energy domestically, but its domestic production capacity is outdated and limited. It will have to import more from other parts of the world. According to some analysis, China has two prevailing oil and gas strategies in the first two decades of the 21st century: increasing Middle East oil imports, and purchasing foreign oil properties.[42] This helps explain why Chinese companies are purchasing oil assets globally, including the China National Offshore Oil Corporation (CNOOC)'s failed bid to buy the California-based oil company Unocal in the summer of 2005.[43]

The Middle East as a whole has become one of China's major trading partners. Being so late in entering the region—and having less to offer in economic or technological terms than the United States, Russia, Japan, and Europe—China must go after marginal or risky markets including Iran, Iraq, and Sudan where others cannot or will not go, supplying customers no one else will service with goods no one else will sell them.[44] For example, the China-Iran military relationship began in the Iran-Iraq war in the 1980s, when Iran was desperate for any supplies given US sanctions and Soviet reluctance to provide weapons. For China Iran's pariah status was an opportunity to exploit a market that would otherwise not exist. China's arms sales to Iran continued until 1997 when Chinese President Jiang Zemin visited the United States and pledged to stop any military sales to Iran. China's arms purchase from Israel and its alleged weapons sales to Middle Eastern countries are a constant irritant for the United States. China's growing presence in the region has become a source of concern for American policy makers.

Nevertheless, China's influence in the Middle East is still limited and is overwhelmed by America's stronger ties with key players in the region. For example, in 2000, Israel bowed to US pressure and cancelled its plan to sell $1 billion worth of Phalcon early warning planes to China. For Israel, its relations with the United States are still more important than any other set of relations Israel has. Israel-US relations are built upon shared democratic values and common strategic interests. But in the future, as Chinese-Israeli relations continue to strengthen, Israel risks finding itself between a rock and a hard place. And as some have suggested, for its own interests Israel should examine the possibility of contributing to the reduction of misunderstandings between China and the United States.[45]

US war in Iraq meant that China lost supplies from a 26-year oil production field contract it had signed with the Baghdad government in 1997.[46] Financial and technical shortages restrict China from building an ocean-going navy to defend its sea-lanes to the Middle East. China remains uncomfortably dependent on US naval power to ensure the safety of its tankers to and from the Middle East.

As China continues to expand economic and diplomatic activities in the Middle East, Middle Eastern countries expect China to play a bigger role in local issues. Increasingly Middle Eastern countries are beginning to turn to China for help in conflict resolution. For example, Egyptian assistant Foreign Minister Ezzat Saad said that "China has become very much involved in the Middle East process and (Egypt) expects it to play a more active role."[47] Israeli President Moshe Katsav has also remarked that China has very good relations with both Israel and the Arab world. It can contribute positively to the relations between Israel and the Arab world.[48]

IMPLICATIONS FOR US-CHINA RELATIONS

On the one hand, China wants a peaceful and stable Middle East to ensure a steady source of oil and to avoid entanglement in regional conflict. It focuses on trade and economic development and does not intend to undermine US interests in the region. On the other hand, China does not want to give up lucrative relationships with Iran, Sudan and Iraq, or see a region so dominated by the United States that there is no room for a Chinese economic or diplomatic role. It is this ambivalent attitude that contributes to the complication of US-China relations.

Huge energy demand is drawing China into deeper involvement in politically volatile regions around the world. From the US perspective, China's foray into traditional America's spheres of influence—the Middle East, Latin America, and Africa—is worrisome, to say the least. Already, many conservative forces in the United States are debating over what to do about this new type of "China threat". Strategically speaking, the United States is deeply uncomfortable with China's growing activities in regions where the United States has enjoyed a near monopoly on international influence since the end of the Cold War. China's energy deals and good relations with "pariah states" such as Sudan have complicated US efforts to stop what it calls a state-sponsored genocide in the Darfur region of the largest country in Africa.

However, China is also trying not to confront the United States directly in the region. For example, despite its long-standing opposition, along with Russia's and India's, to UN sanctions on Iran for Iran's alleged nuclear program, China agreed with other four permanent members of the UN Security Council and Germany to report Iran to the Security Council over its nuclear program when Iran failed to account for its alleged nuclear activities to the International Atomic Energy Agency by March 2006.[49] This is encouraging for the United States in its efforts to prevent nuclear proliferation.

Should the United States be concerned about China's activities in the Middle East? When the oil prices have skyrocketed in recent years and the United States has an unfinished business of fighting against terrorism in the region, China's involvement in the region, especially its close relations with countries hostile to America, may harm US interests. Should the United States become paranoid and attempt to drive China out of the Middle East? The answer is no. And if it chose to do so, it would be unlikely to succeed since no country in the region or elsewhere is going to join the United States in its effort.

Despite Washington's concerns over China's outreach to the Middle East, the Untied States and China share several key interests in the region: seeking energy security, opposing terrorism, and supporting Arab-Israeli peace. And most importantly, both countries support a stable Middle East where their economic and strategic interests can be protected. The US-Chinese competition is clearly not built on the zero-sum model of the US-Soviet conflict during the Cold War. Today, China and the United States depend on each other for economic prosperity and international security. This interdependent relationship compels them to seek cooperation, not conflict.

Is there anything the United States can do to alleviate its own concerns and help overcome the energy shortage in China? Absolutely. For one thing, the United States can help China become more energy efficient. If China used its energy more efficiently, it would have less need to obtain oil from countries that the United States wishes to contain. The US-China Energy Efficiency Steering Committee was established as a result of the Protocol for Cooperation in the Fields of Energy Efficiency and Renewable Energy Technology Development and Utilization signed in February 1995 between US Department of Energy and China's State Science and Technology Commission. Such efforts should further be promoted.

China is already a key player in the global energy equation. The growing threat of United Nations sanctions on Sudan and Iran, which between them supply some 20 percent of China's oil imports, puts Beijing in an awkward situation of having to choose between safeguarding its economic interests and protecting the country's international image. If oil from Iran and Sudan were cut off by sanctions, China would have to increase its demand on other overseas suppliers and look for oil elsewhere. The United States may well take a more active step to collaborate with China in developing alternative energies. Nuclear energy and liquefied natural gas are two obvious options. With its advanced technology, the United States is well positioned to provide assistance to China in the fields of new energy and environmental protection. In his 2006 State of the Union address, President George Bush also proposed to develop alternative energy sources and wean America from oil addiction. The two countries should expand their cooperation on energy issues.

China's global hunt for energy is clearly driven by its domestic growth needs. At present its activities in the Middle East are motivated by economic goals rather than political ambitions. There is no evidence that China is engaged in a strategic competition with the United States in the Middle East now. However, if its key interests are undermined by the United States, China may be forced to become more aggressive in its foreign policy such as being more active in its pursuit of oil from Iran and Sudan, which may pose a more serious challenge for the United States. CNOOC's bid to acquire Unocal in 2005, which eventually failed with strong opposition from US Congress, feeds the fear that the United States does not allow China equal and reliable access to the world oil market. The United States has to work with China to give it a sense of energy security and shared interests in a stable energy market.

China's thirst for energy is also a common development problem for the international community. Even without China, energy demands from India and other emerging markets are expected to jump up drastically in the next few decades. So for the United States and the international community, how to help developing countries reduce the cost of modernization and improve development efficiency has become a serious challenge.

CONCLUSION

The era of China's passive role in the Middle East is over. China's diplomatic and economic efforts in the Middle East are relatively successful, especially since it maintains good relations with virtually every country in the region, ranging from America's close allies such as Israel, Saudi Arabia and

Turkey to intensely anti-American countries such as Iran, Sudan and Libya. Though China's efforts in the region are commercially driven, it has the potential to play a much larger political role.

From the US perspective, China's involvement in the Middle Eastern political economy may have some negative and destabilizing effects. But the United States and China share many common goals in the region and there are prospects for cooperation between them on energy, peace, religion, and other issues in the region. Most significantly, the two countries have a common interest in the stability of the Middle East. Hardly any evidence shows that China is engaged in a strategic competition with the United States in the region. It is pre-mature to declare that the Middle East will become a new battleground for China and the United States to compete for influence and control.

US-China relations are arguably the most important bilateral relations in the 21st century. Many international and regional problems cannot be solved without cooperation between the two great powers. For the United States, paranoia about a coming China threat and a misguided policy based on this assumption will be the wrong choice.

China is already heavily involved in the Middle Eastern political economy. The US strategic calculations in the Middle East will have to take Chinese interests into consideration now. It is impossible for the United States to exclude or isolate China from the region. What the United States can do now is to actively engage China, address China's legitimate needs and concerns, and work together with other powers to ensure a peaceful and responsible China in the future. Only by doing so can the two countries establish a constructive relationship and lay a solid foundation for future cooperation in international and regional affairs, including the Middle East issue.

Notes

[1] Thomas L. Friedman, "The World is Flat," a talk given at Yale University, April 15, 2005.

[2] Some scholars believe that due to political developments in Taiwan in recent years, Taiwanese independence movement has lost its momentum. See Robert S. Ross, "Taiwan's Fading Independence Movement," *Foreign Affairs,* March/April 2006.

[3] For a discussion of the transformation of Chinese foreign policy, see Evan S. Medeiros and M. Taylor Fravel, "China's New Diplomacy," *Foreign Affairs*, Vol. 82, No. 6 (November/December 2003): pp. 22-35. Also David Shambaugh, "China Engages Asia: Reshaping the Regional Order," *International Security,* Vol. 29, No. 3 (Winter 2004/2005): pp. 64-99.

[4] *China Youth Daily (Zhongguo Qingnian Bao),* February 18, 2004, http://www.cyol.net

[5] For a historical survey of US-Middle East relations since 1949, see Guang Pan, "China's Success in the Middle East," *Middle East Quarterly,* December 1997, accessed from the Middle East Forum website at http://www.meforum.org/article/373

[6] David Zweig and Bi Jianhai, "China's Global Hunt for Energy," *Foreign Affairs* Vol. 84, No. 5 (September/October 2005), p.28.

[7] Ibid, pp. 28-9.

[8]John Calabrese, "Saudi Arabia and China Extend Ties Beyond Oil," *China Brief,* Vol. V, Issue 20, The Jamestown Foundation, September 27, 2005, pp. 3-4.

[9]"Saudi Arabia Seeks Big Business From Asia Tour," *Reuters,* January 20, 2006.

[10]"Saudi Arabian Ambassador Designate on King Abdullah's Coming China Trip," *Xinhua* news, January 21, 2006. Accessed from http://news.xinhuanet.com/english/2006-01/21/content_4080120.htm

[11]Jianjun Tu, "The Strategic Considerations of the Sino-Saudi Oil Deal," *China Brief,* Vol. VI, No. 4 (February 15, 2006), the Jamestown Foundation, Washington, D.C.

[12]"China's Oil Ties to Sudan Force It to Oppose Sanctions, *Sudan Tribune,* October 20, 2004. Accessed from http://www.sudantribune.com on November 3, 2005.

[13]"China Invests Heavily in Sudan's Oil Industry," *The Washington Post,* December 23, 2004, p. A01.

[14]Jin Liangxiang, "Energy First: China and the Middle East," *Middle East Quarterly,* Spring 2005, accessed from http://www.meforum.org/article/694 on October 25, 2005. The Gulf Cooperation Council, set up in 1981, is composed of Saudi Arabia, Bahrain, Kuwait, Oman, Qatar and the United Arab Emirates (UAE).

[15]"Robert E. Ebel, "US Foreign Policy, Petroleum and the Middle East," testimony before the subcommittee on Near Eastern and Asian Affairs, US Senate Committee on Foreign Relations, October 31, 2005.

[16]Xiaojie Xu, "China and the Middle East: Cross-investment in the Energy Sector," *The Middle East Policy Council Journal,* Vol. VII, No. 3 (June 2000). Accessed from http://www.mepc.org on November 2, 2005.

[17]The Associated Press, August 24, 1997.

[18]Guang Pan, "China's Success in the Middle East," *Middle East Quarterly,* December 1997, accessed from the Middle East Forum website at http://www.meforum.org/article/373.

[19]Ibid.

[20]China's position on the Middle East issue is summarized by Kong Quan, Chinese Foreign Ministry spokesman as follows: 1) Israel's occupation of Arab territories should be ended in line with related UN resolutions and the legal rights and interests of the Palestinian people should be restored. Meanwhile, Israel's security should be ensured. 2) the "land for peace" principle should be respected. 3) China opposes Israel's use of force and its violent actions against innocent civilians. 4) China appeals the international community to focus more attention and efforts on the Middle East issue. The UN is expected to play a bigger role in settlement to the issue. See *Xinhua* news, February 7, 2002, accessed from http://www.china.org.cn/english/FR/26692.htm on November 2, 2005.

[21]"China Urges Hamas to Negotiate with Israel," *Reuters,* January 27, 2006.

[22]Secret official contacts and exchanges between the two sides started in the early 1980s, leading to the establishment of semi-official China International Tourist Service in Israel and the Beijing Liaison Office of the Israel Academy of Sciences and Humanities in 1990. See E. Zev Sufott, *A China Diary: Towards the establishment of China-Israel diplomatic relations,* London: Frank Cass, 1997.

[23]"China to Declare Israel a Preferred Tourist Destination," *Globes,* August 1, 2005, accessed online from www.globes.co.il the same day.

[24]"China Voices Concern About Business Interests in the Middle East," *China Daily,* April 10, 2002, accessed from http://www.china.org.cn/english on October 25, 2005.

[25]See for example, "China Calls on US to Stop Punishing Companies Accused on Proliferation," Forbes news at www.forbes.com, October 25, 2005, accessed the same day.

[26]"China Invests Heavily in Sudan's Oil Industry," *Sudan Tribune,* December 23, 2004. Accessed from http://www.sudantribune.com on November 3, 2005.

[27]"Down the River Nile: China Gains Influence in Egypt," *China Brief,* The Jamestown Foundation, Vol. V, Issue 22, October 25, 2005, p. 9.

[28]According to Chinese language sources, Taiwan President Chen Shui-bian stopped by the UAE on his way home after completing a visit to Central America at the end of September 2005. While in the UAE, Chen met with President Sheikh Zayed bin Sultan al-Nahayan's brother. See "Taiwan Plans to Sell Weapons to the UAE," Duowei news network, accessed at www.duoweinews.com on October 1, 2005.

[29]*The People's Daily (Renmin Ribao),* January 25, 2002, http://english.peopledaily.com.cn.

[30]The Shanghai Cooperation Organization (SCO) is an intergovernmental organization which was founded on June 14, 2001 by leaders of the People's Republic of China, Russia, Kazakhstan, Kyrgyzstan, Tajikistan and Uzbekistan co promote security, economic, cultural, military, and other cooperations aming the member states.

[31]Chinese Foreign Ministry news conference, September 17, 2002.

[32]Jin Liangxiang, "Energy First: China and the Middle East," *Middle East Quarterly,* Spring 2005, accessed from http://www.meforum.org/article/694 on October 25, 2005.

[33]*China Daily,* February 2, 2004.

[34]"China, Egypt and the World," *Beijing Review,* May 15, 2005. Accessed from http://www.bjreview.com.cn on November 16, 2005.

[35]"Down the River Nile: China Gains Influence in Egypt," *China Brief,* The Jamestown Foundation, Vol. V, Issue 22, October 25, 2005, p. 10.

[36]Ibid, p.10.

[37]*The People's Daily (Renmin Ribao),* April 20, 2004, accessed from http://english.people.com.cn on November 2, 2005.

[38]China Self-supplies 94% of Energy Need," *China Daily,* September 22, 2005. Accessed online from http://www.chinadaily.com.cn/english/doc/2005-09/22/content_480021.htm.

[39]Jeffrey A. Bader and Flynt Leverett, "Oil, the Middle East and the Middle Kingdom," *Financial Times,* August 16, 2005. Printed from the Brookings Institution's website at http://www.Brookings.edu on November 2, 2005.

[40]Ibid.

[41]"China and the Middle East," *AME Info,* September 5, 2004, accessed from http://www.ameinfo.com on November 2, 2005.

[42]"China's Oil and Gas Import Strategies to 2020," Global Energy and Utilities Market Research, Washington, D.C., April 2001. Executive Summary and Table of Contents of the report can be found on Global Energy and Utilities Market Research's website at http://www.emerging-markets.com

[43]CNOOC eventually withdrew its bid due to fierce political opposition in Washington, D.C. Members of Congress publicly opposed the Chinese bid on national security grounds.

[44]Barry Rubin, "China's Middle East Strategy," *Middle East Review of International Affairs,* Vol. 3, No. 1, 1999.

[45]See for example Shai Feldman, "China's Security: Implications for Israel," *Strategic Assessment* Vol. 2, No. 4, Jaffee Center for Strategic Studies, Tel Aviv University, February 2000.

[46]"China and the Middle East," *AME Info,* September 5, 2004, accessed from http://www.ameinfo.com on November 2, 2005.

[47]"China's Participation in Middle East Peace Process Welcomed: Egyptian assistant FM," *The People's Daily (Renmin Ribao)* at http://english.people.com.cn, November 23, 2004, accessed on November 2, 2005.

[48]"Israeli President Expects China to Contribute More to Mideast Peace Process," *The People's Daily (Renmin Ribao)*, December 14, 2003, accessed from http://english.people.com.cn/200312/14 on October 11, 2005.

[49]"Iran to Be Reported to Security Council," *The Washington Post*, January 31, 2006, http://www.washingtonpost.com

Chapter 9

The Energy Factor in China's Foreign Policy

Charles E. Ziegler[*]

INTRODUCTION

Rapid economic growth has made China dependent on the global economy for a range of raw materials, from iron ore and steel to cotton and wood. Of the various resources China needs to power its economic miracle, none is more important than oil. From 1992 to 2005 the People's Republic of China went from self-sufficiency in petroleum to dependence on imports for over one-third of total consumption. China is the world's second largest energy consumer, and in 2004 it surpassed Japan as the world's number two oil importer. Petroleum imports are projected to continue to increase at a rapid pace. At the same time, China is evolving into a global power, with national interests beyond the East Asian region.

This conjunction of growing energy dependence and rising economic influence and military raises the following questions. How has China's foreign policy behavior changed during a period of growing energy dependence? Will China pursue energy security through strategies that result in conflict, as realist theory would predict, or will its energy vulnerability lead it toward cooperation with rival oil consuming nations through participation in multilateral organizations or other forums, in line with liberal explanations? Finally, to what extent might China's energy interests bring it into conflict with other major importing nations such as Japan and the United States?

The following section sets out the argument for the strategic nature of energy for major powers, with a specific focus on oil.[1] Then I present data in China's increasing energy dependence, setting it in comparative perspective with China's East Asian neighbors, and evaluate Beijing's efforts to shift

[*]The author thanks the following journal for permission to reprint previously published article: "The Energy Factor in China's Foreign Policy," *Journal of Chinese Political Science*, vol. 11, no. 1 (Spring 2006), pp. 1-24.

China's energy balance. China's energy diplomacy with the Middle East, Russia and Central Asia, the Asia-Pacific, Africa and Latin America constitutes the subject of the next section. Beijing's efforts toward greater energy security through multilateral organizations are discussed, with particular attention to China's participation in the World Trade Organization and the Shanghai Cooperation Organization. The evidence suggests that energy demands have indeed accelerated China's rise to global prominence and, at least in the short term, appears to reinforce the cooperative aspects of Chinese foreign policy. The liberal argument that economically interdependent states tend to avoid costly conflicts appears more persuasive than does realism in conceptualizing China's foreign policy in its search for energy security.

Oil and Foreign Policy

Øystein Noreng has argued that for governments, energy is a politicized commodity, critical to economic and military strength and therefore vital to national security. The significance of energy as a component of foreign trade far outweighs its proportion of the total value of turnover. Simply put, political leaders view oil in a different category than footwear, electronics, or automobiles.[2] Energy, and in particular oil, is too important to be left to market forces alone.[3]

Considerable attention has been paid in the international relations literature to the link between economic interdependence and conflict. Liberalists in the field, going back to Kant, argue that greater economic interdependence moderates the prospects for conflict, while realists contend that economic ties exacerbate conflict by increasing a state's vulnerability in an anarchic environment.[4] Surprisingly few academic studies have focused on oil in foreign policy despite the strategic nature of this commodity. Logically, support for either realist or liberal theories from a study of energy interdependence should be particularly persuasive, given the vital importance of oil for national security. For example, oil dependence heightens uncertainty, and there is evidence that major powers in the past have gone to great lengths, including war, to ensure oil supplies. If the world's major rising power is employing cooperative strategies rather than using military means to ensure energy supplies, that choice may have significant theoretical and policy implications.

The vulnerability of oil consuming states depends on whether they have alternative forms of energy available either domestically or in the international environment. Consumer states can reduce dependence on oil through various strategies, with resort to war as only the most extreme measure. Domestically, states can provide incentives for exploration and enhanced production, assuming that sufficient reserves exist or are suspected to exist, to make such efforts worthwhile. Governments can also adopt conservation policies to reduce consumption. A third strategy to reduce strategic dependence is to shift from imported oil to alternate fuels—coal, natural gas, nuclear power, wind or solar energy—wherever possible. Finally, states may establish strategic reserves to dampen the shock of unexpected supply interruptions or to even out severe price fluctuation.

Internationally, consumer states may improve their energy security by diversifying imports, obtaining oil from as many suppliers are possible. Second, they may form or join multilateral organizations in order to bargain more effectively with supply cartels or with major producers. Third, states may encourage oil majors within the country to acquire oil properties abroad, to control upstream production. States that do not have nationalized oil companies may enter into corporatist arrangements with private companies, since the interests of the government and those of private energy companies overlap significantly. Finally, states that are sufficiently powerful may use military force to ensure the flow of oil.

For modern industrial and industrializing states oil is a vital component in economic growth. Oil prices are closely tied to inflation and economic growth rates. For example, the Energy Information Administration estimates that doubling the price of oil 1999-2000, from $11 to $22 per barrel, resulted in a .50% increase in inflation in the United States in 1999, and a .75% increase in 2000 The same price increase resulted in a .50% decline in GDP for growth 1999, and a full 1.0% decline in GDP in 2000. The surge in world oil prices to over $65 per barrel in 2005 has further constrained growth and fueled inflation. Given the strong emphasis China's leaders place on social stability and continued rates of high economic growth, steep price increases and shortages threaten domestic order.

Since oil is so important to the economic health of nations, policy makers will accord high priority to ensuring secure supplies at relatively stable prices. Small, militarily weak oil importers can do little to affect the global market. Membership in consumer organizations and stockpiling oil in strategic reserves may dampen the impact of fluctuation in the oil markets, but for the most part these states are highly vulnerable. If an oil importing state is relatively small and militarily weak, then it will tend to rely on multilateral cooperation and stockpiling.

Large, militarily powerful states, however, have more options. First, large consumer states like China or the U.S. are more likely to be home to one or more major energy companies. Even in neo-liberal capitalist systems such as the United States, the interests of these companies and the state overlap to a large degree. By importing and distributing large volumes of foreign oil, preferably at fairly consistent prices, energy companies earn huge profits and preserve market share. Political leaders, of course, have as a major goal strong economic growth and modest inflation, each linked to stable oil imports. Oil companies, then, become an integral component of state energy policy, in a corporatist relationship. This relationship is quite different from that posited in the pluralist model, where large powerful corporations pressure a reactive government.

Most large states also have relatively powerful military forces, which can be used to protect supply routes, or employed in times of crisis to secure oil supplies, either individually or, more likely, in tandem with other large oil importing powers. Certainly this describes the United States as the world's current hegemon, but one could also include Japan, Germany, Britain and France in the past, and China and India as significant emerging oil consumers in the present.

China's Oil Dependence

Concurrent with increasing oil dependence, China has come to be viewed as a great power, not merely a regional actor.[5] China's quarter-century of rapid economic growth and its relative openness to the outside world have forced others to take it seriously. Relatively neglected in the assessment of China's rising global influence is how the country's rapidly growing demand for energy might affect China's foreign policy.[6] In 1971 China's share in the world's primary energy demand was a mere five percent (with 23 percent of the world's population); in 1995 China's share of the world's population slipped to twenty-one percent, while its share of energy demand more than doubled to eleven percent. China's consumption of oil surpassed its domestic production in 1993, and imports have grown rapidly in recent years. In 2003 China's imports of crude oil increased by 31 percent over 2002, and demand for crude rose by 35 percent in 2004.[7]

Unless China's economy experiences a dramatic meltdown, the country will continue to consuming increasing amounts of energy. The International Energy Agency estimates that by 2020 China's share of primary energy demand will increase to sixteen percent, while its share of population shrinks to nineteen percent.[8] Beijing is promoting the exploration of new oil and gas fields within the PRC, but specialists agree that imports will constitute an increasing share of the country's energy consumption. China's energy needs may heighten the potential for competition and conflict with other oil importing nations, most notably the United States and Japan. Conversely, China's vulnerability as an energy importer could lead toward greater cooperation and integration within multilateral institutions.

In this paper I suggest that (a. China's rapidly growing energy demands mesh closely with broader foreign policy goals of promoting a stable international environment conducive to economic development. Cooperative approaches will therefore prove more likely than competitive ones, at least in the near future; (b. The major actors in China's energy policy are largely in accord on the goal of developing reliable sources of imported oil, although differences of emphasis between domestic development and foreign imports can be discerned; (c. The principle of non-interference in other countries' internal affairs confers an advantage in China search for reliable energy suppliers, while Western industrial democracies, most notably the U.S., often find their stated policies at odds with authoritarian, repressive oil producers.

CHINA'S ENERGY BALANCE

China's oil strategy for the 21st century calls for diversifying oil imports, cooperation on developing oil and gas wells in other countries (the "going abroad" plan), establishing a national oil reserve, increased efficiency in oil and coal consumption, reforming the National Energy Commission and tasking it with responsibility for oil security, creating a national oil foundation to develop oil finances and futures, and reducing the volume of oil imports carried by foreign tankers from 90 to 50 percent. Increasingly, Chinese publications are referring to securing oil supplies as a vital component of the country's national security.[9]

China is the largest producer, and the largest consumer of coal, in the world. The country holds 33 percent of the world's coal reserves, and currently produces more coal than it consumes, but as demands for electricity continue to increase coal exports have been reduced. While Chinese consumption of coal is expected to increase along with other sources of energy, much of China's reserves are sulfur-rich brown coal. Extensive use of coal contributes to extraordinarily high levels of pollution—China's largest cities are among the most polluted in the world, especially in levels of sulfur dioxide and particulates. In order to combat air pollution, China's energy strategy calls for decreasing the share of coal in the energy balance from 77.9 percent in 1995 to between 60.8 and 63.3 percent by 2015.[10]

Oil and natural gas consumption are expected to rise dramatically in the future, along with nuclear and hydroelectric power projects such as the Three Gorges dam. But China's domestic deposits of oil and gas are limited. China has less than two percent of the world's total oil reserves, and only about one percent of proven natural gas reserves. The older oil fields in northern and eastern China face declining output, while newly discovered fields in Xinjiang are remote from population centers, relatively small, and expensive to develop. Consequently, China's oil companies since 1997 have embarked on an aggressive campaign to secure properties and rights to oil and gas around the world, in Russia, Kazakhstan, Sudan, Azerbaijan, Indonesia, Iraq, Iran, Venezuela, and elsewhere.

In recent years, between 50 and 60 percent of China's oil imports have come from the Persian Gulf states, making that volatile region vitally important to China. In addition to being overly dependent on one region, China has no strategic oil reserves, and it is vulnerable to fluctuations in price and supply resulting from crises around the world. Like the United States, China is seeking to reduce its dependence on Middle Eastern oil. America's strategic domination of the Middle East constitutes an additional vulnerability for China. Beijing's frequent calls for a more multi-polar world order are understandable in the context of the country's vulnerable energy situation.

Although China is trying to enhance its energy security through expanded domestic production, it simply does not have the oil reserves to meet growing demand. In 2001 China produced 3.2 million barrels per day (bpd) of oil, and

Charles E. Ziegler

imported no less than 1.4 million bpd. In 2003-2004 China experienced phenomenal growth in both oil consumption (from 5.56 million bpd to 6.53 million bpd) and imports (from 2.02 million bpd to 2.91 million bpd). In just one year, the percentage of oil imported increased from 36 to 45 percent.[11] A rapidly growing reliance on imported oil has thrust China into the role of a major actor in world oil markets.

Table 9.1 Energy Production and Imports in Northeast Asia, 2003-2004

	China	Japan	South Korea
Oil consumption, million barrels per day	6.53 mln bbl/day	5.57 mln bbl/day	2.1 mln bbl/day
Net oil imports, million barrels per day	2.91 mln bbl/d	5.45 mln bbl/day	2.1 mln bbl/day
Percent of oil Imported	45%	97.8%	100%
Natural gas production, trillion cubic feet	1.21 tcf	0.09 tcf	0
Net gas imports, trillion cubic feet	0	2.57 tcf	.816 tcf (all LNG)
Percent of natural gas imported	0%	96.3%	100%
Coal production, million short tons	1630 mmst	3.5 mmst	3.7 mmst
Net coal imports, million short tons	0	175.8 mmst	76 mmst
Percent of coal Imported	0	98.%	95%

Source: U.S. Department of Energy, *Energy Information Administration Country Analysis Briefs,* China (2005), Japan (2004), and South Korea (2005), at www.eia.doe.gov.

As is clear from Table 9.1, China is much better off in terms of energy resources than the other major countries of Northeast Asia. However, Japan's energy demand is stagnant, while China's is growing rapidly. And unlike its neighbors Japan and South Korea, who have strategic reserves of 100 days or more of oil, China has no more than a week's worth of domestic consumption held in state-owned facilities. Spurred by uncertainties in the international market, the Chinese government in 2003 announced plans to improve its energy security by building a national oil reserve. Scheduled for inauguration in 2005 and completion by 2010, the strategic reserve would provide China with 70-75 days' worth of oil at the current level of consumption.[12]

Oil consumption in China, as in most countries, is closely linked to the transportation sector. Much of the growth in oil consumption over the next decade will be the result of increasingly affluent Chinese consumers purchasing automobiles. In 1999 China had only 5.34 million private automobiles, or about one for every 250 Chinese By comparison, in the US in 2000 there were about 210 million private vehicles (automobiles and light trucks), or 72 for every 100 Americans.[13] But the automotive industry in China is growing rapidly; projections anticipate 140 million vehicles on the road by 2020. Car sales in 2004 alone were five million, making China the third largest car market, after the United States and Japan.[14] The government has encouraged automobile consumption as a means of stimulating the economy, to restore growth rates that weakened following the 1997 Asian crisis. Beijing's policy makers are clearly more concerned with keeping the population quiescent in the short term, than with the long-term energy and environmental consequences of promoting private transportation.

Demand for natural gas is increasing rapidly in China, as it is in much of developed and developing world. Gas is much cleaner in generating electricity than either coal or oil, releasing far less carbon monoxide, carbon dioxide, sulfur dioxide and particulates. China has extremely high levels of sulfur dioxide and particulates in its urban areas, resulting from heavy reliance on coal, which accounts for about three-fourths of China's current energy balance. The share of natural gas in China's energy balance is projected to grow from about 3 percent in 2002 to about 8-9 percent by 2010, as the share of coal decreases.

China inaugurated the domestic West to East Pipeline in July 2002 as one of several major projects that Beijing is promoting to increase the supply of natural gas flowing to power generation plants in the more populated and developed coastal areas. Originating in the Tarim basin of the Xinjiang-Uighur autonomous republic, the pipeline will cover some 4200 kilometers en route to Shanghai, and is designed to deliver 12 billion cubic meters of natural gas per annum. Total estimated cost is over $18 billion, including $12 billion for exploration and development of fields and retail chains, and $5.6 billion for the pipeline. The eastern 1500 kilometer segment of the pipeline was completed and gas started flowing to Shanghai in late 2003. China's state company PetroChina had initially formed a consortium with Russia's Gazprom, Royal Dutch/Shell, and Exxon Mobil, but the deal foundered on pricing issues and domestic political support for the project. By August 2004 PetroChina had terminated its agreements with all three foreign partners.[15]

To summarize, China's energy strategy calls for decreasing the proportion of coal in the energy balance, increasing the share of natural gas, and developing nuclear and hydroelectric power to deal with frequent shortages of electricity brought about by rapid economic growth. To maintain social stability the government is actively promoting automobile ownership, so demand for oil has soared. Domestic exploration and production are a priority, but limited reserves of both oil and gas are making China increasingly dependent on imports. Energy needs have integrated the China into the global economy. To cope with China's energy demands, the government and state oil and gas companies have partnered their diplomatic efforts.

ENERGY AND DIPLOMACY

China's limited supplies of oil and natural gas have played an important role in broadening that country's interests beyond the East Asian region.[16] China's state-run oil companies, supported by the government, have pursued a strategy of buying energy properties around the world in an attempt to secure oil and gas supplies. Chinese foreign policy has focused on developing bilateral ties with important selected countries, but it is increasingly willing to work through multilateral institutions with other oil consuming nations. As a major energy consumer and importer, China shares America's goals of ensuring reliable energy supplies at moderate supplies. Of course, Beijing is competing with the United States and other energy importers for these finite resources. Moreover, China's pursuit of energy security frequently clashes with U.S. national security interests, as Beijing courts oil-rich countries regarded as pariahs by Washington, such as Sudan, Venezuela, Burma, and Iran.

Liberal theories of international relations would predict that growing interdependence should motivate Chinese leaders to eschew military instruments of statecraft in favor of diplomacy, markets, and participation in international organizations. The realist perspective would place more emphasis on how China's growing energy dependence generates insecurity. Realism would predict an inclination to develop military forces capable of defending the vital sea lanes of communication, particularly the Strait of Malacca, through which 80 percent of the country's oil imports transit. Other evidence supporting the realist approach would include a demonstrated willingness to intervene militarily in oil supplying countries. However, China as yet has shown little inclination to task its modernizing military with ensuring energy supplies. This may be simply a nod to reality, since the PRC is far from being able to challenge the United States globally, or it may be a rational calculus that non-military means are more cost-effective and present a greater likelihood of success than using armed forces. Evidence from Chinese activities around the world suggests that Beijing is utilizing political, diplomatic and economic levers to secure long-term energy supplies from a wide range of sources.

The Middle East

As noted earlier, China is heavily dependent on the Middle East for oil imports, with Oman, Yemen, Iran and Saudi Arabia as the largest suppliers.[17] At the present time virtually all of China's imported oil comes via ocean going tankers, and supply routes could be interdicted either at the source (the Strait of Hormuz) or in transit, at the Straits of Malacca.[18] China faces uncertainties--deliveries could be disrupted and prices affected by conflicts or instability in the Middle East, as in 2003 and 2004. Security experts have raised the possibility of terrorist actions against tankers transiting the Straits of Malacca, or against ports adjacent to the narrow waterway. Even with its recent growth in military spending and the development of its navy, China still must rely on the United States to protect these vital sea lanes.

Beijing's planners are considering many alternative sources of energy. For China, the Middle East will remain in first place as a supplier of crude oil for the indefinite future. This region has about two thirds of the world's reserves, combined with low production costs. Chinese domestic oil costs about 25 percent more per barrel to produce than the average production costs of the world's large petroleum companies.[19] The strategy of Chinese oil companies has been to invest in upstream and downstream of Middle Eastern production (especially in Iran, Iraq, and Kuwait) to reduce possible disruption of oil supplies. China's foreign policy seeks to strengthen political relations with the Middle Eastern oil-producing states, while courting additional suppliers who would not impose the Asian premium of $1-2.00 per barrel.

China's energy needs, combined with the Persian Gulf countries' demand for technology and consumer goods, have elevated the region in China's foreign policy priorities. Former President Jiang Zemin visited Saudi Arabia in 1999 and signed an oil cooperation agreement providing for Saudi participation in Chinese refining in exchange for the kingdom opening its markets to Chinese investment. The Saudis, however, have restricted foreign participation in oil exploration and development. Jiang visited the Middle East again in April 2000, and in November 2002 Beijing sent a Mideast peace envoy to Israel, Syria and Palestine to demonstrate China's commitment to stability in the region, and a small flotilla completed China's first naval tour of the Arabian Sea since the 16th century. In August 2002 the Chinese National Petroleum Corporation (CNPC) announced a $230 million contract to build twin 500 kilometer oil and gas pipelines in Libya, and in 2004 Syria concluded a joint venture with CNPC, forming a Syrian-Chinese oil company (Kobab) to develop the Kbibah oil field in northeast Syria.[20]

Chinese companies have also sought entree to Iraq's oil fields, which account for ten percent of the world's reserves. In 1997 China signed a deal with Iraq to develop the Al Ahdab oilfield in central Iraq, and in 1998 began negotiations for the Al Halfayah field, in the expectation that they would be well-positioned once the sanctions were lifted.[21] The U.S occupation of Iraq and the ensuing instability placed these expectations on hold. In February 2004 Zhongxing Telecom won China's first postwar contract in Iraq, a $5 million deal to supply telecommunications equipment, reportedly in the face of resistance from the Coalition Provisional Authority.[22] As of late 2004 China had not concluded any energy deals in Iraq, but the Chairman of China Petrochemical Corporation had indicated his company's readiness to take advantage of any business opportunities there.[23]

Poor relations between Iran and the United States have provided an opening to Chinese companies. President Hu Jintao has praised Iran and indicated

China's readiness to work with Iran to purchase LNG and develop the upstream sector of Iran's oil industry. Iran is China's second largest supplier of oil, after Saudi Arabia, and the two countries have concluded oil and gas deals worth $70 billion. In addition to cooperating on oil and gas, Chinese firms are working on mine projects, port and airport construction, electricity and dam building, cement, steel, and railway industries in Iran, and the two countries are promoting tourism. Hu has emphasized Beijing's willingness to cooperate with Iran on building regional stability and dealing with the situations in Afghanistan and Iraq, and Iran's Ambassador to China has described political relations as "excellent."[24]

China's energy dependence on Iran has made relations with that country a matter of significant national interest. The energy relationship has made Beijing less willing to support American efforts in the United Nations to pressure Teheran to compromise on its nuclear weapons program. China has rejected U.S. proposals to refer Iran to the UN Security Council for possible sanctions, expressing instead a preference for resolving the issue within the UN's International Atomic Energy Agency.[25] Beijing would apparently prefer not to be forced to choose whether or not to exercise its veto in the Security Council, an action that would be sure to strain ties with Washington.

Given the complementarity of Chinese and Gulf state economies, trade, investment, tourism, and other forms of economic cooperation will continue to grow, as will Chinese political influence in the region. However, it is unlikely that China will seriously challenge America's dominant position in the Middle East any time soon.

Russia, Central Asia, and the Caucasus

Russian and Central Asian energy resources could help China reduce its dependence on Middle Eastern oil, and thus enhance its security. Pipelines, after all, are generally a more reliable form of transportation than tankers. Central Asian and Russian oil occupy the second tier in Chinese priorities. These regions have substantial deposits of oil and natural gas, and China views the development of these resources as key to its energy security, a "strategic backup" to other sources. However, the costs of extraction and transportation of oil are considerably higher than Middle Eastern crude. More importantly, Russia and the Caspian states combined account for less than ten percent of the world's reserves, compared with the Middle East's two-thirds.

Russia and Central Asia do have a key advantage in natural gas, though, since their reserves, at 37 percent of the global total, far exceed those of the Persian Gulf states. At present gas accounts for only a small fraction of China's energy needs, but as the energy balance changes and pipelines come onstream this will change. Russia will likely provide an increasing share of China's energy needs. But in the more distant future, China is also looking to import gas from Turkmenistan, Kazakhstan and Uzbekistan. As Russian and Central Asian gas becomes available via pipelines, it could displace more expensive liquid natural gas (LNG) imported from Indonesia and Australia.[26]

In 2001 President Vladimir Putin and former President Jiang Zemin agreed to build a 2300 kilometer oil pipeline that would run from Angarsk, north of Irkutsk, along the south of Lake Baikal and then skirt Mongolia, dropping southward to terminate at Daqing, northeast China. The Yukos oil firm was to provide most of the oil, which would supply idle refineries in the northeast Daqing region. The pipeline was expected to supply 20 to 30 million tons of crude per year, nearly one-third of China's imports at 2004 rates.

In 2003 several events conspired to undermine the original plan. Japan challenged the Daqing route, proposing the pipeline terminate at Nakhodka on the Pacific coast. This route would prove more costly, but it would have the advantage of giving Russia several buyers (Japan, South Korea, China, Taiwan and the United States) in place of a single customer. To sweeten the deal, Japan offered to invest as much as $7 billion to underwrite construction costs. Second, the Nakhodka route would benefit the economically depressed Russian Far East, through construction of the pipeline, refurbished terminals, and transport tariffs, and so fit more closely with President Putin's goals of raising living standards in Russia's poorer regions. Finally, the government's attack on Yukos and its founder and CEO Mikhail Khodorkovsky in 2003-04 effectively quashed that company's ability to carry out the project, leaving the state-owned monopoly Transneft to construct the pipeline.

Political competition between China and Japan may be nearly as important as economic incentives in securing Russian oil. Chinese-Japanese tensions are on the increase as growing Chinese influence in the Asia-Pacific confronts rising Japanese nationalism. China is intensely suspicious of Japan's intentions, and has criticized the Japanese government for sending Self-Defense Forces to Iraq to assist the American campaign. The Xinhua News Agency accused Japan of seeking to become a military power, and to secure its oil interest in the Gulf.[27]

The controversy suggests that while economic considerations dominate energy planning in Putin's Russia, Chinese energy diplomacy is more a mix of politics and economics. Chinese officials were reportedly furious when Moscow revisited the 2001 agreement, seeing it as a violation of the spirit of their proclaimed "strategic partnership." Curiously, Japan's maneuvering also seems influenced by politics. Japan can certainly use the oil, and would prefer to diversity its supplies (about 80 percent of its imports now come from the Middle East), but domestic Japanese demand has been stagnant for some years now. In any case, Japan will receive increasing amounts of Russian oil and gas from the Sakhalin I and II projects as they reach maturity over the next three decades.

Central Asia may prove a more attractive energy source than Russia. China has concluded projects of varying sizes with the various Central Asian states and Azerbaijan in recent years. In May 2003 China Petroleum and Chemical Corporation (Sinopec) and China's National Offshore Oil Company (CNOOC) bid to acquire a 16.67 percent share in the North Caspian Sea PSA. The deal foundered when five of the six partners—Shell, Exxon-Mobil, TotalFinaElf, Conoco Phillips and Italy's ENI—exercised their pre-emption rights and purchased the share from British Gas. Had the Chinese companies succeeded in their bid, they would have acquired a significant share in one of the world's largest fields, which includes the huge Kashagan oil field in addition to several others. The Kazakh government had enthusiastically supported China's involvement in the project and, when this did not work out, claimed a sovereign right to purchase the BG share.[28]

Chinese interest in Central Asian oil stems from a desire to promote overall economic regional integration, and to build a land bridge between Central Asia and Russia that would be more reliable than Persian Gulf crude. CNPC initially made headlines in 1997 with a deal with Kazakhstan in which China was expected to invest $9.7 billion to update the Uzen oil field and construct a 3200-kilometer pipeline from the western province of Aktobe into western China. However, the Kazakh fields held reserves that failed to justify such investment, and CNPC put the project on hold in 1999. The issue was raised again during Nazarbaev's December 2002 visit to Beijing, when the Chinese proposed that Kazakhstan supply them with up to one million barrels per day of oil. Kazakh energy minister Vladimir Shkolnik has said that construction of a pipeline system that could eventually supply China was continuing.[29] Record oil prices have made the project more feasible. In addition, China has the option to pump the oil through the Caspian pipeline to Novorossiysk via a swap arrangement.

China's strategic interests in the Central Asian region—maintaining stability, preventing terrorism, separatism and religious extremism, and controlling narcotics trafficking--coincide with those of Russian and Central Asian leaders. Neither Russian nor Central Asia can meet all of China's growing oil needs, so competition is muted. For China, closer economic integration with the Central Asian states in the form of rail, road and air links, oil and gas pipelines, and electrical grids, is an important element in Beijing's strategy to diversify energy supplies, while neutralizing the potential for instability in Xinjiang.[30]

The Asia-Pacific Region

As Table 9.1 demonstrates, Japan and South Korea are energy-dependent countries, and so are competitors with China for scarce energy resources. In addition to the rather bitter competition between Japan and China to determine the route of Russia's Siberian pipelines, the two nations have also clashed over plans to exploit a natural gas field which straddles their exclusive economic zones in the East China Sea.[31] However, China, Japan and South Korea have through the Committee on Northeast Asian Cooperative Initiative discussed the possibility of coordinating purchases of oil from the Middle East to eliminate the Asian premium.[32] With South Korea, energy ties have to this point been more cooperative than competitive, as evidence by plans to extend Russian gas pipelines through China to South Korea via an underwater spur. India, with its high recent growth rates and limited energy supplies, is another competitor for oil and gas.

Southeast Asian oil and gas have played an important role in China's energy balance, but exports to China have declined significantly in recent years as Indonesian and Malaysian reserves become depleted. In 1996 the Asia Pacific accounted for 36.3 percent of China's imported oil; by 1999 the share had dropped to 18.7 percent.[33] Nonetheless, China remains one of Indonesia's top four markets for crude, and Chinese firms are eager to cooperate on energy projects. In 2002 the China National Offshore Oil Corporation (CNOOC) purchased most of the Spanish firm Repsol-YPF's assets in Indonesia for $585 million, making it the largest offshore oil producer in Indonesia. However, Indonesia's oil production is declining and domestic demand is growing, so the potential for growth in energy imports in limited. Estimates are that by 2010 Indonesia will become a net oil importer. Planning ahead, Jakarta is seeking to diversity its export base away from oil products.

Prospects are more favorable for natural gas. In 2002 Beijing and Jakarta concluded several memoranda of understanding that enhanced energy cooperation, and Indonesia bid on a multi-billion dollar contract to supply Guangdong province with LNG over a twenty-five year period. Australia won the bid, but China and Indonesia subsequently signed a contract valued at $8.5 billion to supply liquid natural gas to Fujian province, starting in 2007. Energy cooperation is a factor dampening decades of hostility between the two Asian giants, granting China new opportunities to develop political and military relations. For example, Indonesia is considering purchasing arms from China, which is eager to sell military equipment. Beijing's diplomatic approach to Jakarta in recent years has been skillful.

The U.S. approach toward Indonesia, by contrast, is often contradictory, and has earned it considerable resentment. Congress, which had restricted military assistance in 1992, severed all forms of contact with the Indonesian military in 1999, after troops engaged in human rights abuses in East Timor. At the same time, the U.S. is pressuring Indonesia to cooperate in the war on terror. Chinese leaders are not troubled by human rights issues, nor do they exert pressure toward democratization. In Southeast Asia China is increasingly viewed as a positive force, a status quo power, rather than a revolutionary troublemaker as in past years.

The huge LNG contract Australia landed with China in August 2002 was billed as Australia's single largest trade deal. North West Shelf Venture agreed to supply over three million tons per year of LNG to Guangdong province for 25 years, generating export earnings of approximately one billion dollars annually. Although considerable smaller than Australian LNG exports to Japan ($2.6 billion annually), the sales would increase total exports to China by about 15 percent.[34] However, leadership changes in Beijing, the SARS outbreak, revisions to China's energy strategy, and delays by the Guangdong local government on approving the receiver terminal hindered progress on the agreement.[35] In addition, China will be competing with the west coast of the United States for Australian LNG. Starting in 2007, Chevron Texaco is planning to import LNG from Australia's Gorgon project to a terminal in Mexico, and then pipe the gas north to California.[36]

China has also worked with the Association of Southeast Asian Nation (ASEAN) to ensure stable energy supplies by creating regional oil stockpiles. In July 2003 China joined the ASEAN nations, Japan and South Korea to set up an ASEAN Plus Three Energy Partnership, a governing group to explore ways to ensure stable energy supplies for the region, including coordinating on oil stockpiling. Japan and the Republic of Korea were to fund the group's research programs. The first formal meeting of the Energy Partnership was held in June 2004, where members discussed how to improve energy security, enhance exploration, share information, and develop stockpiling.[37]

Common energy needs may lead China's foreign policy to be more accommodating in East Asia. One example is in the six-nation dispute over the Spratly and Paracel islands in the South China Sea, where a militant Chinese posture has led to repeated armed clashes in the past. China does not plan to give up its extensive claims to the oil and gas-rich waters of the South China Sea, but Beijing's leaders appear to be substituting a policy of engagement for confrontation. In late August 2003 the Chairman of the National People's Congress, Wu Bangguo, who was in Manila for an Association of Asian Parliaments for Peace conference on economic development and terrorism, proposed that China, the Philippines, and other claimants to the Spratlys engage in joint oil exploration and development. In March 2005 national oil companies of China, Vietnam and the Philippines signed an agreement to conduct a joint survey of oil deposits in the South China Sea. Political and corporate officials hailed the accord as an historic event that would contribute to peace and stability in the region.[38]

While Chinese leaders are increasingly willing to grant major state oil firms economic autonomy, their activities are expected to mesh with Beijing's foreign policy strategy. When China's oil companies seek to acquire holdings in oil-rich states around the world, these acquisitions serve the twin goals of strategic energy diversification and expanding political presence. Government and corporate interests are not identical in China, but there is considerable overlap. China's political officials are well aware that their country needs increasing supplies of raw materials, above all energy, to continue to maintain high economic growth rates, and they are using statecraft to help China's energy companies acquire properties across the globe.

Africa and the Americas

With the Middle East in turmoil, and Russian pipelines uncertain, Chinese companies have increasingly sought out business opportunities with African and Latin American oil producing states. The share of China's crude oil imports from Africa increased from 8.5 percent to 28 percent from 1996 to 1999.[39] East Asian imports of crude from West Africa for the first three months of 2004 were 1.3 to 1.4 million bpd, considerably higher than the one million bpd average in 2003. Most of this was driven by China's surging demand for sweet crude.[40]

China's interest in Africa during the Cold War was to present an alternative to the superpower rivalry of the United States and the Soviet Union. Competition then was for ideological influence with the developing world, through such projects as the Tanzania-Zambia railway and aid to Mozambique, in which China presented itself as a defender of the poorest Third World states. This ideologically driven approach declined after Deng's pragmatic market reforms were begun, and policy toward the African continent now is driven more by a blend of political and economic interests.

The political side of China's recent attention to Africa is a response to Taiwan's efforts to spread largesse in exchange for diplomatic recognition from smaller nations on the continent.[41] China's search for new energy supplies also accounts for a significant part of Beijing's Africa policy. In 2002 China provided $1.8 billion in development assistance to African countries, while China's trade with the continent reached $12.4 billion.[42] China can help Africa's energy exporting states by providing direct investment and technology. In turn, China receives much-needed oil and other raw materials, in addition to a more visible presence on the continent.

In February 2004 President Hu Jintao visited Algeria, Egypt and Gabon, all major oil producers. In Algeria, Hu and Algerian President Abdelaziz Bouteflika signed a framework energy agreement and accords on technological cooperation and educational exchanges, and China extended a preferential loan worth $48 million. Major Chinese projects in Algeria include a CNPC refining agreement worth $350 million, a $525 million contract with Sinopec to develop the Zarzaitine oil field in the Sahara, and a contract for China National Oil and Gas Exploration and Development Company to build an oil refinery near Adrar. Chinese firms are involved in the construction of an air terminal at Hourari Boumedienne airport, a teaching hospital in Oran, and some 55,000 apartments. Algeria is eager to increase its output from the current one million bpd to 1.5 million bpd, and China is a willing customer.[43]

Gabon has far less oil than Algeria (current production, at 270,000 bpd, is down more than a third from the peak year 1997), but it is still important given China's status as a latecomer to the ranks of oil importing nations. During Hu's 2004 visit Total Gabon and China's Unipec (a subsidiary of Sinopec) signed the first contact for the delivery of Gabon crude, and Sinopec has exploration plans for the West African nation.[44]

Sudan is a key energy producing state for China in Africa. Government-sponsored massacres in the western region of Darfur have resulted in U.S. economic sanctions, and most major oil companies have reduced their presence in this troubled country. China resists criticism that its energy investments in Sudan have funded the brutal Janjaweed militias, arguing that China and Sudan have normal business relations. Sudan has received the bulk of Chinese investment in Africa, but Beijing argues this is simply normal business relations. China's National Petroleum Corporation has developed a plan to invest $1 billion in upgrading Sudan's refineries and pipelines. Approximately $700 million of this would go toward constructing a 750 kilometer pipeline from the Kordofan field to the coast, while the remainder would be used to increase capacity at the Khartoum refinery.[45] Sudan only supplies a small fraction of China's oil imports, but it is crucial as a base for energy development in Africa.

The African oil producing states have relatively backward energy technologies and need foreign investment to modernize their facilities. In some cases, such as Sudan, U.S.-imposed sanctions and pressures from human rights organizations have led Western oil firms to pull out, giving Chinese companies a chance to establish a foothold. The Chinese government provides foreign assistance to complement the investment from its oil companies. For example, the Chinese have financed administrative offices in Gabon and the Ivory Coast, an airport terminal in Algeria, and communications networks in Ethiopia.[46]

Chinese involvement in Latin America is small but growing, and much of the interest can be attributed to the continent's raw materials, including oil and gas. Beijing has requested permanent observer status in the Organization of American States. In 2004 the Brazilian oil major Petrobras invited Sinopec to bid on an offshore bloc, to conduct oil exploration. Petrobras' plan is to contribute technology, while the Sinopec Group would provide funding for the joint exploration venture. China is reported willing to contribute one billion dollars to refurbish Brazilian ports, in exchange for oil and raw materials. Brazil's President Luiz Inacio Lula de Silva provided political support for the project during his May 2004 visit to Beijing.[47] China is Brazil's third largest trading partner, after the United States and Argentina.

Venezuela is South America's largest producer of crude, and PetroChina has identified Venezuela as one of the top four countries from which it expects to obtain oil over the next seven years. Venezuela under President Hugo Chavez is highly critical of the United States, although the country continues to supply well over one million barrels of oil per day to the U.S. In 2000 Venezuela signed an agreement to export 6.5 million tons per year of orimulsion, a coal substitute, for use in China's thermal power plants and steel mills. The deal was touted as greatly expanding Venezuela's exports of this unique form of energy. However, the Venezuelan Energy Ministry suspended orimulsion production in mid-2004 as unprofitable.[48] In June 2004, China's ambassador to Caracas has public reiterated his country's goal of developing large-scale energy projects with Venezuela. But this country, like Middle Eastern oil producers, is volatile, with major labor unrest cutting oil production sharply in 2002 and 2003.

Chinese oil companies have even sought to acquire major holdings in North America, the most notable of which was the 2005 attempt by China's National Offshore Oil Company (CNOOC) to purchase the American oil company Unocal. The CNOOC bid, valued at $18.5 billion, resulted in a firestorm of criticism from the U.S. Congress amid fears that U.S. energy security would be compromised. CNOOC's chairman Fu Chengyu insisted his company's attempt to outbid Chevron was purely commercial, but the process collapsed amid charges that the Chinese government was subsidizing the purchase to enhance its leverage over oil and gas producers in Central and Southeast Asia.[49] Chevron lobbied Washington far more effectively than did CNOOC, and acquired Unocal for nearly two billion dollars less than the Chinese offered. Clearly, politics and security issues shaped the behavior of leaders in both countries.

Chinese companies will continue a long-term strategy of acquiring energy assets around the world. The Unocal experience may lead China to focus on the more unstable or politically unsavory oil and gas producers. China's arrangements with individual producers—Iran, Saudi Arabia, Russia, Kazakhstan, Indonesia, Azerbaijan, Sudan, Brazil and Venezuela—are promising, but each of these countries faces serious domestic or international problems. The uncertainty of bilateral energy ties has contributed to a new appreciation for multilateral organizations in Beijing's international energy policy.

CHINA, ENERGY, AND MULTILATERAL ORGANIZATIONS

China's growing involvement in the global economy, and its more active diplomacy, provide Beijing's leaders with a new perspective on participation in multilateral institutions. The organizations that are of greatest relevance to China's energy strategy are the World Trade Organization (WTO), the Shanghai Cooperation Organization (SCO), and the International Energy Agency (IEA).

Securing membership in the World Trade Organization has been an important component of Chinese foreign policy, although it is a mixed blessing for Chinese businesses and the Chinese people. The open market provisions of the WTO will pay the greatest dividends in areas where China has a comparative advantage—textiles, clothing, processed foods and leather goods. China's agricultural sector will be hit hard, as will much of China's energy industry. Expectations are that output of all energy sectors will be reduced, with the greatest impact falling on downstream industries. Many of China's inefficient refineries, which rely on outmoded technology, will be forced to close or will be forced to join with foreign partners. Retail sales outlets will be taken over by the larger multinationals as non-tariff barriers fall. The impact will be lower on upstream oil and gas, including exploration and development.[50]

Tariff cuts under the WTO mean that Chinese companies will have to reduce production costs in order to compete with imports. Under WTO China was required to phase out its trade barriers to the import of oil products by the end of 2004. In addition, restrictions on distribution will be lifted, allowing U.S. and other foreign firms the right to sell gasoline and other oil products in the Chinese market. Royal Dutch Shell, Exxon Mobil and BP are now retail marketing in China; these companies own some 300 of China's 75,000 gasoline stations. The number of retail gasoline stations will increase as car ownership continues to grow.

By lowering import barriers and tariffs WTO membership will encourage gasoline consumption in China. In 2003, China had some 96.5 million motor vehicles on the road, of which about 80 percent were publicly owned. But China's affluent middle class is purchasing automobiles at a furious pace--car sales increased by 75 percent in 2003, and production for 2004 is expected to be 40 percent higher than the previous year.[51] Imports are also expected to increase as WTO regulations force price reductions. Imported cars had been taxed at 80-100 percent tariff rates, which allowed domestic manufacturers to keep automobile and parts prices high. Shortly after joining the WTO, prices on Chinese-made cars dropped as much as 20 percent. Tariffs on imported cars are projected to decline to 25 percent by 2006, and tariffs on spare parts will drop to 10 percent.[52] Lower prices, together with the government's policy of promoting private automobile ownership, virtually guarantees continued growth in demand for oil.

Energy cooperation through the Shanghai Cooperation Organization has recently gained in importance for China. Originally formed to deal with territorial issues arising from the breakup of the Soviet Union, the SCO, whose members also include Russia, Kazakhstan, Uzbekistan, Kyrgyzstan, and Tajikistan, has in recent years focused more on problems of terrorism, religious extremism, and narcotics smuggling. China and Russia have used the organization to gain Central Asian support in their campaigns against separatism in Xinjiang and Chechnya, and both Moscow and Beijing view the organization as a possible counterweight to American influence in the region.

China's new focus on SCO energy cooperation derives from its concern over instability in the Middle East, and the goal of securing both Russian and Kazakh oil and gas.[53] Within the SCO Russia, Kazakhstan and China appear to be forming an energy and security triangle. Kazakh oil is currently exported through the Caspian Pipeline Consortium, which runs through southern Russia and terminates at Novorossiysk, and there are plans to ship Kazakh oil through the Baltic pipeline when it is finished. Russia's state natural gas monopoly Gazprom has secured rights within Kazakhstan, as it has within all five of the Central Asian states. Russia's Unified Energy Systems, the electricity monopoly, has tied Kazakhstan and its neighbors into an electrical power grid.[54] Kazakhstan continues to negotiate with China on an oil pipeline eastward, while the government suppresses Uighur separatists and leases agricultural land to ethnic Chinese.[55] Trade among the three continues to grow. Government officials and political observers in Kazakhstan are increasingly worried that economic and political pressures are forcing Astana to tailor its policies to suit Moscow and Beijing.[56]

Emphasis on energy cooperation within the SCO could lead to conflict with the United States, since American oil companies have been actively developing Kazakhstan's oil sector for over a decade. Kazakhstan's western fields already pipe about 300,000 bpd through the Caspian Pipeline Consortium, in which Chevron has a leading interest, and the Kazakh government plans to export up to ten million tons of crude oil per year through the Baku-Tblisi-Ceyhan pipeline. Washington adamantly supported the BTC pipeline's route through the Caucasus, in part because it skirts Russian territory.[57] And the U.S. has worked hard to consolidate support among its new Central Asian allies in the war on terror. Defense Secretary Donald Rumsfeld visited Kazakhstan and Uzbekistan in February 2004 to discuss expanding military relations and ensuring security in the oil-rich Caspian region.

China is not a member of the International Energy Agency, but it (along with Russia and India), has signed a memorandum of policy understanding to strengthen cooperation with the agency. The IEA, created after the 1973-74 oil crisis, seeks to develop rational energy policies, and to help its members cope with supply and price disruptions and with environmental issues relating to energy use. Based in Paris, the IEA is linked to the OECD and its members are the OECD countries. China's goals mesh closely with those of the IEA, including security of supply, more efficient use of energy, technological advances, regulatory reform of the energy sector, environmental sustainability, and producer-consumer dialogue. The IEA works with China and countries in Eastern Europe, Latin America and Africa through its Committee on Non-Member Countries.[58] The IEA has held conferences on natural gas use in China, seminars on energy efficiency standards, energy modeling and statistics, and developing emergency oil stocks.

CONCLUSION

The evidence presented in this article suggests that China's foreign policy on energy security is accurately described by the liberal perspective on international relations. China, at least at this point in time, has pursued a cooperative path in the energy field. Beijing is critical of the United States over its Middle East policies, but Chinese leaders appear willing to work together to keep energy producing regions quiet and stable. And China is actively cooperating with other importing nations through various multilateral forums. In line with liberal theory, energy dependence appears to have exerted a moderating influence on Chinese foreign policy, leading Beijing toward cooperative strategies. This does not preclude the possibility that military force could become a viable option in securing energy supplies. But at present, the Chinese military does not have the projection capabilities that would allow it to intervene militarily in oil producing states, or to protect the vital shipping routes in the South Pacific.

Securing reliable and diversified energy supplies is central to China's security today, and the need will become even more pressing in coming decades. As a net energy importer, China has a stake in the stability of neighboring oil and gas producing regions, which China's leaders perceive as linked to domestic economic growth rates and societal quiescence. As a major oil consuming nation, China has shared interests with other major oil and gas importing nations, such as the United States, Japan, South Korea, and members of the European Union. These include securing stable and diversified supplies, maintaining stable and moderate prices, and protecting the transportation routes through which oil and natural gas flow.

The driving elements in China's foreign policy since the Deng era have been continued modernization and development of the economy, a focus on the regions bordering China, and promoting nationalism as the leading ideological current.[59] China's foreign policy is concerned above all with preserving national sovereignty and national security.[60] Economic development and maintaining domestic stability are a high priority of the regime, and readily available supplies of energy are critical to keep economic growth rates at their recent high levels, as well as to provide the capabilities needed to strengthen China's international role and preserve the country's historic boundaries (that is, to prevent Taiwan's independence). The country's national interests are increasingly difficult to protect, as China's growing dependence on imported oil and gas make it more vulnerable to the vagaries of the international energy market and global instability.

China's energy requirements constitute one significant factor driving Beijing to move beyond regionalism; China is indeed becoming a global power. This study suggests that energy demands have caused China's business elites and government officials to move beyond a regional focus on the Asia-Pacific, developing joint ventures and acquiring properties in Central Asia, Africa and Latin America. Politics and economics are still mixed in China's unique brand of capitalism, so it is difficult to separate the interests of China's petroleum firms from those of the Chinese state. In many instances, as in Western capitalist countries, government officials have close ties to the oil industry, and their goals mesh closely with those of business.

China's emergence as a global energy actor has had a major impact on the world economy, and will continue to do so in the foreseeable future. Energy policy in China, as in the United States, is focused on increasing supply rather than curtailing demand through conservation, mass transportation, and alternative technologies. China's foreign energy policy is critically important to economic development, and sustained economic growth is vital to maintain social stability. Chinese officials are positioning their country, economically and politically, to meet its rapidly growing energy needs in the coming decades. Energy dependence, in turn, constitutes a powerful incentive for a constructive, cooperative Chinese foreign policy.

Notes

[1] While this paper will discuss China's imports of oil and natural gas as they relate to Chinese foreign policy, the chief focus here will be on oil. As noted in the section on China's energy dependence, the share of natural gas in the country's energy balance is growing, but remains relatively small. China is self-sufficient in coal, and its imports of electricity are negligible.

[2] Richard Rosecrance argues just the opposite, that importing energy is no different than importing fashions or automobiles. *The Rise of the Trading State: Commerce and Conquest in the Modern World* (New York, Basic Books, 1986), pp. 233-36.

[3] Øystein Noreng, *Crude Power* (London: I.B. Tauris, 2002), p. 42.

[4] Edward D. Mansfield and Brian M. Pollins, "The Study of Interdependence and Conflict: Recent Advances, Open Questions, and Directions for Future Research," *Journal of Conflict Resolution* 45 (December 2001), 834-859; Katherine D. Barbieri, "Economic Interdependence: A Path to Peace or a Source of Interstate Conflict?" *Journal of Peace Research* 33 (1996), pp. 29-49; Dale C. Copeland, "Economic Interdependence and War: A Theory of Trade Expectations," *International Security* 20 (Spring 1996), pp. 5-41.

[5] See Evan S. Medeiros and M. Taylor Fravel, "China's New Diplomacy," *Foreign Affairs* (November-December 2003), pp. 22-35.

[6] Two of the best studies are Philip Andrews-Speed, Xuanli Lia, and Roland Dannreuther, *The Strategic Implications of China's Energy Needs*, Adelphi Paper #346 (London: IISS, July 2002), and Bernard D. Cole, *'Oil for the Lamps of China'—Beijing's 21st-Century Search for Energy* (Washington, D.C.: National Defense University, 2003).

[7] *The Financial Times* (21 January 2004); People's Daily Online (14 January 2004); China Economic Net (9 June 2005).

[8] China's Worldwide Quest for Energy Security, International Energy Agency, 2000, p. 14.

[9] *People's Daily* (14 November 2002), http://english.people.com.cn/200211/14/eng20021114_106819.shtml); and *People's Daily* (9 January 2004), http://english.peopledaily.com.cn/200401/09/eng20040109_132208.shtml.

[10] Gao Shixian, "China," in *Rethinking Energy Security in East Asia*, Paul B. Stares, ed. (Tokyo: Japan Center for International Exchange, 2000), p. 48.

[11] Energy Information Administration, Department of Energy, Country Analysis Brief for China, 2005, http://www.eia.doe.gov/emeu/cabs/china.html.

[12] Michael Mackey, "China Setting up a Strategic Oil Reserve," *Asia Times* (7 February 2004), http://www.atimes.com/atimes/China/FB07Ad02.html.

[13] *People's Daily* (6 October 2001); US. Department of Transportation, Office of Highway Policy Information, http://www.fhwa.dot.gov/ohim/onh00/onh2p3.htm.

[14] *Financial Times* (24 March 2004); Asia Pulse (5 August 2004). *The Economist* (5 June 2005).

[15] Premier Zhu Rongji, who stepped down from his position in 2003, had been an enthusiastic supporter of foreign participation in the project. *Financial Times* (4 August 2004); *Russian Oil and Gas Report* (4 August 2004).

[16] The US Department of Defense Annual Report to Congress, *The Military Power of the People's Republic of China 2005*, refers to resource demands, particularly energy, as a "driver" of Chinese strategic behavior. Accessed at http://www.dod.gov/news/Jul2005/d20050719china.pdf

[17] Steven W. Lewis, *China's Oil Diplomacy and Relations with the Middle East* (Rice University: James A. Baker III Institute of Public Policy, September 2002), p. 7.

[18] Sergei Troush, "China's Changing Oil Strategy and its Foreign Policy Implications, *CNAPS Working Paper*, Fall 1999.

[19] Comprehensive production costs (production plus discovery) for a barrel of oil lifted by Chinese corporations was $12.30 at the end of the 1990s, compared with $9.40 per barrel for non-Chinese oil majors. Shi Zulin and Xu Yugao, *The Impacts of China's Accession to the World Trade Organization (WTO) on China's Energy Sector* (Berkeley, CA: Nautilus Institute, 2002), p. 13.

[20] Ed Blanche, "Chinese Oil Diplomacy Focuses on Middle East," Lebanonwire, 27 November 2002, http://www.lebanonwire.com/0211/02112716DS.asp; MENA Business Reports (27 July 2004).

[21] Global News Wire (26 September 2003).

[22] AFP (10 February 2004).

[23] China Post (2 August 2004).

[24] IRNA (9 April 2004; 24 March 2004).

[25] Statement by Zhang Yan, China's permanent representative to the UN: "China Calls for Resolving Iranian Nuclear Issue within IAEA," People's Daily Online, http://english.peopledaily.com.cn/200409/19/eng20040919_157555.html.

[26] Shell Vice President F.K. Lung calculates that pipeline gas is generally cheaper if the distances involved are less than 3000 kilometers. Between 3000 and 9000 kilometers LNG and gas offer similar prices, depending on construction costs, and beyond 9000

kilometers LNG is cheaper than piped gas. F.K. Lung, "Clean Fossil Energy—Roles for Natural Gas and Coal," http://apec-egcfe.fossil.energy.gov/7thtech/p206.pdf.

[27] Japan Economic Newswire (9 December 2003).

[28] Dan Roberts, "Western Oil Majors Flex Their Muscles," *Financial Times* (10 May 2003); Lina Saigol, "Battle Lines Drawn for Caspian Oil," *Financial Times* (8 May 2003); AFX European Focus (7 May and 12 May, 2003). Ibragim Alibekov, "Kazakhstan Asserts State Interests in Kashagan Oil," Eurasianet.org, http://www.eurasianet.org/departments/business/articles/eav070904.shtml. The sixth partner in the joint venture, Japan's Inpex, declined to increase its stake.

[29] Interfax-Kazakhstan, in Global News Wire-Asia Africa Intelligence Wire (29 January 2003). The perception that a Kazakhstan to China pipeline would eventually be constructed was reinforced by a series of interviews conducted by the author in Kazakhstan in June 2003.

[30] On Xinjiang's links to the Central Asian region, see Sean R. Roberts, "A 'Land of Borderlands': Implications of Xinjiang's Trans-border Interactions," in *Xinjiang: China's Muslim Borderland*, S. Frederick Starr, ed. (Armonk, NY: M.E. Sharpe, 2004).

[31] Mariko Sanchanta, "Gas Provokes Japanese Clash," *Financial Times* (7 July 2004).

[32] Karen Teo, "Big Three to Fight 'Asian Premium' on Saudi Sales," *The Standard* (Hong Kong, 25 November 2004, accessed at the Energy Bulletin, http://www.energybulletin.net/3349.html

[33] Yanjia Wang, "Oil Security in China," Institute of Energy Economics, Japan Symposium on Pacific Energy Cooperation 2003.

[34] "China LNG delivers Australia's largest ever trade deal," Australian Trade Commission, 8 August 2002, http://www.austrade.gov.au/corporate/layout/0,,0_S1-1_-2_-3_PWB1655449-4_-5_-6_-7_,00.html.

[35] Nigel Wilson, "LNG on a Slow Boat to China," *The Australian* (18 March 2004).

[36] Nick Muessig, "LNG: Where Will it Go?" Neftegaz.ru, http://neftegaz.ru/english/analit/comments.php?one=1&id=1250.

[37] Pacific Forum CSIS 3rd quarter 2003, http://www.csis.org/pacfor/cc/0303Qchina_asean.html; Alexander's Oil & Gas Connections (29 June 2004), http://www.gasandoil.com/goc/news/nts42644.htm.

[38] Radio Free Asia (14 March 2005), http://www.rfa.org/english/news/business/2005/03/14/china_vietnam_spratlys/

[39] Wang, "Oil Security in China."

[40] "China Boosts Asian Demand for African Crude" Reuters (9 April 2004), http://www.gulf-news.com/Articles/Business2.asp?ArticleID=117383

[41] Richard J. Payne and Cassandra R. Veney, "China's Post-Cold War African Policy," *Asian Survey* 38 (September 1998), pp. 867-879.

[42] Carter Dougherty, "China, Seeking Oil and Foothold, Brings Funds for Africa's Riches," *The Boston Globe* (22 February 2004).

[43] AFP Algiers Petroleumworld.com (4 February 2004), http://www.petroleumworld.com/story3469.htm)

[44] AFP Algiers Petroleumworld.com (3 February 2004), http://www.petroleumworld.com/story3461.htm)

[45] BBC News (19 May 2003).

[46] Ibid.

[47] AFX News (3 August 2004); Financial Times Information (23 July 2004). Energy cooperation was just one component of the meeting, to which da Silva took 400 officials and nine ministers. The Brazilians also pledged to expand agricultural and mineral exports, and concluded deals on aircraft, steel, and automobiles. U.P.I. 28 May 2004.

[48] Inter Press Service (30 June 2004). China agreed to provide two-thirds of the financing needed to modernize the emulsion plant in Venezuela.

[49] Unocal's holdings include production and operations in Thailand, Indonesia, Burma, Bangladesh, The Netherlands, Congo and Azerbaijan. The company is conducting exploration in Vietnam, and has a significant interest in the Baku-Tblisi-Ceyhan pipeline.

[50] Shi Zulin and Xu Yugao, *The Impacts of China's Accession to the World Trade Organization (WTO) on China's Energy Sector* (Berkeley, CA: Nautilus Institute, 2002).

[51] *People's Daily* (8 February 2004).

[52] "WTO Fulfills the Chinese People's Dream of a Family Car," China Today (30 March 2002), http://www.china.org.cn/english/2002/Mar/29796.htm.

[53] Sergei Blagov, Asia Times Online (27 February 2004), http://www.atimes.com/atimes/Central_Asia/FB27Ag01.html.

[54] See Gregory Gleason, "Russia and the Politics of the Central Asian Electric Grid," *Problems of Post-Communism* 50 (May-June 2003), pp. 42-52.

[55] Robert M. Cutler, "Emerging Triangles: Russia-Kazakhstan-China," Asia Times Online (15 January 2004), http://www.atimes.com/atimes/Central_Asia/FA15Ag03.html.

[56] This perception came up repeatedly in interviews conducted by the author in Almaty, Atyrau, and Karaganda in June 2003.

[57] Another reason cited is the powerful U.S. business and legal interests that are profiting from the pipeline, including BP, ConocoPhillips, Unocal, and the Baker Botts law firm, the family firm of former Secretary of State James Baker III, which is representing the consortium.

[58] See the IEA website, at www.iea.org.

[59] Quansheng Zhao, "Chinese Foreign Policy in the Post-Cold War Era," in *Chinese Foreign Policy in Transition*, edited by Guili Liu (New York: Walter de Gruyter, 2004), pp. 295-322.

[60] See Yong Deng, "The Chinese Conception of National Interests in International Relations," *The China Quarterly* 154 (June 1998), pp. 308-329.

Chapter 10

Increasing Interdependence between China and the U.S. and its Implications for Chinese Foreign Policy

Chenghong Li

RISING CHINA AND THE CURRENT DEBATE

Since the early 1990s, with China's increasing economic and comprehensive powers, how to deal with China has become a very heated topic among American policy-makers and Chinese observers alike. *The National Interest* editor Owen Harris even termed 1999 as "a year of debating China."[1] Scholars and strategists are occupied with many questions surrounding the issue of rising China: what kinds of role will a rising Beijing choose to play in the coming years? How will the U.S.-China relations evolve? Will China become a partner of the U.S. or will it aggressively seek regional dominance and challenge American supremacy in world affairs? Among them, what kinds of strategy the United States should choose to handle a rising China has also attracted a lot of interests from scholars. "Engagement" and "containment" are two of the most prevalent approaches propounded by scholars.[2] Scholars of engagement emphasize the importance of contacts with China, by which they contend that China would be able to be integrated into the world system peacefully. For the scholars of "containment," they argue that with China's power increasing so quickly, sooner or later China will inevitably challenge the supremacy of the United States. What the United States should do to avoid this scenario is to adopt the "containment" policy just as it did to the former Soviet Union to prevent the further increase of the Chinese power.

Those scholars supporting the "containment" approach endorse a realist approach in their studies. The underlying logic is a typical power struggle and balance of power. Whether intentionally or inadvertently, the "Cold War complex" is apparent in their analysis: China is just another rising Soviet Union and the best strategy for the United States to deal with a rising China is just like what the United States did to the former Soviet Union: containment. For example, Richard Bernstein and Ross Monro maintains that it is true that China's current international engagement is thicker than at any time since the communist revolution of 1949. Nevertheless, those two writers contended that since the late 1980s, in part driven by nationalist sentiment to redeem the humiliations of the past, in part by the simple urge for international power, China is seeking to replace the United States as the dominant power in Asia. As a consequence of this logic, they asserted that America's conflict with China is coming and inevitable. To gain an upper hand over the future potential conflict with China, those two journalists suggest that America needs to set a plan to derail China's quest for a 21st-century hegemon.[3] John Mearsheimer articulated a similar view in an even more straightforward way. In an interview with *Foreign Affairs*, professor Mearsheimer contends that the United States has a deep-seated interest in making sure that China does not become a wealthy country and the best way to protect American exalted supremacy in the world system is to slow down China's economy development. Mearsheimer even predicted that if failing to prevent the rise of a peer competitor, then "the United States will move to contain China, much the way it contained the Soviet Union in the Cold War."[4]

Is that analogy enough? Is China really another equivalent of the pre-Soviet Union and U.S.-China relationship is really another version of U.S. –Soviet Union? Is containment a wise policy choice for the United States? First, the analogy of equating China with the former Soviet Union ignores many differences between China and the Soviet Union. Among them, one of the most distinctive differences lies in the ideological realm. Despite the fact that superficially, just like the former Soviet Union, China officially claimed to be a socialist country, in reality as many Sino-observers would agree that China has gradually given up its obstinate radical Maoism through its three decade's policy of "reform and opening to the outside world" as initiated by Deng Xiaoping in 1978. Presently, pragmatism, as demonstrated in Deng Xiaoping's "Socialism with Chinese Characteristics", and Jiang Zemin's "Three Represents" as well as Hu Jintao's "Building a Harmonious Society," is the ideology in China. In contrast with the previous socialistic ideology as adopted by both the Soviet Union as well as Mao's China, China's pragmatism-oriented ideology focuses more on the issue of how to maintain domestic stability while aiming at achieving economic development. There is no proclamation of universal superiority in China's pragmatism ideology, thus making it less likely to serve China's possible expansion ambition, which consequently further makes China less likely to get involved into conflict with the United States in the future.[5] If considering the possible impact of China's traditional pro-peace Confucian culture, then the rationale of containment approach becomes even more problematic.

More than the inside difference, what is more relevant here is the current configuration of the China-U.S. relations. A comprehensive examination of the China-U.S. bilateral relationship will reveal that realists' analogy of the relationship between China-U.S. with that of the U.S.-Soviet Union in the Cold War period is not very solidly founded. The increasingly thickened trans-Pacific interdependences raise doubt about the viability of projecting the future of U.S.-China relations based on the former U.S.-Soviet Union relations. Here by interdependence we mean something more than mutual economic transactions such as bilateral trade and investment, it also includes cultural, educational, and other people-to-people communications such as student exchanges, family adoption, missionary activities, and films interchanges etc.

In terms of scale and intensity of mutual transactions and interdependence in the domain of economic exchanges, people-to-people communications as well as other transboundary interactions, the former relationship between the U.S. and the Soviet Union does not match that between the present relationship between China and the U.S. By the end of 2005, cumulatively there were close to 58,000 U.S. direct investment projects in China, with a total contracted value of $94.7 billion and the actually invested value of $ 50 billion, which comprised nearly 10 percent of China's total FDI (Foreign Direct Investment) Currently, more than 20 percent of China's exports go to the United States (according to the statistics of U.S. Department of Commerce, America's share of China's exports is almost close to 40%). The United States persistently ranked as one of China's top two trade partners in the past five years.

Instead of the cold number, James Watson's personal Beijing impression might give us a more vivid picture concerning the increasing interdependence relationship between China and the United States. Watson keenly observed, "Looming over Beijing's choking, bumper-to-bumper traffic, every tenth building seems to spot a giant neon sign advertising American wares: Xerox, Mobil, Kinko's, Northwest Airlines, IBM, Jeep, Gerber, even the Jolly Green Giant. American food chains and beverages are everywhere in central Beijing: Coca-Cola, Starbucks, Kentucky Fried Chicken, Häagen-Dazs, Dunkin' Donuts, Baskin-Robbins, Pepsi, TCBY, Pizza Hut, and of course McDonald's."[6] Even today, needless to say in the Soviet Union period, we might not spot such a live picture in Moscow, the capital of the former Soviet Union and its successor Russia.

We have observed a realist view in our current debate about China-U.S. relations, neglecting the other side of actual picture regarding China-U.S. bilateral relations. Some analysts constructed their arguments and policy suggestions simply based on their ideal type rather than the real picture of China-U.S. bilateral relations. By following Karl Deutsch's transatlantic community studies as well as Nye and Keohane's case studies of the complex interdependence between the U.S.-Australia and U.S.-Canada in their influential monograph *Power and Interdependence*, this chapter will focus on the increasing interdependence relationship between China and the United States, and attempts to present a different view. It intends to provide the other side view of the configuration of China-U.S. relations.[7]

The chapter will address two main questions. The first and also the most focused one is: to what extent the current Sino-U.S. relation is interdependent. This study will look over a wide range of issues between China and the United States, striding from the most notable economic communications in trade and investment, to people-to-people contacts across the Pacific, such as tourists, student and scholar exchanges and other cultural interchanges in an extensive way. The study will examine those issues in a comparative way: to contrast the present with the past, and to contrast Sino-U.S. relations with U.S.-Soviet Union relations.

Another focus of this chapter is to identify the possible impact of the growing interdependence between China and the United States on Chinese foreign policy. As the long lasting debate between realism and liberalism demonstrates, the controversy surrounding the relationship between interdependence and conflict is far from settled. One strand of scholars, mainly realists, argue that economic interdependence does not prevent conflicts by pointing out the history of pre-World War I as a supporting empirical case. Another strand of scholars maintain that economic interdependence has the ability of pacifying the conflict tendency between nation-states. One more strand of scholars suggest that there is no liner relationship between economic interdependence and conflict. Economic interdependence's impacts on political conflicts are conditional, depending on anticipated change in streams of benefits. [8] This chapter observes that China's increasing integration into the world, especially its enhancing ties with the United States since 1970s has led to several changes in Chinese foreign policy. These changes range from the redefinition of national interest to the incorporation of more and more liberal components in its foreign policy, from more decentralized decision making to more cooperative foreign policy in some issue areas.

Nevertheless, the transformative effects of increasing transactions across the Pacific on the Chinese foreign policy are not as comprehensively as envisioned by liberalist. In some issue areas such as Taiwan, China remains unchanged in its position of "non-excluding of resorting to military means to prevent the Taiwan independence," despite the fact that technically China has adopted a softened policy to Taiwan as adroitly embraced and implemented by the present Chinese President Hu Jintao. Given the mixed results of the increasing interdependence on the Chinese foreign policy, how to construct effective policy which can encourage positive impacts while inhibiting negative effects will be a big challenge facing two countries' leaders in the coming years.

INCREASING INTERDEPENDCE BTWEEN CHINA AND THE U.S.

Pioneering the study of the formation of the Atlantic Security Community, Karl Deutsch constructed a number of indicators to illuminate the degree of interdependence across those countries, which provides a very good example for us to follow in the study of transnational transactions across the Pacific. Deutsch argued that transnational transactions could be shown by all sorts of interactions, including written and spoken messages (mail and telephones frequency etc), face-to-face contacts (tourism) and dealings such as trade as well as the work of international organizations—both governmental and non-governmental. In addition, international reading of each other's publications, listening to each other's radio programs, or viewing each other's moving pictures and television shows are also important indicators. Finally, how much attention was devoted to the volume of foreign news columns in each other's newspapers was also a very important component to be examined. To illuminate the degree of interdependence, Deutsch suggested looking over the ratio between domestic and foreign mails, the ratio of domestic and national income to total foreign trade, etc. [9]

Although we will look at all these issues in this chapter, we will focus on two major issues regarding transnational communications across the Pacific. The first is the economic relations between China and the U.S. The second is the People-to People contacts between China and the U.S.

Economic Ties: Trade and Investment

Economic and trade issues were not the primary motivations for thawing relations in the early 1970s for Beijing and Washington. As Henry Kissinger told Mao Zedong in February 1973, "Our interest in trade with China is not commercial. It is to establish a relationship that is necessary for the political relations we both have."[10] However, since the establishment of Sino-U.S. diplomatic relations, economic and trade relations between the two countries have developed rapidly. Over the past two decades, trade volume between China and the United States has increased tremendously. According to Chinese customs statistics, Sino-U.S trade in 2005 was valued at $211.6 billion, 85 times that of 1979's $2.5 billion when the bilateral relationship was normalized. The average annual rate of increase during that period was over 20 percent. As recorded by U.S customs statistics, the 2005 trade volume between the two countries was $285.3 billion, which was 120 times that of 1979 ($2.38 billion). Between 2000 and 2004, U.S. exports to China have increased 114 percent. Just in 2005, the United States recorded $41 billion exports, an increase of 19 percent over 2004. Through May 2006, U.S. exports to China have grown 37 percent over the same period of last year. These statistics report the average annual rate of increase as 19.9 percent, which is much higher than the average rate of U.S. trade growth as a whole. China now is the third largest trading partner of the United States (after Canada and Japan) and the fourth largest export market of the U.S. The United States is China's largest export market and the second largest trading partner, just behind the European Union. The following Table 10.1 will provide a more detailed picture regarding the Sino-U.S. trade relationship.

It is easy to note that there is a big discrepancy between China and the U.S.'s data on the bilateral trade. For example, in 2004 China reported an $80 billion trade surplus while the United States recorded $600 billion trade deficit, with $520 billion difference. Several factors might contribute to the discrepancy in recording the trade imbalance. First, China and the U.S. used different computation system in reporting the volume of imports and exports. China measures and reports its exports on a *fob* (free on board) basis, the U.S. however, records its exports on a *fas* (free along side) and *cif* (cost, insurance,

Table 10.1 The China-U.S. Trade (1978-2005) (million)

Year	Total	U.S. Export	% of U.S. Export	Chinese Export	% of Chinese Export (China Data)	% of Chinese Export (U.S. Data)
1978	1,181	***	0.6	271	2.8	3.7
1979	2,380	1,724	0.9	595	4.4	4.8
1980	4,919	3,755	1.7	983	5.4	6.4
1981	5,665	3,603	1.5	1,505	7.0	9.6
1982	5,414	2,912	1.4	1,761	8.1	11.4
1983	4,650	2,173	1.1	1,713	7.8	11.2
1984	6,385	3,004	1.4	2,313	9.3	13.6
1985	8,080	3,856	1.8	2,336	8.5	15.5
1986	8,347	3,106	1.4	2,633	8.4	16.7
1987	10,407	3,497	1.4	3,033	7.7	17.5
1988	14,278	5,017	1.6	3,399	7.1	19.4
1989	18,708	5,807	1.6	4,414	8.3	24.4
1990	21,103	4,807	1.2	5,314	8.5	25.9
1991	26,592	6,287	1.5	6,198	8.6	28.2
1992	34,883	7,470	1.7	8,599	10.1	32.1
1993	39,950	8,767	1.9	16,976	18.5	34.0
1994	50,649	9,287	1.8	21,421	17.7	34.2
1995	60,270	11,749	2.0	24,744	16.6	32.6
1996	66,387	11,987	1.9	26,731	17.7	36
1997	78,637	12,805	1.9	32,744	17.9	36
1998	85,410	14,241	2.1	37,976	20.7	38.7
1999	100,900	13,100	1.9	41,947	21.6	42
2000	123,900	16,300	2.1	52,099	20.9	40
2001	128,600	19,200	2.6	54,283	20.8	38.5
2002	155,600	22,100	3.2	69,946	21.2	38.4
2003	191,700	28,400	3.9	92,467	21.1	34.8
2004	245,200	34,700	4.4	124,942	21.1	33.2
2005	285,300	41,800	5.0	162,900	21.4	32.0

Sources: The United States –China Business Council, the U.S Department of Commerce; China Statistics Yearbook 2005; U.S. Census Bureau.

and freight) basis which includes the cost of insurance and freight. According to one study, if counting both exports and imports on a *fob* basis, the trade imbalances between China and the United States might be reduced as much as 20 percent. [11] The second problem concerns the role played by Hong Kong as an intermediary in handling re-exports to and from China. China's statistics on exports to the United States exclude goods sold to Hong Kong or to a third country for reexportation to the United States, while the U.S. statistics include such reexports as being from China. In addition, U.S. Customs calculations of imports from China ignore the value added from reprocessing by Hong Kong's middlemen for the purpose of reexports. If taking into account those two factors related to Hong Kong, almost three-quarters of the trade imbalance will be reduced. Thirdly, Foreign Invested Enterprises (FIEs) in China further complicates the issue of trade discrepancy between China and the U.S. Various data sets reveal that FIEs play an increasingly important role in the expansion of China's overall trade. According to China's General Administration of Customs (GAC), in 2004, the exports of foreign-funded companies accounted for 57.1 percent of China's total exports, up 9.2 percent point from 2000. In the first nine months of 2005, foreign funded companies enjoyed a trade surplus of $31.89 billion, 87 times more than that of the same period in 2004. They also accounted for 57.6 percent of China's total exports.[12] On the other hand, the 2005 White Paper of American Chamber Commerce of China (AmCham-China) indicates that 62 percent of its members operating in China mainly produce goods or services for the China market, which can be somewhat accounted for as American exports to China. Therefore, China-U.S. trade deficits should be considered as a result of internationalization of production and economic globalization, in which China just plays a linking role in the production chain for FIEs competing for out-sourcing

Finally, in the commercial service trade sector, the United States is the most developed in the world and has enjoyed increasing surpluses. Statistics show that the United States enjoyed consistent trade surplus with China in commercial services, rising from $0.5 billion in 1992 to around $2 billion in 2002. With China's rapid economic growth and increasing integration with the world economy, the commercial services will become increasingly important to China, which will naturally benefit the U.S. more due to their relatively strong comparative advantage in this segment.

The significance of Sino-U.S. trade becomes even more apparent if compared with that between the U.S.-Soviet Union during the Cold War period. Because of political division, international trade between the United States and the Soviet Union closely paralleled the division of the world into two major political-military blocs. Almost without exception, member states of the North Atlantic Treaty Organization became signatories of the General Agreement on Tariffs and Trade, while members of the Warsaw Pact joined the Council Committee for Mutual Economic Assistance. In turn, the Coordinating Committee for Multilateral Export Controls (COCOM), essentially a subset of NATO, controlled trade between East and West. This can be illustrated with the geographical distribution of the Soviet Union's foreign trade by the following Table 10.2. It shows that in 1970, 1975, 1980, as well as 1983, the Soviet Union's major trade partners were mainly other socialist countries, consistently maintaining more than 52% volume in both imports and exports. The Soviet trade with the developed West was increased, but still accounted for below 30% of the Soviet Union's whole trade. Examination of the bilateral trade between the Soviet Union and the United States can show this trend even more clearly. Table 10.3 shows that the Soviet Union's imports from the United States only account for at most 4% of its total imports. Indeed, in 1970 the figure was only 1%. On the other hand, the Soviet Union's exports to the United States were consistently below 1% from 1970 to 1989. In 1985 the number was even reduced to only 0.4% of its total exports. The same thing is seen in the United

States. As we can see in Table 10.4, the U.S.'s imports from the Soviet Union comprised from 0.1% to 0.4% of its total imports. The highest level occurred in 1978, with a record of only 0.7%. Regarding exports, the numbers were also very low, with the highest level reaching 1.6% in 1978.

Table 10.2 Geographical Distribution of Soviet Union's Foreign Trade (% share)

	1970		1975		1980		1983	
	export	import	export	import	export	import	export	import
Socialist Countries	65.4	65.1	60.7	52.4	54.2	53.2	55.6	56.5
Developed West	18.7	24.0	25.6	36.4	32.0	35.4	28.9	31.4
LDCs	15.9	10.9	13.7	11.2	13.8	11.4	15.5	12.1

Source: *CMEA* Statistical Annual, Various Years.

Table 10.3 USSR's Trade with the United States (in % share)

	1970	1974	1978	1985	1989
Import	1%	3%	4%	3%	4%
Export	0.5%	1%	0.8%	0.4%	0.8%

Source: UN International Trade Yearbook, Various Years.

Table 10.4 USA's Trade with the USSR (% share)

	1970	1974	1978	1985	1989
Import	0.2%	0.3%	0.7%	0.1%	0.2%
Export	0.3%	0.6%	1.6%	1%	1.2%

Source: UN International Trade Yearbook, Various Years.

Therefore, the present Sino-U.S. economic trade ties are enormously stronger than those between the United States and the Soviet Union during the Cold War period. In exports, Table 10.1 shows that the U.S. exports to China have consistently occupied around 2% of its whole exports since 1993, with the highest record of 5% in 2005. In the context of having more than 20 percent growth rate, the proportion of U.S. exports to China will become even larger in coming years. As for China, its exports to the U.S. have consistently accounted for more than 20 percent of its whole exports since 1998 according to the Chinese data. This number raises close to 40 percent of Chinese exports according to the United States data. Either way, the above clearly shows that the bilateral trade relationship between China and the U.S. is substantially more intimate than that between the U.S. and the former Soviet Union.

The growing trade relationship between China and the U.S. has become increasingly important and central to the economies of both countries. China's economy has been growing at roughly ten percent a year for more than two decades, which is closely tied to the open trade and investment regimes of the major economies of the world. Analysis shows that exports which help spur the modernization of Chinese economy and support improved standards of living account for 40 percent of China's gross domestic product (GDP). The World Bank estimates that during the past two decades (1980s and 1990s), nearly 400 million people in China have been lifted out of poverty. According to the Chinese data, the United States market has directly accounted for 22 percent of China's phenomenal export growth over the last twenty years.

Similarly, the United States has also derived great benefits from the trade relationship. American manufacturers, service providers, and farmers continue to eye China's increasingly fast growing middle class and new businesses as potential consumers of U.S. products, including capital equipment, financial services, high-quality and efficiently produced brand name and specialty consumer products, services, agricultural products, and technology. Between 2000 and 2004, U.S. exports to China have increased 114 percent. Just in 2005, the United States recorded $41 billion in exports, an increase of 19 percent over 2004. American businesses also make huge profits. Some data sources even suggest that China helped create 4 to 8 million jobs for the U.S. in 2004 alone. [13] Data shows that a total of 19,028 U.S. firms are known to have exported merchandise to China in 2003, a 16 percent increase from 2002 and a 27 percent increase from 2001. Over the 1992-2003 period, the number of small and medium-sized enterprises (SMEs) exporting to China rose faster than the number of SMEs exporting to any other major markets. SMEs exported merchandise to China from every state and the District of Columbia in 2003. Just in California, there are 5,464 SMEs exporting merchandise to China, followed by New York (1,969 firms), Texas (1,459 firms), Illinois (1,394 firms), and New Jersey (942 firms). In addition, American consumers now have access to a wider variety of less costly goods from China, which have helped spur U.S. economic growth while keeping a check on inflation. A report by Morgan Stanley shows China's low-priced quality products have saved American consumers over $600 billion over the last ten years and $100 billion in 2004 alone. Just in children's clothes, data shows that young American parents spend $400 million less because of purchasing Chinese goods. Also, the close economic ties between China and the United States jointly help maintain the driving forces for the world economy. Some data suggest that together the United States and China have accounted for roughly half of the world economic growth in the past four years (2002-2005).

Mutual Investment between China and the United States

With respect to FDI (Foreign Direct Investment), the U.S. investments in China began in 1980 and then experienced rapid growth in the 1990s. By the end of 2005, there were nearly 58,000 U.S direct investment projects in China, with a total contracted investment of $94.7 billion and an actually invested value of $50 billion (See Table 10.5). The U.S. has remained the country with the largest direct investment in China through 1999-2002. The U.S. direct investments are distributed over 26 provinces, municipalities, and autonomous regions in China and cover a wide range of industries, including automobiles, pharmaceuticals, petrochemicals, chemicals, textiles, machinery, electronics, telecommunications, light industry, food, agriculture, and such service sectors as tourism, real estate, and financial services. An increasing number of American multinational corporations are showing optimism about China's markets. By 2002, there were already more than 300 Fortune 500 companies investing in China, many of which are American conglomerates.[14] The Fortune Global Forum '99 was convened in the Pudong Area of Shanghai on September 27, 1999. Among the executives of the more than 300 transnational corporations represented at the forum, many were entrepreneurs from American multinational corporations. American businesses see generous returns from investments in China. According to Chinese statistics, American-funded businesses in China sold goods worth $75 billion in the Chinese market in 2004 and sold about the same amount of goods to other markets. The U.S. Chamber of Commerce in China released a white paper on American businesses in China recently. Its survey of its member companies shows that 93 percent of American-funded businesses in China believe that the Chinese economic reform has improved business environment for American businesses. 92 percent said their forecasts of business in China are optimistic or cautiously optimistic at least for the next five years. 86 percent of those surveyed have seen improved returns, 68 percent either are making money or have very high rate of profitability, while 42 percent report profitability higher than their global average.[15]

Consequently, China represents a strategic decision for many of the United States' largest multinational corporations. The American auto industry (Ford, GM, and Chrysler), for example, competed fiercely for entry into the auto assembly and auto parts arenas, believing that their foothold in the Chinese market was a key to maintaining production scales that would keep them competitive in the twenty-first century. According to Automotive Resources, as of 2005, GM sold to China more than 26,000 GL8, a GM's Buick Minivan, giving GM a 21% share of minivan sales in China. In 2005, sales by GM's joint adventures with state-owned Chinese vehicle manufacturers increased more than 35 % to 665,390 vehicles. GM's share of China's passenger-vehicle market rose to 11.3%, making it only second to Volkswagen AG. For 2005, GM reported preliminary profit of $327 million from its affiliates in China, compared with $417 million the year before.[16]

In addition, with the growing economic strength, both Chinese government and Chinese companies started to invest in the United States. According to U.S. government data, Chinese direct investment in the United States is small compared with other countries. By 2004, China had a total direct investment of $490 million in the United States, which represented only 0.03 percent of the total inward FDI in the United States. Even including Hong Kong's direct investment in the Untied States, it only amounted to $2.199 billion, 0.15 percent of the total FDI in the United States (see Table 10.6).

Table 10.5 American Enterprise Investments in China (1982-2005)

Year	Number of Approved Projects	Contracted Value (millions of U.S. $)	Utilized Value (millions of U.S $)
1982	23	247.00	118.68
1983	32	477.52	256.52
1984	62	165.18	256.25
1985	100	1152.02	357.19
1986	102	541.48	326.17
1987	104	342.19	262.80
1988	269	370.40	235.96
1989	276	640.52	284.27
1990	357	357.82	455.99
1991	694	548.08	323.20
1992	3265	3121.25	511.05
1993	6750	6812.75	2063.12
1994	4223	6010.18	2490.80
1995	3474	7471.13	3083.01
1996	2517	6915.76	3443.33
1997	2188	4936.55	3239.15
1998	2238	6483.73	3989.44
1999	2028	6016	4216
2000	2609	8001	4384
2001	2594	7505	4858
2002	3364	8200	5400
2003	4060	10160	4200
2004	3925	12170	3940
2005	3714	NA	3060
Total	58,000	94720	49565

Source: Ministry of Commerce, People's Republic of China

Table 10. 6 Direct Investment of China and Hong Kong in the United States, 1989-2004 (US $ Million)

Year	Direct Investment Position (Historical basis)		Income	
	China	Hong Kong	China	Hong Kong
1989	87 (0.02%)	1,124 (0.30%)	-60	-15
1990	124 (0.03%)	1,511 (0.38%)	-20	-16
1991	192 (0.05%)	1,162 (0.28%)	2	-48
1992	167 (0.04%)	1,358 (0.32%)	-2	-64
1993	109 (0.02%)	1,518 (0.32%)	19	44
1994	244 (0.05%)	1,505 (0.31%)	61	51
1995	329 (0.06%)	1,511 (0.25%)	59	20
1996	197 (0.03%)	1,711 (0.29%)	69	82
1997	182 (0.03%)	1,656 (0.24%)	17	84
1998	251 (0.03%)	1,458 (0.19%)	59	64
1999	295 (0.03%)	885 (0.09%)	41	125
2000	277 (0.02%)	1,493 (0.12%)	-22	12
2001	535 (0.03%)	1,292 (0.10%)	-12	21
2002	412 (0.03%)	1,888 (0.14%)	14	58
2003	309 (0.02%)	1,831 (0.12%)	-22	73
2004	490 (0.03%)	1,709 (0.12%)	58	105

Source: U.S. Department of Commerce

Table 10.7 Value of Foreign Holdings of U.S. Long-term Securities by Major Investing Countries, as of March 31/2000, June 30/2002, 2003, 2004, 2005 (Billion of US$)

Country	2000	2002	2003	2004	2005	Rank in 2005
United Kingdom	534	368	390	488	560	2

Japan	431	637	771	1019	1091	1
Canada	209	208	260	291	308	7
Germany	207	145	154	190	NA	NA
Switzerland	187	168	180	199	238	9
Netherlands	140	142	163	203	262	8
Cayman Islands	127	160	242	376	430	5
Luxembourg	107	229	297	392	460	4
China	92	181	255	341	527	3
Rest of world	1415	1925	2025	2200	NA	
Total	3,558	4,338	4,979	6,006	6,864	

Source: U.S. Department of the Treasury

On the other hand, Chinese official data indicates that up to 2002, cumulative approved Chinese direct investments to the United States amounted to $835 million (approved rather than realized). Still, investment from relatively underdeveloped China has attracted American's attentions. For example, China's Haier and other big companies built factories in the United States. Also China's largest computer firm Lenovo, acquired IBM's PC hardware division with a value of $1.75 billion in early 2005, which many Sino-observers considered as a watershed event in Sino-U.S. economic relations.[17] In July 2005, China's third largest oil (gas) company, China National Offshore Oil Corporation (CNOOC), tried to compete with Chevron in bidding for U.S. energy company UNOCAL. Due to the intervention of the United States government, Chevron won the deal with a lower offer.

In addition to direct investment, China also holds a large amount of U.S. treasury securities, primarily through the People's Bank of China and four other commercial banks. According to the data set, since 1999 China has remained one of the top purchasers of U.S. treasury securities among foreign central banks for 6 years. Presently, two-thirds of China's foreign exchange reserve, which is more than $800 billion, is in dollar-denominated securities, including treasuries, government agency debt and corporate debt. As of June 2005, American data shows that China's holding of U.S. long-term securities is $527 billion, ranking behind Japan and Britain (see Table 10.7). If adding Hong Kong's holdings of U.S. treasury securities, then the number will become even larger. If China sold these securities, especially in a disorderly way, then such action will affect the U.S. economy significantly.

It is exactly due to the intimate economic and financial ties between China and the United States, the outgoing Harvard president, former Treasury Secretary Lawrence Summers, calls the evolving U.S.-China relationship "a balance of financial terror," echoing the U.S.–Soviet "balance of nuclear terror" in the Cold War period. Summers contended that just like the terror balance that existed between the United States and the former Soviet Union due to what become known as MAD, or "mutually assured destruction," there is a similar "mutually assured economic destruction" existing between present China and the United States: if either side initiated a trade or financial war, both would be economically devastated, thus neither side could win. To illustrate his points, Summers raised the issue concerning the large amount of American treasury securities held by China. He argued that if China stopped buying billions of U.S. dollars each month, it could prompt a dollar collapse and consequently undermine the American consumer and global stability upon which the China's economic miracle rests. On the other hand, Summers contended that if the U.S. chooses to implement tough sanctions to punish China's undervalued currency or other options, it could also trigger inflation, higher interest rates and finally economic recession in the United States. [18]

People-to-People Contacts across the Pacific

Thirty-five years ago, some American Ping Pong players were invited to visit China, which signaled the starting of the normalization efforts between China and United States. Now that more than 30 years have passed, China-U.S. relations are undergoing development; contacts between the Chinese and American people are expanding in a continuously deepening way. On February 21, 1972 when President Nixon first stepped on the soil of China, there were very few Americans in China. Over the past 30 years, according to Chinese statistics, the number of Americans coming to China on visits has been on the increase each year, to an excess of 1,500,000 at present. While the statistics provided by the United States show that with the expansion in China-U.S. economic and trade ties, the number of Americans coming to the Chinese mainland on business activities had exceeded 280,000 in 2000. Meanwhile, there were massive groups of Chinese students and business people going to the United States for study and business investigation.

Over 30 years ago, there were virtually no student exchanges between China and the Untied States. This situation was finally changed on December 26, 1978 when China dispatched 52 students and scholars to the U.S. for academic studies. Similarly, the United States also sent 8 students and scholars to China for academic training in the same year. Since then, bilateral education exchanges have increased tremendously. According to data from China's Education Ministry, between 1978 and 2005, in total 933,400 Chinese went abroad to study, with close to 35 percent going to the United States. Figures also show that by the end of 2001, the number of Chinese students that have studied or are studying in the United States reached 190,000. According to

China's Ministry of Education, just in 2001, there were 78,000 students studying in the U.S. Data provided by the American embassy in Beijing indicated that in 2005 alone the United States issued 25,600 student visas to Chinese applicants, 40% more than that of 2002. Most of the students were master or doctorate degree candidates. Their studies cover almost every major.[19]

Table 10.9 gives us a clear picture with regard to the Chinese students in the United States. From this table, we can see that since 1994, the registered Chinese students constitute almost 10 percent of the international students in the United States every year. According to data from the Institute of International Education (IIE), since 1998/99, China has been the top two leading senders of students to the U.S. (In 1998/99, China overtook Japan as the leading sender, and remained in the number one position until being overtaken by India in 2001/02). The majority of the Chinese students study at the graduate level. In the academic year of 2003/04, among 61,765 enrolled Chinese students, 79% are graduate students, while 13% are undergraduates.

Table 10.8 Students Exchanges between China and U.S. (1994-2005)

Year	# of Students From China	% of Total Foreign Students in US	# of US Students Studying in China
1994/95	39,403	8.7%	1,257
1995/96	39,613	8.7%	1,396
1996/97	42,503	7.8%	1,627
1997/98	46,958	9.8%	2,116
1998/99	51,001	10.4%	2,278
1999/00	54,466	10.6%	2,949
2000/01	59,939	10.9%	2,942
2001/02	63,211	10.8%	3,911
2002/03	64,757	11.0%	2,493
2003/04	61,765	10.8%	4,737
2004/05	62,523	11.1%	n/a

Source: Institute of International Education (IIE), www.iie.org

China's top two universities, Peking University and Tsinghua University, perhaps best illustrate the ever increasing trend of going abroad to study in the United States. Some numbers indicate that over 50 percent of Tsinghua bachelors degree holders and over 30 percent of the graduate degree holders are abroad five years after graduation. A similar situation happened with Beijing University. The chief of the Foreign Affairs Department of Beijing University confirmed that in the Physics Department alone, since the restoration of the university entrance examination in 1977, one third of the graduates from the Physics Department have not returned to China. In the United States alone there are 500 graduates of the Beijing University Physics Department. Furthermore, he verified that in 2001, of the 170 students in the Chemistry Department, 60 have applied to go abroad; of 80 physics students, 40 applied to go abroad. Among the graduate students, one out of three leaves.[20] Obviously, the majority of those students come to the United States to pursue their career dreams.

At the same time, more and more American students choose China as a place to study. In 1992, there were only 768 American students studying in China, but by 2004, the number reached 4,737, increasing over 6 times within 10 years. According to the Chinese education resource, in 2005, the number of American Students in China is 5,400, which is more than the American statistics. And with the increasing commercial contacts, the education exchange potentials between China and the United States will be even higher.

The student and scholar exchanges between China and the United States benefit both countries very much. From the perspective of the United States, although international students comprise only over 4% of America's total higher education population, the Open Doors 2002 report shows that they contribute nearly $12 billion dollars to the U.S. economy in money spent on tuition, living expenses, and related costs. Nearly 75% of all international students' funding comes from personal and family sources or other sources outside of the United States. Also, Department of Commerce data describe U.S. higher education as the country's fifth largest service sector export. More than the economic benefits, China's most talented students and scholars contributed a lot to the technological and social development of the U.S. According to statistics, Chinese engineers and software programmers account for 20 percent of the employees in Silicon Valley in California. Just in the field of political science, data shows that by 2003, there were forty-four PRC-born political scientists teaching and doing research in American institutions of higher education, excluding those Chinese political scientists who are working in U.S. government agencies, think tanks, or private companies. They provide a variety of special courses on Chinese politics, Comparative politics and East Asian Political Economy, which help significantly enhance the diversity of American higher education. In addition, those PRC-born political scientists in the United States have authored fifty-six books in English on Chinese politics, Chinese foreign policy, East Asian politics, and U.S.-China relations, which also considerably increase the understanding of China for the American students and people in general. [21]

From the perspective of China, overseas students, especially those coming to study in the United States, exert even greater influence on China in various respects. They help increase China's overall science research and technological development. They also bring the most advanced management experience to

China. According to an empirical study on the effect of Chinese national-support overseas studies, public-dispatched overseas students and scholars make great contribution to the buildup of many new fields in China. They help initiate far-reaching changes in Chinese academic realms as well as in other societal respects. New academic fields such as public relations, MPA and MBA, have been established essentially on the basis of American models. [22] Kathryn Mohrman traced how China's education exchanges with the United States influenced the direction of Chinese university reforms, especially the most recent Chinese endeavors of building "World-Class Universities". [23] In the International Relations field, exchanges with the U.S. through scholar visits, curriculum transplant and classic works translations, help mold the shape of this field in China completely. Before the early 1980s, virtually no IR theory was taught in China, and there were almost no institution focusing on American studies. But by the end of the 1990s, courses on IR theories had been offered almost in all esteemed universities in China. As for American studies, in 1990, more than seventy institutions, research centers and departments were established in China. [24]

Many returning overseas Chinese students and scholars become key players in their respective fields. According to a systematic study on the effects of returning overseas Chinese students and scholars on China's scientific development by Beijing University and Zhongshan University, returning overseas Chinese students and scholars contributed 81% of the members of the Chinese Academy of Science (CAS), and 54% of the Chinese Academy of Engineering. In addition, 94% of the CAS's institutes' leaders and projects' directors have overseas studying experiences.[25] Individually, Tian Suning, a graduate of Texas Technological Institute, and Ding Jian, a graduate of University of California, introduced internet to China and became the founders of China's internet. Zhang Chaoyang, a Ph.D from MIT, founded sohu.com, which turned into one of the most popular websites in China.

Also, many returning overseas students join the government and some of them even become high level Chinese government officials. Among those entering into the government, Zhou Ji, a graduate of the State University of New York at Buffalo, became China's Education Minister; and Wan Exiang (JD, Yale University) assumed the vice presidentship of the Supreme Court. As more and more Chinese have come to study and work in the United States in recent years, their future impacts on China's economy, science, technology, politics as well as culture will become even more extensive and profound. As a result of this increasing transaction trend, some pundits even predict that around 2030, the top leader of China will likely be a U.S.-trained returning student, perhaps a classmate of the incumbent U.S. president. [26]

The exchanges and cooperation between China and the United States in the cultural field have also brought closer ties between the two peoples. Following President Nixon's "ice-breaking tour" of China in 1972, the first group of Chinese cultural envoys stepping onto the soil of the United States were Chinese acrobatic performers. In 1973, the Philadelphia Symphonic Orchestra paid its first visit to China, which captivated thousands upon thousands of Chinese audiences with their Beethoven symphonic music. Statistics show that from its founding in 1957 to the end of 2001, the Chinese Foreign Performing Company alone has received 1,623 American artists. It also has simultaneously sent out 3,436 Chinese artists to the United States, performing 15,000 times in 850 different cities and areas with a total audience over 20,500,000. [27] China also gave film shows in the United States. Well-known personages Yu Yang, Feng Xiaogang in the Chinese film circle went to the United States. The United States imports a considerable number of Chinese films each year. There is a large cinema at the center of New York City, which screens Chinese films all year round.

The American cultural products are exerting even broader and deeper influence on Chinese people, especially the young generation. The American pop music and fancy films are so influential in China that almost in every big city, there is a special channel broadcasting exclusively English pop songs and films which are very well-liked among Chinese youths. In the middle of 1990s, the Chinese government made a deal with the United States that China would import 10 films each year from the Untied States. Since 2002, after China's entry into WTO, the number of importing films from the United States has increased to 20 per year. Almost without exception, all the imported films have made a large profit in China. According to some statistics, in China's ten largest cities, the income from 23 nationally produced movies can not match even one imported movie. Before China's entry into WTO, over two-thirds of China's movie industry income come from the imported movies; China's own 80 domestic movies could only account for one-third. After China's entry into WTO, more Hollywood films were imported into China and they definitely helped to exert even greater influence on China's young generations. [28]

The cultural exchanges are not very balanced: China imports significantly more than the U.S. Just in 2004, China imported 4,068 books from the Untied States while only exporting 14. With regard to movies, from 2000-2004, China has imported 4,332 films while exporting very few. [29]According to the most recent development, in addition to producing good movies for export to China, this fast growing movie market, big American movie corporations started to build joint-venture companies with their Chinese counterparts. For example, Time Warner has built a "Yonghua Movie City" in Shanghai with Shanghai Yongle Limited Company, with Time Warner sharing 49% of the capital. [30] However, the wide-spread piracy in China is becoming a big concern to both countries. According to a survey conducted jointly by the Center for American Studies of the Chinese Academy of Social Sciences and the American Motion Picture Association, just in 2005, piracy led to $2.7 billion loss for the film industry in China. According to this study, in total China maintained 747 DVD/CD production lines which have the capacity of making nearly 2.7 billion pieces of DVD/CD in 2003, much higher than China's officially acknowledged 0.35 billion. [31]

In addition, more and more Americans choose China as a place for vacation. During the period of 1949 when PRC was founded to 1972, in total there were only roughly 1,500 Americans visiting China. With China's opening to the outside world and the increasing connections between China and the United States, more and more American and Chinese people visit each other. Table 10.9 shows that over the period of 1990-2000, the number of China's American tourists has increased roughly 4 times. In 2005, China hosted 1,555,000 American tourists, with an increase of 19% over the same period of the previous year. At the same time, 530,000 Chinese visited the United States, a 20 percent increase over 2004. As China's economy continues to grow very quickly, more and more Americans will choose China as their preferred destinations for vacation, doing business, or making investments. Chinese officials in charge of tourism predict a 10 percent increase per year for American tourists in the coming years.[32]

Also, more and more United States people, single, or married, choose to adopt children from China. Intercountry adoption from China by U.S. families has grown from 201 children in 1992 to 5,203 children in 2000. As of 2002, adoption from China accounted for 3.5 percent of all adoptions in the United States. Using INS (Immigration and Naturalization Service) immigration visas as a tally, from 1985 through 2000, 23, 093 Chinese children, mostly girls, were adopted by U.S. parents. Since 1991, when China loosened its adoption laws to address a growing number of children abandoned because of its national one-child policy, American families have adopted more than 55,000 Chinese children, almost all girls. Just in 2005, more than 7,900 children were adopted from China by American families. [33]

Table 10.9 Number of American Tourists to China and Its Percentage of Total China's Foreign Tourists (Ten thousand)

Year	# of American Tourists	Percentage of China's Total Foreign Tourists
1990	23.32	13.30%
1993	39.97	8.60%
1994	46.98	9.10%
1995	51.49	8.70%
1996	57.64	8.50%
1997	61.64	8.30%
1998	67.73	9.5%

1999	73.64	8.70%
2000	89.62	5.30%
2001	94.92	8.30%
2002	112.12	8.40%
2003	82.25	7.30%
2004	130.86	8.40%

Sources: China's Statistics Yearbook, Various Years.

INTERDEPENDENCE AND ITS IMPACT ON CHINESE FOREIGN POLICY

In discussing the influence of transnational communications on international relations, Deutsch constructed a new concept "security-community" to capture the new features of international relations with a high density of communications and exchanges. By "security community," Deutsch refers to "a group of people which has become integrated." By integration, he "means the attainment, within a territory, of a 'sense of community' and of institutions and practices strong enough and widespread enough to assure, for a long time, dependable expectations of 'peaceful change' among its population." Community "means a belief on the part of individuals in a group that they have come to agreement on at least this one point: that common social problems must and can be resolved by process of 'peaceful change.'"[34]

Similarly, in discussing the relations between power and interdependence, Keohane and Nye introduced a concept of "complex interdependence" to capture the changing facets of international politics at the end of the 1970s. According to Keohane and Nye, "complex interdependence" entails three main characteristics: 1) state policy goals are not arranged in stable hierarchies, but are subject to trade-offs; 2) the existence of multiple channels of contact among societies expands the range of policy instruments; and 3) military force is largely irrelevant. This last point suggests that deep interdependence between states will reduce the likelihood of war. Therefore, under "complex interdependence," Keohane and Nye contended that countries whose economic and political interests are deeply entangled with one another's are less likely to use force to solve their disputes.

With respect to the Sino-U.S relations, given the complexity of the bilateral relations, the political impacts of interdependence between China and the Untied States are mixed. As the previous examinations reveal, communication and exchanges across the Pacific are very thick and increasing exponentially. However, compared with Deutsch's "security community" as well as Keohane and Nye's "complex interdependence," Sino-U.S. relations are still in the pre-integration stage, and the discrepancies as well as potential conflicts between two countries in some issue areas, especially the sensitive Taiwan problem, are still high, and thus cannot be overlooked. Nevertheless, with China's increasing contacts with the outside world, especially the United States, several noticeable changes can be observed in China's foreign policy, ranging from the redefinition of China's national interests, to the incorporation of more liberal components into China's foreign policy, from the decentralization of foreign policy decision making, to increasing cooperation in some issue areas.

Changing Conception of National Interest

In order to look at whether the increasing interdependence between China and the United States has any feasible influence on China's foreign policy, we can first examine the evolution of the concept of national interest in China's IR scholarship as well as policy areas. Many scholarly analyses in North America have pointed out that China holds a hard-core, well-entrenched realpolitik world view with little in-grained liberal thinking.[35] China is said to hold an outdated Westphaliaian notion of sovereignty and an obsolete definition of national interest in a world of growing interdependence and globalization. Actually, in the 1980s, Chinese IR scholars' primary interest lay in realist and neorealist variants of IR theory. Most of the English-language IR books which had been translated and published in Chinese at that time belonged to the realist camp, including those authored by Hans Morgenthau, Kenneth Waltz, and Robert Gilpin. Hans Morgenthau's classic realist statement, *Politics among Nations: the Struggle for Power and Peace* became the canon for Chinese IR scholars and students.[36]

However, with the implementation of the open-door policy and the following increased communications and transactions with the outside world, China's foreign policy incorporated more and more liberal elements in the Chinese conception of national interest in world affairs. This not so-trivial shift can be firstly shown in the works of Chinese scholars in the international relations field. According to Yong Deng's study, in 1990s, liberal values were expanding their space in China's discourse on international relations. The late 1980s and 1990s saw highly frequent references to interdependence in international relations, in contrast to the complete absence of the concept of "interdependence" in earlier Chinese writings.[37] With the increasing interdependence with the world, China's IR scholars began to pay more attention than ever before to economic issues as well as "globalization" in the post-Cold War era. For example, Yan Xuetong, a UC Berkeley trained hard realist published an influential book in 1996 focusing exclusively on the notion of Chinese national interest. In spite of the well-known fact that Yan is a hard realist in China's IR field, still in this book, Yan argued that with the end of the Cold War and the restarting of "globalization," the priority of China's national interest was shifting from ideology and security interest to economic interest.

Therefore, Yan asserted that "to attain economic interests should become the main task for China's foreign policy" and "realizing economic interests should be taken as the standard for judging the rationality of a foreign policy (in China)." [38] On the other hand, Wang Yizhou, the deputy director of the Institute of World Politics and Economy of the Chinese Academy of Social Sciences (CASS) published his highly influential book *Analysis of International Politics* in 1995, wherein Wang examined the impact of interdependence and globalization on international relations. He listed ten factors that are challenging the traditional notion of state sovereignty, including incongruence between the nation and the state, the weakening of state capacities and responsibilities, the rising importance of NGOs (Non-governmental Organization) and IGOs (Inter-governmental Organizations) in world politics, etc. [39]

China's changing attitude and notion regarding national interest can also be reflected in its concrete policies. One of the most evident signs in this respect is China's departure from the traditional emphasis on political-military relations in favor of greater economic competition as a fundamental dynamic of international relations. Civilian economic development is becoming more of a top policy priority in China's sorting of national interests. China's decision to make the concessions necessary to join the WTO in spite of severe domestic opposition clearly demonstrated the priority shift in China's foreign policy. Some might contend that China's policy shift was intended to increase its economic capability so it will be able to pursue great power aspirations in the future. Nevertheless, it is still difficult to ignore the significance of China's changing priorities. As long as economic growth is on the top of the list for Chinese leaders, Beijing will be prone to maintain positive relations with the outside world, especially the United States, which is one of the largest sources for China's phenomenal economic growth. On the security issue, somewhat liberal views are evident too. A growing number of Chinese analysts are starting to advocate multilateral collective security, or a "new notion of national interest," as it is believed to serve China's national interests. For example, *China's White Paper on National Defense*, released by the Information Office of China's State Council in July 1998, reaffirmed that China supports this "new mode of security thinking" and China seeks to enhance "mutual security" without targeting against any third country. [40]

China's "Peaceful Rise" or "Peaceful Development" thesis as recently revised demonstrates most the impacts of the increasing interdependence on China's foreign policy thoughts and behaviors. The "Peaceful Rise" thesis was first propounded by the Chinese government in the 2003 BoAo Forum. It states that with the end of imperialism and the deepening of globalization, China must take a different path for development which none of the other late emerging countries has taken in the contemporary world. As a result of the rising new trends in world politics, China will adopt a peaceful development strategy which is inherently different from the traditional confrontational way as taken by other newly rising powers like imperial Japan and Germany. That is, China will focus on development, which essentially depends on a stable world system as presently dominated by the United States. As a result of this choice, China will have no interests to challenge the predominance of the United States, therefore leading to its peaceful rise. In the words of Zheng Bijian, a close associate of President Hu Jintao and the originator of China's "Peaceful Rise" thesis, "despite widespread fears about China's growing economic clout and political stature, Beijing remains committed to a 'peaceful rise': bring its people out of poverty by embracing economic globalization and improving relations with the rest of the world. As it emerges as a great power, China knows that its continued development depends on world peace—a peace that its development will in turn reinforce." [41]

China's redefinition of its national interests can also be shown in China's changing attitude to international norms and international organizations. As summarized by Samuel Kim, since its foundation, China's attitude to the international system evolved from a system transformer in the 1950s-1960s, to a system reformer in the 1970s, and further changed to become a system keeper in the 1980s.[42] More and more international organizations accepted China as a member state. In the 1970s, China belonged to 21 international government organizations and 71 international non-governmental organizations; by 1997 the respective numbers were 52 and 1,163. Gradually, China's views on multilateralism and international institutions also shifted from cautious suspicion to "conditional" embracement.[43] Increasingly China takes part in more and more regional and global security missions. For example, China cooperated well in the Cambodian peace process; China also willingly joined the South China Sea workshop. China supported peacekeeping operations in East Timor and the Congo. In Central Asia, China even led the establishment of the region's first multilateral organization, the Shanghai Cooperation Organization. In 1995, China started holding annual meetings with senior ASEAN officials. In 1997, Beijing helped initiate the "ASEAN+3" mechanism, a series of yearly meetings among the ten ASEAN countries plus China, Japan, and South Korea. One of the distinctive examples in this regard is China's active broker role in the Six Party talks on the North Korean nuclear issue.

Allen Carlson's detailed studies of China's shifting positions on sovereignty and intervention through the 1990s also convincingly reveal that even in those two traditionally very sensitive issue areas, China shows more and more signs of "learning" and becoming more "socialized" to the international norms by gradually modifying its intransigent stance and playing a more active role in peace-keeping as well as multilateral endeavors concerning sovereignty. [44] As a result of the transformation of Chinese foreign policy, Medeiros and Fravel concluded that "in contrast to a decade ago, the world's most populous country now largely works within the international system. It has embraced much of the current constellation of international institutions, rules, and norms as a means to promote its national interests. And it has even sought to shape the evolution of that system in limited ways."[45]

Decentralization of Foreign Policy Decision Making

In addition to the redefinition of national interests, another observable change in China's foreign policy which can be partially attributed to the increasing interdependence with the outside world, especially the United States, is the growing decentralization trend in China's foreign policy making. China's open door policy has increased its international interaction abroad at a very high speed. In 1978, China had relations with 113 countries, in 1999 with 161—a 42 percent increase. In 1978, foreign trade constituted 10 percent of China's GDP; by 1995, it had reached 40.4 percent. At present, some data suggest that it has increased to 70-80 percent. By 2010, some data project that the number will grow to 80-90 percent. [46]

More importantly, with the increasing economic interaction with the outside world, China's local authority enjoys greater economic power and autonomy which was unimaginable under the traditional Mao's central planning economy system. In 1978, the proportion of total government expenditures controlled by Beijing was as high as 47.4 percent; in 1996, the ratio fell to 27.1 percent, whereas provincial control increased from 53.6 percent to 72.9 percent. Over those years many provinces, especially those coastal provinces, achieved even more economic powers thus gaining more latitude over the central government in decisions concerning local interests. Just in 2005, Guangdong province accounted for close to one third of the whole Chinese foreign trade.

With regard to China's U.S. policy, one example of the decentralization influence on China's approach to its foreign policy can be illustrated by the negotiation of the WTO deal with the United States. Several studies on the implications of WTO membership that were commissioned by local governments and ministries recorded the anti-WTO attitudes at the provincial and local levels.[47] They believed that if Beijing adopted universal rules of trade administration they would lose their capacity to extract "rents" for their required approvals. During this process, some provinces not only affirmatively sought permission for policy departures but also tried to prevent the adoption of international economic policies they considered contrary to their interests. Also, broad opposition to the WTO can be observed in various industries, ranging from old, established industries such as machinery and agriculture to growing industries such as automobile manufacture, telecommunications, and chemical production and new industries such as financial services and insurance. Resistance to WTO was particularly strong among SOEs (State-owned Enterprises) and their representative ministries.

The effects of decentralization have also been apparent in the arms sales and technology transfer area. As Bates Gill reported, "China's initial efforts at trade liberalization included the decentralization of trade authority from a handful of centrally controlled foreign trade companies to 'private' foreign trade corporations operating independent of the government's foreign trade plan." The entrepreneurship of these firms in the sale of arms to sensitive countries, however, created foreign policy problems that the central government has had to address in turn by exerting tighter control and oversight.

In addition, as China's ties to the international community proliferated, the highly centralized decision-making process in which only one person, like Mao Zedong or Deng Xiaoping, has the final say was gradually abandoned. More and more new actors started exerting influence over China's foreign policy decision making. The authority is gradually flowing from the core leader to the broader central collective, from the central leadership to the supraministerial and ministerial levels, from Beijing to the provinces, municipalities, and even corporations. Moore and Yang's case study of China's foreign policy decision making in the age of economic interdependence reveals that during the Asian financial crisis period, in defying the central government, particularly the Premier Zhu RongJi's decision of keeping the PRC's exchange rate stable which will put local export targets in jeopardy, local province leaders made their own new policy (most notably GuangDong province, close to Hong Kong) to prevent erosion of their own economic positions.[48] Another two scholars, Cheung and Tang, also found that the local authorities gained more spaces to maneuver or "creatively implement" the policy made by the central government. Sometimes, the local authorities, especially in the border areas, directly seek to influence the central government to get permission for establishing economic, diplomatic, or project relationships with neighboring countries or international agencies to serve their own local interests. [49]

China also started to build interagency coordinating bodies like "leading small groups" for the purpose of managing key policy issues. In late 2000, Beijing established a National Security Leading Group (Guojia Anquan Lingdao Xiaozu) to coordinate the foreign policy making. In addition to the inside information, China has also acted to diversify the information sources and began to get more and more input from outside government agencies. For example, the foreign affairs ministry has begun to hire specialists from outside the government to serve as consultants on technical issues such as nonproliferation and missile defense. Chinese scholars and policy analysts are involved increasingly into the policy discussions.[50] A recent study found out that President Hu Jintao's foreign policy making involves multiple players, ranging from the Politburo, leading small groups, national ministries, think tanks, to citizens as represented by public opinion.[51]

Becoming More Cooperative in Some Issue Areas

A China whose liberal conception of national interests gains ascendancy would mean a China that is more cooperative and less apt to redraft the rules of the game in its foreign relations. Just as Stanley Karnow observed, compared with Mao's China, current China's positions on many international issues are becoming more moderate. He cited the example that former Chinese President Jiang overtly expressed support for the U.S. intervention in Afghanistan—a move that until recently China's spokesman would have excoriated as "blatant imperialism"—to support his points. China has also donated $150 million to Afghanistan's reconstruction. In addition, China has cooperated in the attempt to curb North Korea and has helped to prevent India and Pakistan from stumbling into a nuclear conflict. Karnow attributed China's conspicuous shift within the past generation from a crucible of romantic Maoist ideology to a society run by pragmatists focusing on rapid economic development to China's increasing interdependence with the outside world.[52]

Similarly, Bates Gill noted China's moderate response to the U.S.'s withdrawal from the ABM (Anti-Ballistic Missile) Treaty. According to Gill, compared with Russia, whose President Putin characterized the ABM treaty withdrawal decision as a "mistake," Chinese president Jiang Zemin took the high ground in his officially released statements, expressing China's willingness to "work with other countries to make efforts to safeguard world peace and stability," even though among the nuclear powers China stands to lose the most in the face of U.S. missile defenses. [53]

China's increasingly cooperative behaviors have also been shown in the UN security council by its attitude to the traditionally sensitive UN decision on a wide range of sovereignty-related issues, such as the use of force, humanitarian intervention, and the establishment of international criminal tribunals. According to Samuel Kim's study, in the period of August 1990 to December 1999, China in total had cast no fewer than 41 abstentions, which to some degree can be counted as"acquiescence" if not a full endorsement.[54] China's shift is in stark contrast with its traditional most cherished principle of the nonviolability of state sovereignty. China's views of arms control also transformed from irrelevance to active participation. Michael Swaine and Alastair Johnston show that in the 1970s, China only signed about 10 to 20 percent of all arms control agreements for which it was eligible; however, by 1996, this figure had jumped to 85 to 90 percent.[55] In regard to international environmental protection, Beijing has already ratified all relevant environmental conventions, including the Kyoto Protocol, the Montreal Protocol and others, despite the fact that there is still a big discrepancy between China's promises and its actual performance. Most notably, in the sensitive issue of human rights protection, China signed two keystone human rights covenants (the Universal Declaration of Human Rights and The International Bill of Rights) in 1997 and 1998 respectively, signaling China's willingness to gradually accept international norms.

CONCLUSION

Detailed examination of the bilateral relations between China and the United States demonstrates an increasing interdependence across the Pacific in terms of economic, cultural, educational, and people-to-people contacts. The network across the Pacific is drawing closer two countries and their people. The bilateral trade turnover (the sum of exports and imports) grew from $1 billion in 1978 to $211.6 billion in 2005. Currently, the United States is the second largest trade partner of China, and China is the third largest trading partner of the U.S. In terms of direct investment, the U.S. is ranked second in China's composition of direct foreign investment.

The thickening transnational communications between China and the United States not only form a tighter relationship between each other, they also influence China's approaches to its foreign affairs, particularly its policy toward the United States. Compared with Mao's China which tended to define its national interest in an ideological and military way, post-Mao China incorporates more economic and pragmatic elements into its definition of national interest. More specifically, economic interest is playing an increasingly important role in China's approach to its foreign policy. Consequently, China's foreign policy is becoming more moderate and pragmatic. The moderateness and pragmatism in Chinese foreign policy can be demonstrated in many issue areas. China is becoming more willing to cooperate with the United States in terms of preventing the spread of weapons of mass destruction (WMD) and their means of delivery, adherence to the Non-Proliferation Treaty and Comprehensive Test Ban Treaty, etc. The intimate contacts with the outside world also weaken the central control over certain aspects of foreign policy decision making, which led to both positive and negative consequences for China's approach to the United States.

Sino-U.S.'s increasing interdependence does not influence China's U.S. foreign policy in security areas. The 1996 Taiwan Strait missile crisis, the 1999 Yugoslavia embassy bombing, as well as 2001 Hainan spy plane incident demonstrated the fragility of the bilateral relations. However, it seems that the increasing interdependence and thickening networks across the Pacific do help the two sides to prevent their bilateral relations from worsening further.

Notes

[1] See Owen Harris, "A Year of Debating China," *The National Interest,* Winter 1999/2000.

[2] Two representative scholars of these two schools are Zbigniew Brzezinski and John Mearsheimer, with the former standing for liberalism and the latter for realism. They engaged in an intensive debate in a special issue of *Foreign Policy* centering on the "rising China." See Zbigniew Brzezinski, John Mearsheimer, "Clash of The Titans," *Foreign Policy*, vol.146, no.1 (Jan-Feb 2005); pp.46-50. Also see Aaron Friedberg, "The Future of US-China Relations: Is Conflict Inevitable?" *International Security*, vol. 30, no.2, 2005, pp. 7-45. Thomas Christensen, "Fostering Stability or Creating a Monster? The Rise of China and U.S. Policy toward East Asia," *International Security*, vol. 31, no.1, 2006, pp.81-126.

[3] See Bernstein and Munro, "Coming Conflict with America," *Foreign Affairs,* vol. 76, no. 2, 1997, pp. 18-31; and Richard Bernstein and Ross Munro, *The Coming Conflict with China* (New York: Alfred A. Knopf, 1997).

[4] John Mearshermeir, "The Future of the American Pacifier," and "Interview with the Author," *Foreign Affairs,* vol.80, no.5, 2001.

[5] However, the proposition of "Beijing Consensus versus Washington Consensus" by Joshua Copper Ramo raised an interesting question concerning whether China's growth will finally lead to exportation of its development model to the world in competing with Washington, which might result in conflicts with the United States accordingly. Officially, China's top leadership insist strongly that China has no intention to export its development model abroad and it is in China's own interests to realize its "rise peacefully" as articulated by China's official thinker Zheng Bijian at various places.

[6] James. J. Watson, "China's Big Mac Attack," *Foreign Affairs*, vol.79, no.3, 2000.

[7] David Lampton and Cheng Li provided two very illuminating studies on Sino-U.S. education exchange and its impacts on China. See David Lampton, Joyce Madancy and Kristen Williams, *A Relationship Restored: Trends in U.S.-China Educational Exchanges, 1978-1984* (Washington, D.C.: National Academy Press, 1986); Cheng Li, *Bridging Minds across the Pacific: U.S.-China Educational Exchanges, 1978-2003* (Lexington: The Rowman & Littlefield Publishing, 2005).

[8] For an insightful comprehensive review of the studies of the relationship between economic interdependence and political conflicts, see Edward Mansfield and Brian Pollins, "The Study of Interdependence and Conflict: Recent Advances, Open Questions, and Directions for Future Research," *Journal of Conflict Resolution*, vol. 45, no. 6, 2001.

[9] See Karl M. Deutsch, *Political Community and the North Atlantic Area: International Organization in the Light of Historical Experience* (Princeton: Princeton University Press, 1957)

[10] See David M. Lampton, *Same Bed, Different Dreams: Managing U.S.-China Relations, 1989-2000* (Berkeley: University of California Press, 2000), p.113.

[11] Sarah Y. Tong, "The U.S.-China Trade Imbalance: How Big is it Really?" *China: an International Journal*, vol. 3, no.1, 2005, pp.131-154.

[12] *Xinhua*, "China's Export Increment Heavily Depends on Foreign-funded Companies," November 19, 2005.

[13] Liao Xiaoqi, "Buying Chinese Goods Saves Americans 100 billion a Year," *the People's Daily (overseas edition)*, November 30, 2005.

[14] For a complete list of U.S. Fortune 500 Direct Investment in China in 1995, 1996, 1998, 2000, 2001, see K.C. Fung, Lawrence J. Lau and Joseph S. Lee, *U.S. Direct Investment in China* (Washington D.C.: The American Enterprise Institute Press, 2004), pp.77-83.

[15] Liao Xiaoqi, "Buying Chinese Goods Saves Americans 100 billion a Year," *the People's Daily*, November 30, 2005.

[16] Gordon Fairclough, "The Hot Limo in China? GM's Buick Minivan," *The Wall Street Journal*, March 28, 2006.

[17] Jean-Pierre Lehmann, "China-IBM Computer Deal Marks a New Era," *Yale Global Online*, April 1, 2005.

[18] Frederick Kempe, " U.S., China Stage an Economic Balancing Act," *The Wall Street Journal*, March 28, 2006.

[19] Source: *China News Network*, February 26, 2002, those figures are provided by China's Education Ministry.

[20] *China News Network*, February 26, 2002.

[21] Shiping Zheng, "Sino-U.S. Educational Exchanges and International Relations Studies in China," in Cheng Li, ed., *Bridging Minds across the Pacific: U.S. –China Educational Exchanges, 1978-2003* (Lexington: the Rowman & Littlefield Publishing, 2005), pp. 133-154.

[22] Caroline Haiyan Tong and Hongying Wang, "Sino-American Educational Exchanges and Public Administrative Reforms in China: A Study of Norm Diffusion," in Cheng Li ed., *Building Bridges across the Pacific*, 2005, ibid. pp.155-175.

[23] Kathryn Mohrman, "Sino-American Educational Exchanges and the Drive to Create World-Class Universities," in Cheng Li ed., *Building Bridges across the Pacific*, 2005, ibid, pp.219-235.

[24] Shiping Zheng, "Sino-American Educational Exchanges and Internaitonal Relations Studies in China," in Cheng Li ed., *Bridging Minds across the Pacific*, ibid, pp. 133-154.

[25] "Seven Contributions Made by State-Sponsored Oversea Chinese Students and Scholars to China," *China's Youth Daily*, October 10, 2002.

[26] Cheng Li, "Introduction: Open Doors and Open Minds," in Cheng Li, ed., *Bridging Minds across the Pacific: U.S.-China Educational Exchanges*, 2005, ibid, pp.1-24.

[27] "People-to People Contacts Bring China and US Closer," *People's Daily*, March 01, 2002.

[28] See Yanhua Hu, " I am watching movies—China's entry into WTO and its impact on China's movie market." http://www.phil.pku.edu.cn/personal/zhangzq/files/dianyingmeixue/68.doc

[29] *Lianhe Zaobao (Allied Morning Newspaper, Singapore)*, March 10, 2006.

[30] Xinhua News Agency, June 19, 2003.

[31] Richard McGregor, *Financial Times*, June 19, 2006.

[32] "Learning American experience of developing tourism industry, to promote China's American tourist industry," [Jiejian Meilvyouye Fazhan Jinyan Tuidong Meiguo Lvhua Shichang Kaifa], *Xinhuanet*, August 14, 2006.

[33] Lynette Clemetson, "Adopted as children, Chinese in America," *The New York Times*, March 24, 2006.

[34] See Karl Deutsch, *Political Community and The North Atlantic Area* (Princeton: Princeton University Press, 1968)

[35] See Thomas Christensen, "Chinese Realpolitik," *Foreign Affairs*, vol.75, no. 5, 1996, pp. 37-52.

[36] Alastair Johnston, "Learning Versus Adaptation: Explaining Changes in Chinese Arms Control Policy in the 1980s and 1990s," *China Journal*, vol.35, no.1, 1996, p.31.

[37] See Yong Deng, "Conception of National Interests: Realpolitik, Liberal Dilemma, and the Possibility of Change," in Yong Deng and Feiling Wang ed., *In the Eyes of the Dragon: China Views the World* (Lexington: Rowman & Littlefield Publishers, 1999), pp.47-72.

[38] Yan Xuetong, *Analysis of China's National Intersts* [Zhongguo Guojia Liyi Fenxi], (Tianjin: Tianjin Renmin Chubanshe, 1996).

[39] Wang Yizhou, *Analysis of Contemporary International Politics* [Dangdai Guoji Zhengzhi Xilun], (Shanghai: Shanghai Remin Chubanshe, 1995).

[40] *People's Daily*, July 28, 1998.

[41] Zheng Bijian, "China's Peaceful Rise to the Great-Power Status," *Foreign Affairs*, vol.84, no.5, 2005. On the other hand, Yong Deng's study indicates that in proposing the "Peaceful Rise" thesis China might purportedly intend to defuse the heated "China threat theory". See Yong Deng, "Reputation and the Security Dilemma: China Reacts to the China Threat Theory," in Alastair Johnston and Robert Ross ed., *New Directions in the Study of China's Foreign Policy* (Stanford: Stanford University Press, 2006).

[42] Samuel Kim, "China and the United Nations," in Elizabeth Economy and Michael Oksenberg ed., *China Joins the World: Progress and Prospects* (New York: Council on Foreign Relations, 1999), pp. 45-47.

[43] Evan S. Medeiros and Taylor Fravel, "China's New Diplomacy," *Foreign Affairs*, vol.82, no.6, 2003. Yuan Jingdong, "Asia-Pacific Security: China's Conditional Multilateralism and Great Power Entente," The Strategic Studies Institute. http://www.strategicstudiesinstitute.mil/pdffiles/PUB72.pdf.

[44] Allen Carlson, "More Than Just Saying No: China's Evolving Approach to Sovereignty and Intervention Since Tiananmen," In Alastair Johnston and Robert Ross

ed., *New Directions in the Study of China's Foreign Policy* (Stanford: Stanford University Press, 2006), pp. 217-241.

[45] Evan Medeiros and Taylor Fravel, "China's New Diplomacy," *Foreign Affairs*, vol.82, no.6, 2003.

[46] Yang Fan, "China's GDP Calculation and Its Relationship with Resource Consumptions [Zhongguo GDP Jisuan yu Ziyuan Xiaohao de Guanxi]," *Fenghuang Zhoukan (Phoenix Weekly)*, February 28, 2006.

[47] Margaret Pearson, "The Case of China's Accession to GATT/WTO," in David Lampton, ed., *The Making of Chinese Foreign and Security Policy in the Era of Reform, 1978-2000* (Stanford: Stanford University Press. 2001).

[48] Thomas Moore and Dixia Yang, "Empowered and Restrained: Chinese Foreign Policy in the Age of Economic Interdependence," in David Lampton ed., *The Making of Chinese Foreign and Security Policy in the Era of Reform*, 2001, ibid., pp.191-229.

[49] Peter T.Y. Cheung and James T.H. Tang, "The External Relations of China's Provinces," in David Lampton ed., *The Making of Chinese Foreign Policy in the Era of Reform*, 2001, ibid, pp.91-120.

[50] For a study on the role of think tank in present China, see Murray Scot Tanner, "Changing Windows on a Changing China: the Evolving "Think Tank" System and the Case of the Public Security Sector," *The China Quarterly*, vol. 171, no.3, 2002, pp.559-574.

[51] Lai Hongyi (Harry), "External Policymaking under Hu Jintao — Multiple Players and Emerging Leadership in China," *Issues and Studies*, vol. 41, no.3, 2005, pp.209-244.

[52] Stanley Karnow, "This President Facing a More Moderate China," *Boston Globe*, February 20, 2002.

[53] Bates Gill, "Can China's Tolerance Last?" *Arms Control Today*, Jan/Feb, 2002.

[54] Samuel Kim, "Chinese Foreign Policy Faces Globalization Challenges," in Alastair Johnston and Robert Ross ed., *New Directions in the Study of China's Foreign Policy* (Stanford: Stanford University Press, 2006), p.295.

[55] Michael Swaine and Alastair Johnston, "China and Arms Control Institutions," in Elizabeth Economy and Michael Oksenberg ed., *China Joins the World: Progress and Prospects* (New York: Council on Foreign Relations Press, 1999), p.101.

Index